The Environmental Factor

The Environmental Factor

An approach for managers

D. J. DAVISON

with an Introduction by
BERNARD TAYLOR
Professor of Business Policy, Administrative Staff College
Henley-on-Thames

A HALSTED PRESS BOOK

JOHN WILEY & SONS
New York – Toronto

English language edition except USA and Canada published by
Associated Business Programmes Ltd
17 Buckingham Gate,
London SW1

Published in USA and Canada by
Halsted Press, a Division of John Wiley & Sons Inc
New York

First Published 1978

Davison, D. J.
   The environmental factor

   'A Halsted Press book.'
   Bibliography.
   Includes index.
   1. Pollution – Economic aspects – United States.
   2. Industry – Social aspects – United States.
   3. Environmental policy – United States.
1. Title
HD69.P6D38   1978   301.31'0973   77–20123
ISBN 0–470–99351–0

Typeset by
Computacomp (UK) Ltd., Fort William, Scotland.
Printed by
Biddles Ltd., Guildford, Surrey, England.
Bound by
Mansell (Bookbinders) Ltd., Witham, Essex, England.

Contents

Preface

Business and society

The industrial revolution of the post-war years, with its new technologies and the growth of vast multi-national companies has, predictably, been accompanied by public demands for business to be more regulated and for businessmen to become more socially responsible. Public opinion, as reflected both in the media and in votes, has demanded that business as well as government should be concerned with the solution of social problems such as: equal opportunity for minorities, equal treatment of the sexes, protection of the environment from pollution, protection of the consumer from shoddy merchandise and poor service, and protection of workers from occupational risks. With surprising swiftness social protest groups have been organised, legislation has been enacted and new government agencies have been established to administer the new regulations. In a matter of a decade or so the social, political and legal environment of business has been transformed, the traditional autonomy of businessmen in managing their enterprises has been redefined and the legitimacy of the board of directors itself has been challenged.

The businessman's response to this social and political challenge has varied from passive disbelief to open confrontation. Gradually, however, this emotional reaction is being replaced by a more rational approach — using many of the management techniques which have proved to be effective in other areas of business. Senior management are of necessity spending more of their time communicating their industry's problems and concerns to politicians and government officials and to society at large. Companies are establishing departments of public affairs, or civic affairs, to develop and implement social policies and programmes. Corporate staff engaged in personnel, marketing, manufacturing or finance are finding that their skills in analysis, research and planning can frequently be applied to social and political problems. And operating managers at all levels are realising increasingly that decisions made largely on financial and technical grounds need to be informed by a clear understanding of their likely effects on the local, national and international community.

The Business and Society Series is designed to provide books which will help managers in dealing with social and political problems

— in understanding the basic concepts which are being put forward and debated;

— in identifying and forecasting social and political trends which may be significant for business;

— in developing business philosophies and approaches which take account of the new relationship between business and society;

— in discussing and developing new strategies and programmes aimed at building support for the business, from politicians, government officials, social action groups, and the public at large;

— in organising and implementing systems and procedures which will provide incentives and support for operating managers who need to adjust their traditional management approaches to cope with changed social values and new social and political pressures.

The environmental movement

In the context of this new relationship between business and society, environmentally-oriented planning and management of projects, products and production have become pre-requisites for business success in the 1970s and 1980s. Maintaining and improvising the quality of the environment has become established as one of the major aims of public policy at national and international level. And, despite the energy crisis, hyperinflation, economic recession and increased levels of unemployment there is still profound public concern about conservation of natural resources and the protection of the environment. Government interest in, and regulation of, the environmental impacts of industrial activities continues to broaden and strengthen.

The high cost to business of environmental legislation is well documented particularly in the United States. The United States Commerce Department has calculated that in 1975 capital expenditures for air and water pollution control amounted to $7.7 billion, and the Council on Environmental Quality predicts that in the ten years 1975 to 1984 United States industry will spend $258 billion just to meet the provisions of existing legislation.[1] The Environmental Protection Agency, founded in 1770, estimates that between January 1971 and December 1976 environmental restrictions helped to close ninety-five plants, making 19 250 workers redundant.

---

[1] Statistics quoted in *Business Week*, April 4 1977, pp 72–3.

A recent McGraw-Hill study highlights the particularly high expenditures on pollution control which are required in the major United States process industries (see Table 1).

Table 1   Pollution control expenditures in 5 major US industries

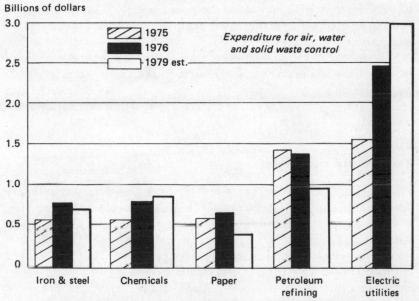

Data: McGraw-Hill Publications Co, Economics Department.
(1) Statistics quoted in *Business Week*, April 4 1977, pp 72-73.

The cost is not only in capital expenditure and in jobs but in delays in launching new products, and in opening new plants. The EPA's programme to re-evaluate by October 1977 250 000 pesticides will probably not be completed for ten to fifteen years and pesticide producers have almost given up hope of getting new products cleared.

Dow Chemical Company recently abandoned plans to build a $500 million thirteen-plant complex near San Francisco which would have brought thousands of jobs and a $15 million a year payroll. After spending two years and $4 million on environmental studies, Dow had obtained only four of the required sixty-five permits and the company took its investment elsewhere.

Arguments over environmental impact held up the Alaska pipeline for five years and now threaten to delay the construction of a tanker terminal which BP Sohio wants to build for Alaskan oil in Los Angeles harbour. In the Eastern States the EPA is holding up Volkswagen's plans for opening a plant in Pennsylvania, and the New York Port Authority has delayed the start of the Concorde service from New York.

In Western Europe environmental issues are equally significant. In Iceland and Ireland there is concern about preserving the fish stock in the North Sea. In Northern Italy a recent disaster in a chemical plant is causing continuing anxiety. In Holland, Hogovens were recently prevented from building a steel plant because of worries about the pollution of the Rhine. In Britain and Norway there are recurrent worries about oil slicks from tankers and oil rigs. In virtually every European nation the public outcry against the dangers of building and operating nuclear power plant has been sufficient to hold back nuclear energy programmes.

It is clear that managers in business cannot afford to leave the management of the environment to politicians, civil servants and citizen action groups. To operate effectively they must understand the issues, make the case for their industry and play a leading role in the process by which the environment is 'managed'.

Environmental management

Environmental management, as a field of concepts, knowledge and methods is advancing rapidly. It is concerned not with halting economic growth and stopping technical advance but with achieving that sustainable rate of economic development which is necessary to meet man's material needs whilst conserving scarce natural resources and protecting both the external environment and the internal (work) environment.

The task for the government official is to manage the process of environmental protection on a regional, national or international level so as to enable citizens to enjoy the benefits of the natural resources available and the advantages of modern science and technology, whilst minimising the social costs which are likely to occur through shortages, pollution and social conflict. To the businessman on the other hand, environmental management means ensuring that critical decisions are taken with the environment in mind. This means 'that he takes his decisions consciously knowing what their impact is likely to be on the environment and ready to defend himself or his company against any attacks that might be forthcoming in relation to the overall benefit he is seeking to achieve'.[2] Both the public official and the businessman are concerned to understand and 'manage' from different points of view the process by which a balance is struck between technological and economic progress on the one hand and the conservation or the improvement of the natural, urban and work environment on the other.

This involves developing innovative approaches to such tasks as:

— assessing the environmental impact of present and new technologies;

— estimating the economic cost of environmental policies and regulations;

---

[2] See Chapter 3.

— forecasting future trends in environmental management as regards both technology and legislation;

— arranging for public participation in planning for new projects;

— resolving or avoiding conflict between various interest groups;

— formulating strategies and plans to achieve social and political support for projects which are economically and technically viable;

— building organisation structures and management systems, and procedures which will enable and encourage management at all levels to make the environment a consideration when taking decisions.

For the student of environmental management the field for study includes topics such as:

— *the state of the environment* in terms of ecology, natural resources and conservation, pollution and pollution control;

— *energy and the environment*, in particular the use of nuclear energy and the alternatives;

— *social and political trends*, changes in social and cultural values, social and political movements and trends in legislation;

— *regional planning*, and the attempt to meet expanding human needs for shelter, food and water, health, education, production, distribution and transportation;

— *public agencies and interest groups*, international, national and local governments, the representation of sectional interests and the functioning of spontaneous action groups;

— *methods for environmental impact assessment*, the potential of and limitations to various techniques for estimating the costs and benefits to society, and for predicting the likely impact of new technology;

— *handling environmental conflict*, identifying potential conflicts, avoiding conflict by consultation and negotiation and various strategies and tactics for public hearings.

The manager and the environment

Much of what is published about environmental management takes the point of view of the conservationist with a cause or the public official who has the problem of recommending or interpreting legislation and assessing social costs and benefits.

This book is written expressly for the manager in business to:

— help him to understand the basic issues and concepts involved in environmental management so that he may develop a balanced and informed point of view

— explain the social political and legislative trends to which he should be prepared to respond

— describe the political processes and the analytical techniques which he needs to understand if he is likely to be involved in environmental conflicts.

The book should appeal to four groups of readers:

Operating managers Project managers, product managers and production management — particularly those concerned with the development of new products or new production facilities;

Specialist staff Corporate planners, environmental coordinators, directors and managers in business, regional and national government officials from environmental ministries, agencies and departments, international civil servants from environmental sections and departments of international organisations;

Academics and consultants Teachers and students of economics, business and public administration — especially those taking courses in policy and planning — management consultants and researchers involved in projects concerned with environmental protection, or health and safety at work;

The general reader The book should also appeal to readers who are not directly involved in management, e.g. trade unionists or members of environmental protection societies who are familiar with the more emotional statements of the case for conservation or nuclear protection and would be interested in a balanced statement of a managerial point of view.

I trust that this practical and well-written book will help in the development of a more rational approach to the problem of managing the environment.
Bernard Taylor
Editor Business and Society Series
Henley-on-Thames
July 1977

Acknowledgements

I am greatly indebted in the preparation of this book for the press to my secretary, Mrs Elise Charles, without whose efforts I doubt whether the task would have ever been completed. I am also most grateful for the assistance given to me by the NCB's library service and, in particular, by Mrs S Simkin, in tracking down information and references from the flimsiest of leads.

The writing of this book has inevitably made massive inroads into my already severely limited free time, so I am more than conventionally grateful to my wife and daughters for the patience, tolerance and support they have given me during a period when perhaps my own patience and tolerance was not all it should have been!

D.J. Davison
Hemel Hempstead
Herts
July 1977

Introduction

We live in a time when the amount of effort being devoted to analysing the problems of management is ever-growing, and yet we seem increasingly unhappy with the results achieved. In Britain, the decade of growth of Business Schools and the legitimisation of 'Management' as a respectable study for university graduates, has (let us hope coincidentally) seen our industrial performance slump to such a degree that we have become the yardstick of warning to many of our friends. In the world at large, the euphoria of the early 1960s, which arose from the prospect of ever-increasing living standards and the progressive elimination of social problems, has totally evaporated. When we dare to look at the future, we now see it in terms of problems and not opportunities. We have become dominated by doubts, rather than hopes. Society's problems seem to become more and more complex in all their aspects.

Many reasons can be advanced for this state of affairs but underlying most of them is our desire to pursue different social objectives simultaneously and our refusal to recognise that some of them are irreconcilable. A number of apparently fundamental problems stem from our reluctance to try and distinguish between differing objectives and establish some acceptable order of priorities. We want a free society, yet we want an ordered society. We want to be able to pursue our own interests (usually perceived in the short term) while wanting long-term planning to avoid tomorrow's potential disasters. We want low prices for the goods we buy but high prices for those we sell, including our own labour. We want industry to take social objectives into account but we do not expect to have to pay the price of it doing so.

The frightening growth in world population, coupled with inevitable pressures for improved living standards, will result in a demand on natural resources which will cause a qualitative change in our environment in many parts of the world. Is this inevitable and is it a problem that has anything at all to do with day-to-day management?

Managers have, as such, tended to opt out of attempts to help define a priority of objectives for society. This has not always been the case and its consequences are becoming apparent. While it would be as wrong for management, as for any other single group, to try to impose its wishes on society, it can be argued that it is equally wrong for management to be above the battle. Despite all the talk about joint approaches to problems we are still too often in the battlefield of adversary politics. Managers have a vital role to play in changing this potentially tragic situation. This book is a look at one area of managerial concern and is an attempt to show how managers add to environmental problems and how they could contribute towards their solution.

It is probably a sign of foolhardy optimism to propose that we should attempt rational solutions in a world which shows increasing impatience and contempt for rationality. It is so much more exciting to press emotional solutions. To be in the protest march releases far more adrenalin than painstakingly trying to find the right course of action. Emotional arguments on either side of an issue (and it must be accepted that they are used as often in defence of an entrenched position as in an attack on it) tend to produce the reaction that our position is sectionally or politically motivated. But despite the attraction of the appeal to the heart and not to the head, we have no real alternative but to press rational solutions to our problems and not to be content with emotional spasms, however personally satisfying they may be. The rule of force or the philosophy of the big battalions, may be hard to resist at times but that is no excuse for embracing it as a desirable objective. Rationality is one of the great distinguishing marks of civilised life and it should never be consciously cast on one side.

This is not an argument for a cold, unemotional world but for one in which humanity and concern for others links genuine emotion with hard, constructive work to find practical solutions. In environmental problems we are faced with a multitude of conflicting objectives which, in many instances, are not even recognised. As more and more examples of apparent failure to meet adequately issues of environmental concern have been forthcoming, many made searching, and often telling, critiques of what has and is being done, but there has been little in the way of constructive criticism. We have many suggestions for new restrictions and regulations but little analysis as to how such an approach will help society meet its other objectives. Naturally, I hope that this book will help to focus attention on the real, as opposed to the apparent, environmental problems and will provide some help and guidance to those in management who have to bear the increasing burden of trying to tackle them with greater insight and understanding.

Although I have learned much of environmental problems and their potential solutions during my work for the National Coal Board, the views expressed in the following pages are mine, and mine alone and in no way represent or reflect the official policies of the National Coal Board.

1 Getting the record straight

What are we talking about?

This is a book about management for practising managers. It makes no
pretentions to be a work of scholarship or original research. It has the modest
aim of trying to help the manager understand what Max Nicholson has called
'the environmental revolution' and to see how it affects his or her particular
job.

So much has been written on the environment in recent years, that it is
legitimate to wonder whether there is a need for yet another book on the
subject. Because there has been little attempt to synthesise the opposing
arguments from the point of view of a practising manager, I believe there is.

In all the voluminous writings on the subject, management tend to get
caught in the cross fire of opposing extremists, and little work appears to have
been done to try to bring about a cease-fire.

The increasing degree of open warfare will not bring about a lasting
solution. There is a crying need to negotiate a Treaty of Co-operation designed
to arrive at mutually agreed aims which will further the overall objectives of
society. This book attempts to provide a first faltering step in that direction.

Much of what has been written on the environment has been exaggerated,
sentimental, one-sided, or just plain wrong-headed. The fundamental issues
have been ignored, and we have been faced almost exclusively with conflicting
cries from the extremists' dugouts. On the one hand, some having no more
basis in fact than some of the excesses of science fiction, while on the other,
having the equally infuriating moral certainty of a disciple of Samuel Smiles'
Self Help. We must never forget that one reason why the environmental
bandwagon has been able to roll so rapidly has been the failure by
management to meet the legitimate requirements of environmental protection
and conservation. Unfortunately, the extremes of the 'doomsday' arguments
have tended to make some managers feel that they are faced with an irrational
opposition that must be beaten at all costs. They live in the hope that 'sound'
economic arguments alone will eventually carry the day. This is a view which
is short-sighted and may well be self-destructive if unmodified.

The following pages are not altruistic in intention. They are based on the solidly practical assumption that, if managers continue to treat environmentalists as people whose eccentric views will be overcome in the light of harsh economic necessity, then this could put the survival of particular firms, or even industries, in jeopardy.

One of the difficulties facing management in modern society is that it tends to be more over-criticised. Whether or not this is justified, would make a subject for a book in itself. Here it is sufficient to note that managers do not have an unblemished reputation in the world at large. Managers know this, and have, in turn, developed a defensive attitude of mind. They expect their motives to be misconstrued and therefore they want to give nothing away. It is hard to win battles, when you are on the defensive. An underlying theme of this book is that management can make a positive contribution to the environment and, by so doing, wrest the initiative from those who wish to place ever-increasing curbs on its activities.

Whom are we talking to?

I have referred to 'managers' in a generic way without defining what I mean. Definitions come in a later chapter but, for the time being, I should make it clear that I am using the term to refer to all the decision takers in society, whatever they may be called. It is a classification by function, rather than status. Decisions do not have to be taken by senior management to have major effects on the environment. One of the sources of our present conflicts has been the failure of senior management to involve itself with environmental matters.

It will become apparent as we proceed that I believe that many decisions which have environmental implications (whether appreciated or not), are taken by people who would not regard themselves as managers in the conventional sense of the word. Any decision which alters, moulds, affects and influences the environment, either physical or psychological, in which we live, and to whatever degree, can be regarded as a managerial decision affecting the environment.

Whenever we come across anything in life that we do not like, we tend to seek to blame the ubiquitous 'they'. 'Why don't "they" do something about it?' We are fond of declaring that 'they' should not be allowed to get away with it. When disaster strikes we want to be able to pin down the culprits — it is always seen as a case of 'Someone has blundered', to quote Tennyson.

We frequently fail to realise that 'they' are merely other decision takers, and that we, ourselves, in our day to day activities are 'they' or 'someone' to other people. Somewhere somebody is wondering why 'someone' is failing to remedy what they regard as an intrusion into their affairs, and that 'someone' happens to be you. In environmental matters, you may only be immune from criticism until they find out who *you* are.

Many managers will be surprised to realise that their everyday actions have environmental effects. It is not something that they normally consider. Even if they did, they would be unlikely to think that such effects should influence their decision taking. There are so many inhibitions and limitations on management action these days, that many would feel it was asking too much to expect management to concern itself automatically with environmental issues. This is surely a matter for government control and regulation. I am concerned in the following pages to examine the validity of such reactions and to ask whether managers should concern themselves with the environment as an act of conscious discipline. Is this either necessary or desirable, and does it have any bearing on the success of the enterprise?

Why should we bother?

It is a fundamental assumption in this book that managers usually give too little time and attention to the environmental effects of their actions. This is not a moral criticism. In fact, many managers are often quite genuinely unaware, either of the immediate or cumulative effect of their day to day decisions on the quality of life. Even when managers have some awareness of the effect that their activities may be having on the environment, they may well consider and argue that there are no viable alternatives which would avoid or even mitigate the effects while, at the same time, enabling them to get on with the job they are paid to do. Many certainly seem unaware that there might be ways of achieving the same objectives, and at the same time causing less disturbance to people's lives.

The reaction of managers when confronted with demands that they take new objectives into account in managing their business, is often to question whether this is yet another nine days' wonder. If they do, then they are unlikely to pay more than lip service to the ideas put forward, no matter how well founded they might be. There is no doubt that, after decades of experience of management techniques, management training and now management schools, at least one thing (perhaps only one!) is clear, and this is that management, like all other facets of human activity, is subject to the whims and vagaries of fashion.

Historically, it would seem that it's never enough to be content with current ideas or methods, no matter how successful they may be or how questionable the alternatives. The appeal of the *status quo* never seems paramount. Those at the rear cry forward and those at the front cry back. Perhaps because things can never be perfect, we are constantly attracted by the idea of change, even if some want to change back to where we once were.

We have become used in the world of clothing to be subjected to the change from narrow to wide trouser bottoms, from mid-calf to mid-thigh skirt lengths, from double-breasted to single-breasted suits, from winkle-pickers to platform shoes and, eventually, just as surely (even though the stark truth may be hidden from us by the cunning devices of advertising agencies) back again to where we started. We tend to think that such illogicalities can only occur in something as 'unimportant' as dress fashion. In fact, some of the more uncharitable of us may have felt (before the advent of women's liberation of course) that such nonsense could only occur where the decision influencers were aiming mainly at the female sex. The rapid growth of interest in men's fashions over the last twenty years, has snown this to be totally untrue. (Historically, of course, it always was. It is hard to think of a more fashion-conscious group than the Cavaliers, and the epitome of high fashion was of course a man — Beau Brummel.) Nevertheless, it is perhaps surprising that, in such an unsentimental world as management and industry, the illogic of fashion has played an equally large part.

Perhaps because management is, and always will be, much more of an art than a science, it is a good target for the 'hard sell' of professionally contrived commercial management packages offering panaceas which somehow will make management problems miraculously disappear.

We have been subjected to 'job analysis', 'work study', 'organisation and methods', 'corporate strategy', 'standard costs', 'the computer', 'operational research', 'management by objectives', 'budgetary control systems', 'discounted cash flow', the transformation of internal into 'operational' audit, 'decision analysis', 'management development', and so on. As each of these techniques have had their fashionable day in the sun, the manager has been subjected to the full onslaught of management messiahs, urging the overwhelming importance of mastering this, that, or the other technique. In so far as his superiors and his company Boards have been converted, he has been instructed, bullied, cajoled and directed into the belief that he must act in a certain way successfully to optimise performance. As mankind has always been a sucker for pills that promise to cure all ills, we have over time attempted to swallow the lot. It is not surprising therefore that having done this and, as a consequence, suffered acute indigestion, managers should be wary of any further doses.

On top of management techniques have come new 'areas of interest' about which the manager is supposed to have, not only a knowledge, but also, all too often a detailed corporate policy. In this category come the efforts to impress upon companies their corporate 'social responsibility', demonstrated in such things as the drive towards 'equal opportunities', whether these are expressed in terms of class, race or social equality. 'Concern with the environment' comes firmly within this category. Are we all environmentalists now? New names have emerged: 'Friends of the earth', 'conservation society', 'Sierra Club' — in Great Britain, even a 'Department of the Environment'. Is this just a fashionable turn of a particular pressure group's screw? Is yet another skilful marketing package which, in a year or two, will have lost its up-market grading, or will it be more enduring? More important, *should* concern for the environment be more enduring? Has it got any political overtones, does it represent real concern or is it a smokescreen disguising a more fundamental attack on industry? These are legitimate questions which must be at least approached, if not answered, in any book which has the audacity to try to deal with the complex subject of the manager and the environment.

It is because I believe that the question of the environment is not merely a fashionable fad, that I have made the not inconsiderable effort to write this book. It is quite likely that some groups are using environmental issues as a way to undermine a system which they are determined to change. But that should not be allowed to detract from the basic hard core of general concern in society about the environment, a concern which demands attention. Put in stark terms, management ignores environmental issues at its own, literal, peril. By that, I mean that some organisations will founder because of the unwillingness or inability of their management to come to terms with the environmental problems of the age. I have in mind the problems that have already been encountered in such as the chemical industry, where the somewhat haphazard approaches of some manufacturers in past years have led to grave doubts being put on their continued acceptability. Similarly, there is now pressure to end the use of all asbestos products. The automobile industry has taken quite a hammering on both pollution and safety standards and, in the United States, the strip mining industry is unable to take full advantage of its potential because of its past environmental record.[1] It follows that I believe that a knowledge of the issues involved is a vital part of the armoury of any manager attempting to carry out his or her day to day functions in the last quarter of the twentieth century.

It is customary for many books aimed at a specialised audience to include the somewhat pious hope that they will also interest that mysterious being, 'the general reader'. True to tradition, I share a similar aspiration. However, I hope in my case that the arguments set out in this book will be of interest not only to managers but to the 'general citizen'. By that description, I mean the individuals who have, in democratic societies, in the last analysis, to form judgements and to take decisions at the ballot box which indirectly determine the manner in which their country shall be governed. There are few fields in which the general citizen has such an opportunity to influence the future, either for good or evil, as in the field of the environment. The reasons for this I shall go into at a later stage; suffice it for the time being to say that, unless management can convince the general citizen of the sincerity of its approach towards environmental issues, legislative control is certain to increase.

In recent years, the average citizen has become only too aware of the way in which his or her whole environment has been affected, sometimes very badly affected, by the activities of governments, industry, and individuals. Notice I have mentioned the activities of governments as being equally culpable. We

---

[1] See Chapter 7.

must not fall into the error of assuming that it is solely the industrialist who can affect the environment adversely. We have only to think of the siting of artillery or missile ranges, or of the policies which have been adopted covering general planning permissions in both town and country, to see how much the environment can be affected by the actions of our political masters. But the end results of such actions can be surprisingly pleasing. For example, the Chemical Defence Research Establishment at Porton Down in Wiltshire has occupied some 4,000 acres of Chalk Grassland for sixty years. This area has therefore been spared the intensive farming techniques of the mid-twentieth century and has become an important centre of wildlife conservation. It is now a haven for wild flowers, insects especially butterflies. (See article in the London *Observer*, 2 May 1976.) The reaction has been predictable and, in many ways, commendable. There has been an upsurge (particularly in developed countries) of interest in 'environmental studies'. Conservation has become very much a fashionable subject and the growth of civic and amenity societies, together with the emergence of groups for the protection of this, and the prevention of that, have flourished. The defence of the environment has provided an outlet for a considerable amount of repressed patriotic feelings. If we cannot protect our land with the rifle and the bayonet, we can at least do it with the pen and the petition!

Let's put a stop to it

If we examine the facts, it would appear that a great deal of effort is being put into trying to prevent change. There is nothing new in this. Machiavelli in *The Prince* written in 1513 commented:

'It should be borne in mind that there is nothing more difficult to arrange, more doubtful of success, and more dangerous to carry through than the initiating of changes in a state's constitution. The innovator makes enemies of all those who prospered under the order, and only lukewarm support is forthcoming from those who would prosper under the new. Their support is lukewarm, partly from fear of their adversaries who have the existing laws on their side, and partly because men are gradually incredulous, never really trusting new things unless they have tested them by experience.'

The explicit approval of a considerable amount of protest against environmental change implies that change must inevitably worsen the existing situation. At first sight, resistance to change is not an attractive cause. The history of the world over the last four hundred years has been one of change, sometimes in some places faster than in others, but change, nevertheless. This is not surprising, as man is the only animal that attempts to adapt the environment to meet his needs rather than adapting himself to suit the environment. The doubling of the population in this period of change has meant a scramble for survival, not always successful, and this in turn has promoted change of enormous magnitude. To compare the world of the 1970s with that of the 1570s removes any doubt on this point. Whether it is possible to erect a dam to prevent further massive change is extremely doubtful. Whether it is desirable, is equally doubtful and this strikes at the root of the conservationists' case.

Opponents of change in the political sphere used to be called reactionaries — a term of immense contempt. The eighteenth century, the age of the fashionable advocacy of fundamental change in man's affairs, was called either 'the age of enlightenment' or 'the age of reason'. It is therefore somewhat ironic that advocates of the *status quo* now regard themselves as being the progressive thinkers.[2]

I have little doubt that many environmentalists do not regard this as being their intention at all and would refuse to recognise this description of their activities. They consider that they are trying to redress the balance and would point to considerable evidence of a total lack of concern with the environmental effects of change. They would claim that theirs was certainly a progressive viewpoint. In so far as this is their aim, I would agree. The problem is, that so many things are done in the name of environmental concern which do have the result that I have described, of creating a barrier to *any* change irrespective of the care that is taken on environmental matters, that it could be said that the overall movement is in danger of becoming a reactionary, rather than a progressive force. I believe that if this happened it would be a disaster. The environmental movement is potentially one of the greatest forces for good in the world if it concentrates on its constructive and not destructive proposals. It must learn to live in the 'real world' as must the industrialist.

I shall be suggesting in the following pages that, in some instances, the pendulum has been pushed too far. More than that, there is some evidence that the people who are endeavouring to swing it have not fully appreciated that they cannot expect to move the pendulum so violently in one direction and still enjoy an accurate clock. In other words, we are failing to realise that most of us are not prepared to pay the price of what some conservationists are trying to do.

At this point, it might appear to a committed environmentalist that I am attempting to produce an apologia for industrialists to be allowed to get on with their businesses without let or hindrance. Nothing could be further from the case. I want to try to illustrate that we have to develop a coexistence between our environmental and our industrial and economic needs.

Both groups, in this particular conflict, need to see that they have a wide

---

[2] Perhaps we should remember Euripides in *Heracles*, 'All is change — all yields its place and goes.' Or, nearer our own times, Bertrand Russell commenting in his *Unpopular Essays* — 'Change is scientific, progress is ethical — change is indubitable whereas progress is a matter of controversy.'

area of common interest. We are all living on the same 'spaceship earth', with finite resources and an infinite capacity for self-destruction. No thinking person could deny that there is an urgent necessity to appreciate and understand the implications of all actions on the future of life on this planet. With the single exception of the possibility that we could drift into nuclear war, there is nothing potentially more dangerous to mankind than a failure to establish the right kind of working relationship between industry and commerce and the environment in which it operates. If we fail to create such a relationship, then the future is bleak indeed.

Am I my brother's keeper?

At one time, man's activity could have little effect on the general environment in which the majority lived. But we have now reached the situation where the quality of our own environment is neither a fixed factor nor, necessarily, controlled by our own environmental restraints and regulations. Pollution knows no frontiers. Poisoning the atmosphere in one state can result in the effects of that poison being experienced in another. The Scandinavian countries claim that the high amount of sulphur which comes down on their shores is put into the atmosphere by electricity generating stations in the United Kingdom. Nuclear fallout from bomb tests in the Pacific does not simply affect the originators of such tests, but contaminates the whole of the world's atmosphere by increasing the total amount of strontium 90 to which we are all subjected. China's atomic test in 1976 raised the levels of contamination in the United States.

Not only is the quality of the environment no longer a fixed factor, but it is also a variable over which we exercise collectively more influence than most of us appreciate. It is true that it is now quite conceivable that we could make our space-ship literally uninhabitable. But this 'ultimate deterrent' argument does not apply to all the environmental changes we may be considering. It is all too easy to drift into the *non sequitur* of assuming that, as we can bring about irreversible changes which could destroy our environment, all change should be avoided. This is a concept dear to the heart of some of the more extreme ecologists who seem to take the view that, as the mechanism of nature is so closely interlinked, no part of it can be changed without destroying the overall effectiveness of the machinery.

If we react from fear and do not seek ways in which we can facilitate those environmental changes which we require to meet our other needs, then we are in equally grave trouble. We could find that, although the environment has been preserved, we have effectively prevented the continued supply of the goods and services on which we have come to rely as essential underpinnings of our civilisation. To the majority of people this will not be desirable. While it is open to doubt as to whether, whatever we do, our standards can be maintained in the long term, we can greatly accelerate such a process of decline. What is most worrying is that we could do this inadvertently. No one wants either a world of massive pollution and despoliation or an ever increasing fall in living standards, but our actions could move us almost irretrievably in one direction or another.

I have said that the specialist audience this book is aimed at is that of the decision-taker, the manager. What am I offering in that direction? No manager needs telling that the only commodity totally restricted (in economists' terms 'inelastic') in supply, is his own time. Whatever we do, we cannot create more than twenty-four hours in a day. All we can do is to try and use every minute to maximum efficiency.In the face of the multitude of completing tasks to be done — papers to be read, people to be seen, meetings to be attended, decisions to be taken, explanations to be made or demanded, any further incursion into management time needs to be fully justified. Why, therefore, should such an individual take the time to read a book about the environment?

At first sight it hardly seems the type of activity that will help in achieving the desired objectives of the organisation, add to the efficiency or profitability of a concern, make the shareholders happier, or even improve the prospects of personal advance. Surely it is a subject for the academics, the long-haired, the do-gooders, the law-makers. It cannot be of interest to those who have to face up to the difficulty of meeting a payroll, keeping men in employment and supplying the goods and services consumers want at prices they are prepared to pay! The point of this book is that it is the managers who should be the most interested. Just as war is said to be too dangerous to leave to the generals, the environment is far too important to leave to the special interests of any individual section of society. We all have to face up to the facts and their implications, and make our own decisions.

There have been so many books on the environment in recent years that at times it would almost appear we have only just discovered that there is such a thing. This would be a very narrow view. You only have to look for a moment at the great nineteenth century novelists to realise that the effect of the environment on the lives of some of the people was very clearly recognised. Virtually the whole of Dickens can be seen in terms of the effect of their environment on people's lives; although the same can be said of Balzac and Zola, and in an entirely different millieu, of Jane Austen. Just consider how Mr. Bennett's daughters in *Pride and Prejudice* were the complete victims of their own environment. In the United States, this type of comment was more muted and came later, but come it did, perhaps initially most effectively with Harriet Beecher Stowe's *Uncle Tom's Cabin*. As industry developed, it can be seen in the works of Theodore Dreiser and Upton Sinclair and it is arguable that there has been no novel with greater environmental effect than Sinclair's classic about the Chicago stockyards, *The Jungle*; and the effect of Engels' *The Condition of the Working Classes in 1844* can hardly be exaggerated in the non-fictional field.

Few doubt that the unbridled explosion of industrial activity from the middle of the eighteenth century until the last half century created totally unacceptable environmental conditions for many millions of people. The housing conditions in which most of the working population of London, Paris, Manchester, New York, Chicago and Pittsburg had to drag out their short lives were haunting memorials to the results of unbridled industrial enterprises which were either unable or unwilling to consider the implications of their actions.

That atmosphere of indifference to environmental conditions has now changed entirely. We are all made aware, month by month, day by day, of the importance of the environment and we are increasingly subject to laws, regulations and controls, all aimed at modifying our actions in such a way that the environment will be protected. As we are all aware of the problem, in what way does this book differ from others on the subject?

Who is responsible?

The clue to the answer to the question lies in the title. This book is based on the proposition that managers, whether they accept it or not, and whether they like it or not, are inevitably creating the future. They are taking a multiplicity of small decisions which, in totality, create the environment in which succeeding generations have to live, and they will be responsible for the legacy they leave.

If we are making the future we should not be content to do it by accident. If we understand what we are about, we will have a better chance of making an acceptable environment for succeeding generations. Should this seem a fanciful conclusion, consider the impact of the industrial revolution on the environment. The unacceptable living conditions which nineteenth century workers had to endure as part of the cost of the industrial revolution were not the malevolent creation of the warped minds of certain profit-mad industrialists. It was simply that the end result was not considered in environmental terms. The concern of mill owners was to get labour; there was none near at hand, therefore housing had to be provided. If this had to be done, then it was sensible to do it as cheaply as possible, just as they would try to acquire any other source of raw material they needed. People took decisions strictly in relation to their own objectives and, as each decision remorselessly piled on top of the previous one, the industrial slums were born. The environmental consequences of management actions were not considered; they were irrelevant. But although they may have seemed irrelevant to the managers of the time, they have led to many of our present day problems.[3]

---

[3] It is worth noting that some industrialists were able to swim against the tide. People like Robert Owen and Titus Salt and the Rowntree family were able to create model villages to house their work people without apparently destroying their profitability. Perhaps these comments should be confined to the UK. Robert Owen had far less success with his attempt at community building at New Harmony in the United States.

Even the sternest critics of the time did not allege that it was the intention of the factory and its owners to create such degradation, it was merely the inevitable result of the system. It produced what could be described as the first unacceptable face of capitalism. The effects were so profound that the very real improvements in general living standards which the system was capable of producing, were, in the long run, overshadowed by the legacy of the unacceptable consequences.

While we can see that our forefathers made a fundamental mistake in not appreciating the fact that, by allowing such conditions to come into existence, they were undermining the foundations of their own prosperity, we are not so adept at drawing similar conclusions relating to our own time. Our inheritance of nineteenth century working class housing seemed to provide visual proof that the system of production of which our forefathers were so proud, could only deliver the goods at what turned out to be an unacceptable social cost. If we are not to make a similar mistake in our century, we have to think and act most carefully and must analyse the effect of our present day decisions on the kind of environmental inheritance we will bequeath. Most of us would want to leave a legacy of which we can be proud. What we might leave and whose decisions will influence the inheritance, are the subjects of this book.

It might be argued that, while this may be a very laudable objective, it has nothing to do with the day to day objectives of management. Many managers will not accept that concern with the environment is any part of their business. They would maintain that their objective is to be profit orientated and they do not see how the environment has any connection with this.

It is useful to examine this case of the manager who genuinely believes that nothing but profitability is his or her concern, since in practice, this view does not bear close examination. If we start at the beginning, profitability must be defined as profitability within the bounds of the law of the particular country in which the company is operating. The legal obligations of the company cannot be ignored (at least, in the long run). This in itself is a major inhibition on the pure profit motive, but one which managers have to learn to live with. The legal obligations of companies have grown very rapidly in recent years. Management is now accustomed to having to operate within legal restraints on such things as price, quality, health and safety of employees, advertising and taxation.

While managers are more than accustomed to having to conduct their affairs within the confines of many kinds of regulation and restraint, a major concern of many is to avoid further legislative controls. Legislation is inflexible and cannot take account of particular circumstances or conditions. It is therefore likely to lead to some irrational situations. The argument goes that the more managers' activities are restricted by the law, the less able they are to achieve their objectives.

For those managers who take this approach, this is the best possible reason for beginning to take a greater interest in the environmental aspects of their activity. There is ever increasing pressure to strengthen the law relating to the environment and to place greater controls over industry and commerce in order to improve the level of environmental protection. This can only be avoided if it becomes clear that industry and commerce themselves are prepared to take positive and effective action to counter the undoubted problems their activities cause. This is not a matter of merely paying lip service to the environment. To avoid further controls and regulations, a genuine concern with the problem must be seen. Unless industry and commerce put their own houses in order, then the law will be invoked to make them do so. This in itself should be a sufficient incentive to get the most anti-environmentalist manager thinking in terms of how he can maintain his independence.

Apart from the law, it is becoming increasingly evident that managers are being asked to take into account far more varied objectives than the simple maximisation of profit that has guided them for so long. The murmurings about 'social responsibility' are turning to more strident cries and managers are asked to take account of more and more 'social-isms' in their day-to-day activities. This growing call for so-called 'social audits' seems unlikely to be reversed. In this context, the manager should take the environmental aspects of existing or proposed operations with due seriousness, if only because, in one way or another, it will soon become reflected in his profit and loss account.

The attitude of the public has also changed. At one time, they regarded the environmental effects of industry as inevitable consequences of the activity, and seemed willing to accept that there was no alternative. This is no longer the case and there is an increasing tendency to question the need for environmental pollution in any form. People have begun to question seriously the need for the existence of a particular factory, or operation, in a particular place. While, as we shall see later, the motivations for such attitudes are often mixed and by no means always socially responsible, nevertheless, they do exist. The effect of public opinion therefore has to be taken into account in looking at the overall long-term viability of the operation. In this context, the potential environmental ill effects are a matter of the utmost importance.

A further consideration which may become increasingly relevant, especially at times when employment prospects are good, is that industries that develop the reputation, whether they deserve it or not, of being socially irresponsible, may find more problems in recruiting and keeping the quality and quantity of personnel they would like. These are sound practical reasons why the manager of today cannot afford to avoid environmental issues.

The 'environment' will be a matter which will increasingly affect the profitability of companies and, as such, is fully worthy of the attention of all managers. The following pages attempt to explain why, and suggest ways in which management can adapt to the new challenge.

2 Would you say that again please — slowly?

What are you trying to tell me?

The modern world has reached a degree of complexity which increases daily and already defies comprehension. Few people have either the time or the motivation to look outside their own narrow everyday affairs. Yet, in order to attempt to make the world more the way we want it, we have to convince others that our particular point of view is the right one. This is the case whether we are talking philosophy or politics, sociology or science, but is most obvious when we are selling products. The degree of sophistication which has been achieved in advertising, in order to influence the motivation of potential purchasers, is well known, if not particularly well or widely understood. We have been more reluctant to accept that similar techniques are used in selling ideas and even people. The 'packaging of the President'[1] or 'the selling of the Senator' should now be an all too familiar concept. In television interviews with politicians or debates between Presidential candidates, we have been taught to accept that it is not what is said, but the way it is said, that matters. We are concerned with the appearance not the reality. What we fail to realise is that this is not just a game for top people: we all try to do it, either consciously or unconsciously. Managers are, in fact, paid to do it — to influence others, to make things happen in the way they think they should.

This determination to press our versions of reality on others is believed to be crucial because it is seen as being the key to success (however you define that seductive siren). It is therefore totally unsurprising to find that, in pursuit of this objective, the means of communication (i.e. the methods of persuasion) employed have become increasingly emotive and blurred. Precision can be dangerous, as it exposes your weaknesses as well as your strengths.

We find ourselves continuously bombarded, openly or clandestinely, with attempts at persuasion in one form or another. The language used frequently conceals rather than reveals the thought behind the message.[2] Words are often

---

[1] See Theodore White's *The Making of the President 1960* and *The Making of the President 1972*.

[2] For a thorough but far from simple exposition of the confusion of thought caused by the careless use of words see *The Vocabulary of Politics* by T.D. Weldon.

used in an emotional rather than a descriptive manner. They are designed to cloud the thought processes and to make you respond with Pavlovian approval or disapproval. This is most commonly done with political words: a proposal will be described as 'communist' or 'fascist', 'socialist' or 'democratic', not because it is necessarily a part of the creed referred to, but because the author wishes to bias your judgement of the actual proposal. Using words in this way has been called the ' "boo" "hurrah" principle'. If the word is one I support, I will mentally cheer and ignore the 'fouls' that might be committed on the way to scoring a goal. On the other hand, if the word is a 'boo' word in my vocabulary, then I shall certainly take no notice of the merits of the play and argue that the goal should be disallowed.

In attempts at persuasion, words are used to make exaggerated claims for the virtues of the idea or product and, as a result, the original meanings become distorted and weakened. Not every idea can be 'great' or every product 'sensational'. If we use these words all the time to describe petty everyday occurrences, what do we say when the truly 'great' or 'sensational' happens?

No comment on 'pop' culture seems to be valid these days without the use of such words as 'fabulous' or 'fantastic'. These words have now lost their previous precise meaning and now are just 'OK' expressions, signifying pleasure, a kind of 'hurrah' approval of the object being described. To ask a disc jockey using the words 'fabulous' and 'fantastic' to describe a record, whether he really means that it gives the kind of experience of which fables are made, or that it is totally beyond the realms of belief, would produce incredulity, to say the least! While it is possible that such a record could occasionally hit the charts, it is asking too much to believe that half a dozen can be produced every week. The question is, what do you say when such a record is produced? You are then truly lost for words.

In this debasing of the coinage of words we do not realise what is happening until the need arises to use the coinage in a new situation, when we find that we do not receive the return expected. We are improverished entirely by our own doing. The language is weakened by this haphazard and careless usage and, at no time do we realise it more than when trying to make our meaning absolutely clear. In the words of Thomas Hobbes 'words are wise men's counters, they do but reckon with them, but they are the money of fools'.

A popular technique of the hidden persuaders is to widen the use of scientific terms into everyday use, until they move from being specialised and precise to being everyday and fuzzy at the edges.

In discussing any topic, it is of great help if we can be precise about the terms we are using. If we can agree on the general way in which to use particular words, this will reduce the possibility of arguing at cross-purposes. This is an essential basis for advancing knowledge in any field. We must agree that this particular colour and no other is aquamarine, otherwise for the whole of our discussion, I may think it blue, and you may think it green. You cannot argue about the financial accounts unless both parties know the meaning of 'debit' and 'credit'. First define and agree your terms, then you might have some chance of understanding the contract.

In this century, the work of the linguistic philosophers has made us very much aware of the importance of analysing the ways in which words are used. They have argued that many fundamental problems of philosophy are based on failure to define rigorously and clearly the concepts under discussion, or to give consistent meanings to words used in a particular train of thought. Their fundamental approach is based on the idea that, if an attempt is made to clear the decks by rigorously analysing the nature of the propositions put forward, many of the so-called problems will disappear.

This is not the place to argue the merits of this view, except to say that it has the virtue of concentrating the discussion on fundamentals. I am not suggesting that all the problems will disappear in a discussion on the manager and the environment if we take care to define our terms with precision. But it should give us a better understanding of which ones really matter. There cannot be a clear understanding of the argument unless the way in which the concepts are being used is understood. So, while I in no way pretend to be a philosopher, or a linguistic analyst, I still think it necessary to try to spell out the way in which I am using the key words and concepts which will recur throughout the following pages.

This book is concerned with the manager and the environment and has, as a basic theme, the concept that each manager, whether he realises it or not, holds a responsibility to posterity for creating some aspect of the environment through his actions or non-actions. In this context, it is necessary first of all to see what we mean by 'manager' and by 'environment'. As the argument develops, there may be other terms equally requiring definition but first, let us try and make sense of these two basic concepts.

What does a 'manager' do?

Ancient philosophers based their approach to knowledge on the belief that words had intrinsic meanings. They thought that there was a 'correct' meaning of each word locked up in the heavens and that the aim of the philosopher was to find the key. The principal exponent of this view was Plato (this concept runs throughout his works but for a clear exposition see Book X of his *Republic*) and we have had seekers after the 'Platonic ideal' ever since. In recent times, much greater weight has been put on the opposite view, that what we need is not an analysis of the intrinsic meanings of words, but an appreciation that words mean what we want them to mean and that the philosopher needs to provide an accurate description of what actually happens to words in use. It is now argued that words like 'justice' or 'freedom' are only part of the verbal apparatus used for describing and criticising certain types of human conduct. It follows therefore that words seldom have a singular nuclear meaning, but can have a whole range of meanings. If in practice this appears to be the case, we need to be sure which meaning we are using.

There are times when it seems that whole libraries have been written in an attempt to establish what is meant by 'a manager' or the concept of 'managing'. Inevitably, the definitions have varied according to the particular aspect which the author wished to pursue. It is quite instructive to glance at random at the shelves of management texts to see how many definitions you can find in half an hour. If the library is reasonably comprehensive, you are not trying if you cannot reach double figures! However I suggest that one common thread running through all the definitions of management responsibility is the notion of control. The idea that the 'manager' has power and authority to get things done and, subject to certain constraints, to get them done in ways that he can either decide or influence.

In a general sense, therefore, someone is 'managing' when he or she takes actions which result in things happening in a way that would not occur simply by chance, or by letting the constituent parts of the organisation act without any overall direction or constraint. We will discuss later this idea that the manager is able to influence the course of events, that he or she is able to make things happen in different ways, which leads on to the concept of responsibility.

It is the overall task of the manager to create within an enterprise the conditions which will help achieve the objectives of that enterprise and I am using the term 'manager'[3] in this sense.

It will be seen that this definition has nothing to do with particular processes or types of activity. Most of the 'management' covered by this definition is done by people who do not have the word 'manager' in their title and, in fact, many of them would be very surprised to be told that they were 'managing'. Nevertheless, they are changing events, and they are therefore 'managers' within the scope of this book.

The manager is not alone in carrying out these tasks. He is charged with the responsibility of undertaking any actions necessary to enable individuals to make their best contribution towards the objectives of the organisation.

No manager can manage adequately without taking account of the external conditions in which he has to operate. The most obvious one of these is the law of the land. The enterprise, we assume, is intended to be carried out in a legal manner[4] and even though there might be actions which managers could take

---

[3] It should now be unnecessary to remind ourselves that one of the primary categories of managers in our present day society is the trade union official. I certainly have this in mind when considering the contribution that 'managers' can make to tackling environmental issues.

[4] This has not always been the case. The entrepreneurs of the last half of the nineteenth century in the United States would not have recognised such inhibitions. Their solution was to try to get control of the law and, for a while, some of them were notoriously successful.

to improve the probability of reaching the organisation's objectives, if these are in breach of the law then they cannot be pursued.

Behind the law there is public opinion.[5] There are areas in which it might be legal to operate, but the weight of public opinion is such that to attempt or to continue to operate in such a way, could well reduce the organisation's chance of reaching its objectives, rather than the reverse. It may result in new laws being introduced to prevent just that kind of operation.

Similarly, the organisation can be restricted, or affected, by the wages and conditions of service negotiated on a national basis by unions and employers' federations, which encompass a wider area of activity than the individual firm. Such agreements again place a restriction on the freedom of action of the individual manager.

These events outside the firm are often referred to as occurring in the firm's external environment. The manager simply cannot avoid being affected by this external environment. In fact, it has been said many times, from Fayol onwards, that managers have a responsibility to form a general acquaintance with matters not necessarily exclusive to their function, and it is becoming increasingly true that no manager can perform his task well, unless he fosters such a familiarity.

What is 'the environment'?

The other major concept we are dealing with is that of 'the environment'. It is a word we all feel we know the meaning of, yet it has so many varied meanings and ramifications, that it will repay us to spend time on a more precise analysis.

The concept of 'the environment' has undergone a radical transformation in recent years. Originally it was used almost exclusively to define physical surroundings. It has the same roots as the word 'environs' and was taken to mean that which immediately surrounds you. Thus the environs of the town was clearly understood as being the neighbouring areas.

The word was then adopted by psychologists and psychoanalysts to describe all those influences that bore upon the individual, other than his inherent nature. The debate as to whether people are more affected by their inherent ability or by the effects of their environment, is one which still proceeds with vigour.[6]

In many ways this use of the word 'environment' has now become the most common. We talk about the need to bring up children in a happy environment, or the importance of a family environment; in terms of public health we refer

---

[5] The connection between the two has probably never been better expounded than in A.V. Dicey's *Law and Opinion in England*, 1914 edition. Despite its age, it still has some useful insights to impart.

[6] See in particular the works of Professor H.J. Eysenck.

to the need for a clean and healthy environment as being those surrounding conditions that affect or influence the development or growth, not only of individuals, but also of species. Reference is made to species having to cope with a hostile environment; and we certainly hear of environments which are allegedly conducive to criminal or anti-social behaviour.

Given that the word can be used in so many different ways, the obvious question is, in what sense am I trying to discuss the manager and the environment? The answer, I am afraid, is that the manager is concerned with all these different types of environment. He is concerned with them because he will be held responsible for the effects that his actions, or the actions of his firm or organisation, have on all these varying types of environment. There is little doubt that if it can be argued that the conditions which he provides in his factory are such that either because of the nature of the work, or the attitude of management, employees become anti-social in their behaviour, then he is open to the charge that he has totally underestimated the environmental effects of his activity. It will be argued by critics of management, that the real cost of the activity is far greater than that shown by the profit and loss account.[7]

This is a particularly important point because, all too often, the word 'environment' is understood to be referring solely to natural phenomena. We expect it to be used in relation to the natural order of things and the way these are being endangered. In this context the word is used to cover such aspects as the pollution of rivers and of the air, the dust bowls created through over intensive and ill-advised farming, or the elimination of species through commercial exploitation. The destruction of the world's whale population partly as a consequence of the increasing demand for pet food, is a classic example of the latter.

Because, rightly or wrongly, managers will be criticised and blamed for the effects, both real or imagined, of their activities on any aspect of the environment, we cannot confine ourselves to considering only the effects on nature. We must accept that the different definitions of environment are all areas of legitimate concern to society. It may be that we would consider that some were of far more immediate importance to management, but this usually reflects the differing responsibilities of particular jobs rather than a fundamental qualitative difference. Whichever definition we are using of 'environment', it is affected each day by the individual actions of the group of people I have called 'managers'.

We are in a situation where the word 'environment' is in regular everyday use and we all tend to assume that we know what is meant when it is used. The problem, as we have seen, is that it conveys a myriad of meanings and it is therefore worthwhile looking at some of them in a little detail.

Most people who describe themselves as 'environmentalists' are people who are concerned with what we might call the immediate physical environment;

---

[7] This approach can be seen in attitudes towards repetitive assembly line work.

the environment that we see, hear or smell from our windows or that which we experience when we walk in the country. It is something which can be directly experienced, touched, smelt or seen. Environmentalists using the term in this way are concerned usually to ensure that nothing happens as a result of man's intervention to unduly disturb this pattern.

Originally, this concern stemmed mainly from appearance — the 'woodman spare that tree' school. It reflected proper concern with the look of the landscape. But increasingly the argument is put in terms of ecological damage leading to impending disaster. We are told that we meddle with things we do not understand, that 'There are more things in heaven and earth Horatio than are dreamt of in your philosophy'. They point to the totally unanticipated effects of the use of the insecticide DDT on the whole ecological system.[8] Nobody foresaw that the very effectiveness of DDT would create new dangers; its massive use throughout the world resulted in a build up of DDT in food chains so that the poison man was using to wipe out the insects affecting his environment, ironically has resulted in poisoning man himself.

It is this concept of environmental protection that has created the pressure for clean air and rivers and an end to the growing pollution of the seas. It had to be highlighted by one or two disasters before much action was taken, but this aspect of environmental control is now familiar to most managers.

However, as we have seen, 'environment' is more than this. We are familiar with the term 'working environment', which describes the conditions under which we labour. These conditions may or may not be injurious to our health, they may be more a matter of amenity and comfort, but nevertheless they are an important part of our lives and we can expect that people will want the best possible 'working environment'.

It is useful to regard the environment affected by managerial decisions as being two-fold: the internal 'working environment', and the external 'living environment. When we are faced with an 'environmental' issue, we have to be precise as to the conditions we are talking about and consider carefully what particular aspects of managerial decisions might be under attack.

The degree of effect on the environment can be very diffuse. It ranges from, at one end of the scale, nuclear contamination, which can harm generations yet unborn, to the other extreme where environmental opposition is based solely on the grounds that a particular activity may disturb the last surviving haven of particular fauna and flora. Between these levels it encompasses health hazards arising from working environments, such as those which in the past have caused scurvy, farmers' lung, pneumoconiosis and asbestosis. The charge that your activities will damage the environment can apply to any of these points. Management must be prepared either to defend itself all

---

[8] As always, the excellence and success of the first contribution in the field, e.g. Rachel Carson's *Silent Spring* and *The Sea Around Us* brought forth a flood of less well informed imitators whose main objective seemed to be concentrated on the more sensational aspects at the expense of a balanced approach.

along the line, or to modify its actions, where this is possible and justified.

I have mentioned the environmental opposition, derived from personal preferences, the 'I like it as it is' approach. This type of objector will often resort to such phrases as 'the need to preserve the quality of life'. The unassailable argument will be employed that happiness or contentment cannot be measured solely on a material scale and that industry and commerce ought to be able to lift their eyes above mere financial reality in order to appreciate the fundamental purposes of human existence. This should strike a response in all of us. The difficulty that arises is that the argument tends to resolve around our differing definitions of 'quality of life'. The fundamental question is whether the concept is definable in any meaningful terms. It is used as a qualitative statement and yet if it is to be used as a guide to action, ought it not to be quantifiable? If it is not quantifiable, then how do we compare one person's 'quality of life' with another's? This is dangerous ground indeed and one which has exercised the minds of political philosophers throughout the ages.[9]

Perhaps the most methodical attempt to solve this eternal problem was made in the first half of the nineteenth century by the school of political philosophers known as the 'Utilitarians'. The Utilitarians were anxious to get away from abstract thought, they valued ideas as means of serving social purposes and felt that philosophy should be based on experience, on the practicalities of human life.

One of the school's founders, Jeremy Bentham, developed the hedonistic concept that the basic guiding lines of human behaviour were 'pleasure' and 'pain'. He assumed that these two sensations were measurable and that a given amount of one would offset a like amount of the other. This 'hedonistic' calculus was developed with some skill by Bentham and by James Mill and his son John Stuart Mill.[10] This is not the place to discuss their philosophy, but their basic approach runs throughout our present day attitudes. They defined the aim of man as being 'the pursuit of happiness' and the 'avoidance of pain'. They were not concerned with the selfish search for individual happiness but rather considered an individual's own 'happiness' can only be attained in conjunction with that of others. The aim has to be to maximise the greatest good for the greatest number. In some sense this underlines much of our unspoken understanding of the nature of democracy. We believe that by giving everyone an equal vote and an equal chance to state his or her views, by some mysterious alchemy the greatest happiness for the greatest number will emerge.

---

[9] It is still salutory to compare the differing approaches of people like F.A. Hayek and R.H. Tawney. The gist of the arguments can be seen in the very titles of their best known works. In fact we could ask whether the only alternative to the *Road to Serfdom* is the *Acquisitive Society*.

[10] For a brief account of the development of these doctrines, see W.L. Davidson's *Political Thought in Britain from Bentham to John Stuart Mill* published by the Oxford University Press.

It would be easy to run through the arguments of the various philosophical schools which have attempted to define what is meant by 'happiness' and, in so far that the argument still continues, it may be safely assumed that no satisfactory answer has been found. Equally, my idea of 'quality of life' is unlikely to correspond with yours. I might see my 'quality of life' as being defined by my control over material possessions — whether I can live in a large house in the country, run three cars and not one, afford to holiday in the South of France each winter, while on the other hand you may consider the 'quality of life' to be the ability to free yourself from such economic pressures as to live a life of the maximum release from timetables, restrictions and the need to earn a living. Who is right? The question only needs asking to illustrate the futility of expecting an answer. To have agreement on what is meant by 'quality of life' would mean uniformity and an acceptance that we should all be alike. Most of us would regard this as being a stultifying philosophy, only acceptable in totalitarian states and only there because people are not given the opportunity to see the grass on the other side of the fence and to judge for themselves whether it is greener.

If we can accept that the 'quality of life' is indefinable and unquantifiable, then it is manifestly not a concept that is likely to be settled by appeals to the evidence. Despite this, much political and social argument is based on the implicit assumption that the protagonists' own views as to what makes an enhanced quality of life are self evident and that they can only be disputed on grounds of perversity or wilful self interest. Its relevance is that it is a notion which affects people's motivations and actions. If I believe that my 'quality of life' is threatened, then I will defend it even if I am unable to convince you what I mean by this concept. This is a laudable reaction: how many of the people who have defended the concept of liberty would have agreed on a definition of that most emotive of words. It is the belief not the rationale that matters. If people are motivated by their own view of the 'quality of life' to accept or reject particular propositions, then it is relevant to the manager. He must be aware of the different varieties of 'quality of life' that people hold dear and which they are prepared to defend. He is not obliged to agree with them, but he must recognise their presence. It is futile to enter into an argument about their respective merits, but essential to understand the power of their driving force.

From what I have said about the nature of management, it could be argued that the environment in its wider sense is the totality of the conditions in which the enterprise has to operate. These conditions may be physical, legal, political, social, or economic. All these various aspects go together to make up the overall environment in which people work. In recent years there has grown up a much more specialised meaning of the word 'environment'; that is when it is used to refer to the totality of the natural physical environment in which we all live and work. Far wider than the immediate physical surroundings of the work or dwelling place, it is concerned with the world environment. If you poison the atmosphere with atomic radiation in one part of the world this will affect, in time, the environment of the world in general. If one country's standards of clean air control are lax, the resulting pollution of the atmosphere could well affect other countries. Environment and ecology have become intertwined. Protection of endangered wild life species has become an environmental issue.

Until recently, the 'environment', in the sense of the immediate physical conditions surrounding the particular operation, was one of the fixed factors in any operation. It was felt that with few exceptions, nothing that the company or manager could do, could possibly have any major and lasting effect on that environment, although the environment could well affect the company. The fundamental cause for the major concern over environmental issues in the last twenty years has been the realisation that, in many cases, individual actions were adversely influencing this 'total' environment.

We have seen that the word 'environment' is used to describe all the individual 'environmental' issues, such as working, social and physical environments, as well as the totality. In any discussion it is important to be clear in which sense the word is being used, as it sometimes alters the weight of the argument. I must take more seriously an accusation that I may be causing physical harm to somebody, than that I am disturbing his quality of life.

Having had a look at what is meant by managing and what is meant by environment, we need to look now at the cement that binds the two together — the concept of responsibility.

Why don't 'they' do something about it?

We have already said that managers have to accept responsibility for their actions or non-actions in the environmental field. We expect 'them' to do something about it. 'How could "they" let this happen.' 'It is about time "they" did something about it.' 'What could you expect from "them"?' are all familiar comments on environmental themes. But who are 'they'? When we look closely, we find ourselves gazing in a mirror, for the final analysis — 'they' are 'we' — you and me. We see environmental faults in others, but not in ourselves and can always find good sound reasons for doing what we have to; but in the case of our opponents we tend to see their attitude as being one of wilful blind self interest!

The whole of the literature of management (and for that matter, political science) is littered with attempts to define authority and responsibility. On the face of it, these are simple concepts which everyone understands but in practice, when they are approached and analysed, then they tend to disintegrate into areas of vagueness. All too often, responsibility is used as a synonym for authority, and the two words are used wrongly in an interchangeable fashion. I can have a duty to do something without being resonsible. A soldier has a duty to carry out his orders, but he is not responsible for them.

Responsibility does *not* mean duty or authority. It is something which arises from the 'superior/subordinate' relationship. In simple language, it means that someone has the authority to require specific services from another person. It is that second person's duty to provide such services as and when they are required.

People all too frequently talk about delegating responsibility. This is a misuse of words. Responsibility cannot be delegated. If I am responsible for the safety of a mine, a ship or a factory, I cannot avoid my responsibilities by attempting to 'delegate' them. What I can do is delegate some of my *authority* to have the required actions carried out. Responsibility is an obligation to perform certain tasks, to behave in a particular way, and it is owed to one's superior.

To take the example of being responsible for the safety of a ship. If I am captain of such a vessel, I am responsible for its safety. I know that certain acts have to be carried out in order for the ship to be safe. I must ensure, for example, that the correct watches are kept and that the navigation is carried out in a proper manner. While I can certainly delegate the authority for ensuring that this work is done, — i.e. I do not need to carry out all the navigation myself or always be on watch — I cannot delegate the responsibility. Having delegated the authority, if the navigation proves to be faulty or the watches are not properly carried out, then the responsibility for whatever disasters overtake the vessel remains mine. You have only to examine the findings of courts of inquiry into shipping disasters to be made aware of this. There is no way in which I can delegate the responsibility. (In the last analysis, all I can do is hand over the total responsibility for the remit to somebody else and this has to be done with the agreement, explicit or implied, of my superiors.) It is the authority to get things done, and not the responsibility, which can be delegated.

So far, I have talked in general about responsibility. However, like the environment, it breaks down into various types and one type needs further examination — social responsibility. Of the various types of responsibility, this is one that increasingly concerns the manager.

Am I my brother's keeper?

The idea of social responsibility is based on the concept that nothing an individual can do can be independent of society as a whole. The actions that a manager takes in his everyday activity inevitably have an effect on society. The most obvious example of this would be the decision of a firm on whether to recruit school-leavers or to run down the labour force. We are all aware of the disruption that can be inflicted on a local community by the decision of the management of the local factory or organisation to cease its operations in that particular locality. Similarly, the possibility that a new process may increase the likelihood of explosions affects the local community and, as such, management has a responsibility (whether it decides to exercise it or not is a different matter) to take the possibility of such effects into account when deciding on a course of action.

If an organisation is sizeable in relation to the locality in which it operates, then most major actions that it takes have an impact on the social environment. These impacts can be positive as well as negative but, even where the organisation believes it is providing something the locality needs, it can still be in trouble. For instance, providing additional employment in the area through expansion could still raise fundamental social problems because of the pressures that this might place on local housing or on the social infrastructure, in the demand for school places, parking, shopping facilities and social amenities in general. Conversely, a decision to close down a factory, office or operating unit could cause social problems of a different kind. Local communities are demanding more and more that these effects be taken into consideration before the decisions are taken and are not impressed by the simple logic of the profit and loss account. This is exemplified in such actions as sit-ins/work-ins where employees refuse to accept the decision of the management that the enterprise must close, and insist on trying to find ways to keep it in operation. This can lead to co-operative ventures being formed, such as the Meridan Motor Cycle Co-operative and the unsuccessful attempt to run the *Scottish Daily News* on a co-operative basis.

Although the pressures of social responsibilities are well known and appreciated, it is only in recent years that there has been a move to try to identify, quantify and evaluate a company's performance in relation to such pressures.

Who is keeping the score?

The move towards 'social audits' is now becoming pronounced, particularly in the United States. The basic concept is that the conventional balance sheet, or the description of a company's performance purely in terms of the profit and loss account, is outmoded and that what is needed is an indication as to how the company or organisation has performed in relation to its social obligations. This has fostered proposals for direct public and consumer involvement in corporate affairs, in order to ensure that the social facets of an organisation's performance are correctly evaluated and understood. For the first time, organisations are becoming subject to the scrutiny of people who want to find fault with the purely traditional objectives of management and to ensure that the social aspects of a company's performance are taken into account in deciding on the merits or otherwise of its achievements.

To achieve given objectives in any form of social grouping, there is inevitably a sense of lost freedom of action. Every time we agree to co-operate in a group, whether as a member of the Cabinet or the local golf or tennis club, we, by definition, give up some of our individuality in order to pursue the interests of the group as a whole. While it might please me as an individual member of a golf club to close the subscription list so that I could be more sure of a game on a Saturday morning, I have to be brought to face the fact that, without a larger membership, I may not have a course to play on at all because the club could go broke. In such an event, I am likely to go along with the body of opinion that argues we ought to have a wider membership list. In this example, the motivation would be economic or commercial. But supposing we then had a further debate. Having accepted that we should widen the list, it might be argued we should not be prepared to accept certain categories of people as members. Supposing we said that we would not admit coloured people or people who are of a particular religion, then this would be regarded by some people outside the club as anti-social. As anti-social, in fact, as not admitting people with brown eyes or blond hair, or below 5ft 10in. While we would see these latter qualifications as being patently absurd, it is one of the tragedies of the modern world that we may not see that the other categories of exemption are equally indefensible. Whatever we may wish to do in that context will now be seen as having connotations of social responsibility and we may find it in our overall interests to modify our instinctive responses.

Why are we in business?

In the past it has often been argued that the purpose of business is to satisfy the economic wants of people for products and/or employment. The implication of this is that the companies concerned carry no social responsibility for the articles they produce. But is that, in fact, the case? Are we saying that, for example, the only reason pharmaceutical manufacturers do not produce heroin and sell it on the market, is that it is illegal? If we are not saying that, then we must be taking the view that heroin is not being sold to the general public because people would regard it as being socially irresponsible. Once this argument is accepted, then it becomes a matter of where the line is drawn on what a company regards as its social responsibility. This is, of course, a constantly shifting line, reflecting to some degree the changing and ethical values of the particular society. An example of this is the reaction in 1975 to the so-called 'Lockheed bribes scandal'. Such a disclosure of payments of the types of 'commission' which caused such a reaction would probably have attracted little attention ten years ago — apart, perhaps, to the size of the amounts involved!

In relation to standards and conditions of employment, many companies pay or provide above the minimum because they believe it to be worthwhile.

While it is true that the point at which enlightened self-interest merges into social responsibility is sometimes hard to judge, there is little doubt that quite a number of actions taken by organisations in the course of a year are motivated mainly by a feeling of social responsibility, rather than just the look of the accounts.

It has frequently been argued that questions involving social responsibility are in fact distractions from the main aim of the enterprise. The supporters of this view would consider that where something needs to be done in relation to a person's housing or working conditions, then the right way to see this carried out is by laying down minimum conditions in law rather than by relying on the attempts of 'do-gooders' to carry out what they see as their 'social responsibility'.

Those who advocate this view consider that these issues should be decided between the government and the company or between the government and the unions. This tends to ignore the areas or the times in which management and men, and now the consumers, have had unequal bargaining power.[11]

The third quarter of this century, has seen increasing comment on what has been termed by the eminent economist Professor Galbraith as, 'private affluence and public squalor'. Insofar as much of the public squalor has resulted from the actions of individual firms and organisations in the past, it is true to say that their reluctance, unwillingness, or inability to exercise some form of social responsibility, has resulted in these particular burdens being placed on the current generation. Coupled with this, there has been an increasing fear of the power of the firm. Up until the 1960s this concern expressed itself in anti-trust and monopoly legislation, aimed at preventing individual companies monopolising the market and then squeezing it in order to make 'unnaturally' high profits.

In the 1970s, fear of the firm has become even more sinister. The misguided attempts by some of the multinational companies to interfere, or at least to seem to be trying to interfere, in the political affairs of their host countries, has led to a widespread suspicion about their aims and objectives.[12] In some circles, they are now widely believed to be merely a coverup operation for the activities of their parent government. However idiotic such views might be, there is no disputing the concern that has been aroused amongst host nations by the activities of the multinational giants. In the last analysis, this could be described as fear that such companies are not acting in a socially responsible manner.

This concern with social responsibility is made more difficult by the almost

---

[11] For an interesting discussion of the strengths and weaknesses of the approach, see J.K. Galbraith *American Capitalism — the Concept of Countervailing Power*. He has since modified some of the views expressed in this relatively early work but the general thesis is a useful one.

[12] See for example Anthony Sampson's *The Sovereign State — the Secret History of International Telephone and Telegraph* and his *The Seven Sisters — a Study of the Great Oil Companies and the World they Made*.

impossible task of trying to define what we mean by the concept. The opponents of the spread of such an idea raise the question — how can a business act in a socially responsible way unless it knows and understands the social objectives and priorities of the particular environment in which it is operating? The problem is even more difficult than that. The company or organisation may fully understand the social objectives and priorities of the particular environment in which it is operating, but such objectives might be totally contrary to the objectives and policies of the government in the parent country. The most obvious example of this is South Africa. It is not difficult to know what the South African Government would regard as being socially responsible acts, but it is very debatable whether the same view would be taken by the parent government if the company happened to come from the United Kingdom or the United States. Is it socially responsible to pay a much lower wage to a coloured worker in South Africa than to a white worker doing a similar job? A moment's reflection will show it depends through which end of the telescope you are looking. There is, however, little doubt that, whatever a company in this situation does, it will be accused by the opposing government of not measuring up to its social responsibilities.

The problem need not be put in such stark terms. Is it socially responsible, for example, to pollute one area of the country in order to provide benefit in another? Or even more pertinently, is it socially responsible to avoid pollution in the parent country by exploiting resources overseas and creating the pollution in the host country? In fact, the view will vary according to the climate of opinion in each of the countries concerned. It is not even helpful to decide to concentrate on your social responsibility purely in relation to one or the other of the countries concerned, because it is at least possible that the social priorities, and therefore the social responsibilities, of any particular country will alter in time, particularly if there is a change in government.

If that is the case, is there much point in pursuing the idea of organisations accepting some form of social responsibility? I think there is, but once again it tends to boil down to individual actions on the part of each member of the organisation. In the same way that responsibility cannot be delegated downwards, it is arguable that, similarly, it cannot be delegated upwards. If I decide that in order to achieve my objectives I am going to act in what might be regarded as a socially irresponsible way then, unless I can show that I have been instructed to so act, the total responsibility must fall on my shoulders. Even where I had been instructed to act in a particular way, it is still my responsibility if I decide to carry out these instructions rather than face the consequences of disobedience. This concept was clearly established in the Nuremberg war trials where those accused of mass murder and extermination of Jews, resorted to the 'excuse' that they were only acting under orders. It was made manifestly clear on that occasion that such orders cannot override the moral imperative on all of us to behave in what could be regarded as a 'morally and socially responsible way'. We have therefore to make some attempt to define our own guidelines in this somewhat uncharted area.

With all the varying social objectives of the groups that make up a community, it is almost impossible for a company to decide on positive courses of action to show acceptance of social responsibility that will not lead to increased problems. However, social responsibility can be seen in a negative way, and that is to avoid actions which unnecessarily prevent people achieving their own objectives and satisfactions. It could be regarded as being a personal obligation of any decision-taker to ensure that when he acts in his company's interest, he does what he can to ensure that the right and legitimate interests of others are not unnecessarily impinged upon. In other words, he may be aware that the actions proposed will affect the achievement of the objectives of some other individuals, but he should make such a decision consciously in full knowledge of the outcome of his actions. He will therefore be able to defend himself or his company against any attacks that might be forthcoming on the grounds of the overall benefits which he is seeking to achieve. He will in fact be echoing Jeremy Bentham's precept of pursuing 'the greatest happiness of the greatest number'.

The term 'responsible' raises difficult ethical and legal questions, many of which are irresolvable, but acceptance on the part of the manager that such issues exist will help in deciding the best course of action.

In considering what society and management might do in these situations, sooner or later the words 'preserve' and 'conserve' are brought into use. Conservation sounds a very acceptable concept, so let us examine it in more detail.

Conservation and preservation

This is a word which, again, is often used in different ways. The concept of conservation is a respectable one. It implies the opposite of waste. The idea that we should conserve our energy until such time as we may need it, that we should conserve our resources so that we are not caught without them, and that we should conserve those things that we wish to keep and protect, is surely a reasonable one?

Unfortunately, the word is often used implicitly or explicitly by some groups, who regard themselves as being interested in conservation, as meaning 'to keep entire, to retain or to preserve'. The basis of my argument is that there is a world of difference between the idea of conservation and that of preservation. Preservation means keeping things as they are on the assumption that any change must be for the worse and therefore avoided. 'Preservation' not only implies a 'no growth' economy, but also almost literally a 'no change' economy.[13] This must be so because growth implies greater use of the natural

---

[13] For arguments in support of changing the emphasis on economic growth, see E.J. Mishen *Costs of Economic Growth* and the profoundly thought provoking contribution by E.F. Schumacher in *Small is Beautiful*.

resources than is already the case and even a no growth economy, if it involves change, will alter the balance in supply and demand of the various resources being used to meet the economic requirements of the world. As it is an impossibility that we can carry on with the same mix of use of resources as we do at present (if only because some of these resources will be used up in the relatively near future), we must change. If we have change, then we cannot have total preservation of the world as it is.

The argument then moves into the realm of what changes are acceptable and what changes are not. In other words, we are back into the familiar territory of alternatives. There is no point in getting out on the limb of asserting that without resource X the world will grind to a halt, because this is not the experience of mankind at present. Similarly, there is no realistic future in spending time trying to preserve the *status quo*, because it simply cannot be preserved. The argument has to be in terms of which changes are totally unacceptable and can be avoided, and those which are necessary but require modification before they become acceptable, and thus turn out to be the lesser of the inevitable evils.

The concept of preservation is entirely removed from that of conservation. Preservation means keeping things as they are — unchanged. It means fighting a perpetual rearguard action with nothing but ultimate defeat facing you. Of course, it will prove possible to win battles here and there, but these would tend to be temporary and, in the last analysis, the war will be lost. To aim at outright preservation is to aim at ossifying a particular structure of the environment at a particular moment in time. This seems to go flatly against the whole nature of human existence and would appear to be a counsel of despair.

Conservation, on the other hand, when correctly used, should be the saving of our resources and our energy, so that we do not dissipate them all at once but make the best possible use of them to meet the legitimate needs of our society. In Max Nicholson's *The Environmental Revolution* he says 'Conservation means all that man thinks and does to soften his impact on his natural environment and to satisfy his own true needs while enabling that environment to continue in healthy working order'.

3   How did we get here anyway?

You can't beat nature!

At some time or other, most of us have looked at a piece of countryside and have rejoiced in the fact that it is 'unspoiled'. By that, we have meant that we felt we were looking at something which was the product of nature, not of man. As 'every prospect pleases and only man is vile',[1] we have assumed that 'natural' is intrinsically better.

This is an attitude which is at the heart of many of the criticisms put forward in relation to visual amenity. 'Natural' must equal 'best', therefore change of any kind should be resisted. It is not immediately apparent why this argument should be taken as self evident. We do not assume that swamplands, tropical forests and deserts, however 'natural', are necessarily environments which would not benefit from change. Much time, effort and skill has been devoted to bring about such changes. (It is noteworthy that most of the people who object to such changes do not have to try and eke a living out of such environments).

Please note that I am not arguing that *all* such environments should be changed or that they make no contribution to the quality of life on this planet. I am simply arguing that, because an environment is 'natural', it is not therefore axiomatic that attempts should be made to keep it in its pristine condition.

Unfortunately, some of the recent popularisations of the ecologists tend to suggest that, because the whole epic of natural selection has brought us to our present state, the current balance of nature must represent the best of all possible worlds. Therefore it must not be disturbed. The impression is given that any change must be for the worse. This is such self-evident nonsense that it is surprising it is implicit in so many of the arguments put forward by so-called environmentalists.

Let us take the argument a stage further and try to establish what we mean by 'natural'. To do this we must look at our landscape in an historical context.

---

[1] Reginald Heber, Bishop of Calcutta

When we do this we find that the fundamental weakness of this approach is that of deciding what is a 'natural landscape'.

With very rare exceptions, there is no such thing as a 'natural landscape' or a 'natural habitat'. When we look closely enough, the effect of mankind is almost always there to be seen. Although, to quote again from Max Nicholson's *Environmental Revolution*: 'Few people have eyes sufficiently trained to recognise many of the more subtle marks which man has left', all too often the results can be seen only too plainly.

Let us start by looking at what the majority of people would regard as being the most natural part of the environment, the countryside itself.

The first effect that man's arrival had was to change the landscape by cutting down trees, both in order to build shelters and to provide fuel. As agriculture began, clearings were made in order to grow crops and little by little the great forests of Britain were eaten into by the impact of man's 'environment'. Over the last 700 years there have always been critics in society who have complained about the erosion of the forest lands of Britain and the reduction in the number of trees. In fact, reading back through the literature, it was at a very early stage indeed that people began to worry about the deforestation that was taking place although, in all fairness, their concern was mainly to maintain the quality of the hunting rather than from any higher ecological motive.[2]

Once the farmer had moved in and begun to clear the trees, his stock helped in the process by eating the young trees and shrubs. This, in itself, resulted in the creation of grasslands. For some centuries, there was the Anglo-Saxon pattern of open-field farming, with each peasant having narrow strips of land in all the fields in order to ensure that no one was unduly favoured or put to a disadvantage. The overall impression of the countryside must have been of wide open spaces. As well as these strips, there were areas of common lands where grazing was free for all and the villagers had a right to seek fuel for their fires.

In the uplands, the pattern of development is clearly visible. It is easy to see the varying limits of cultivation, and to identify those areas which were previously cultivated or used for grazing, now either much less used or fallen entirely into disuse. The pattern of dry walling over the Pennine Hills shows the attempts that were made to use all the moorside for sheepfarming. There was a similar expansion of use of land in Britain in the Second World War when the accent was on growing more food in order to cut down on the need to import during the blockade. The slogan at that time was 'Dig for Victory' and a great deal of money was ploughed into marginal farming in order to try

---

[2] A growing population resulted in pressure to increase agricultural land by clearing forests and the kings were torn between their love for hunting, and their desire to maintain the greatest possible extent of land under 'Forest law', and the needs of the people. They managed to compensate themselves by charging heavily for licences those who wished to plough up forest land — see D.M. Stanton, *English Society in the Middle Ages*, Chapter 3.

to maximise the yield of the land.[3] When the War came to an end, the boundaries of cultivation fell back, as they did in the seventeenth century.

If we look at the historical development of, say, the English countryside in a little more detail, we can make the bold assertion that the countryside of England is in no sense natural. It is, in the words of Henry James, 'a masterpiece of produced beauty', the result of generation after generation of daily work on a natural habitat by ordinary men and women providing their daily bread, coupled with changes made by the owners of the land to improve its productivity and provide them with their own forms of pleasure and relaxation. In a few instances it was the direct result of that great breed of English landscape architects indulging themselves and their masters by consciously trying to create a view or vista that would delight future generations.[4] In most cases, however, this was a by-product, an unlooked for bonus. The main influences were changes in the population and in the demands placed on the land for food, and the agricultural and industrial revolutions.

If we were able to look at the pattern of the countryside in England or, for that matter, any European country, in say the eleventh century, we could see substantial expanses of forest, moor or swamp, with a sprinkling of villages linked together by rivers or unsurfaced roads. These villages would be small and although there would be some towns to be seen, few of them would have more than ten thousand people. Over the next five hundred years, changes took place, but without any tremendous rapidity. The changes were those of degree. There was greater specialisation, the towns increased in size and number and, although the population fluctuated to a considerable extent because of war, famine and disease, this trend continued.

There was a move from a substantial degree of self-sufficiency, whether of the individual peasant or the local community based on the manor, towards the market economy. For most of the period the whole structure of society depended, finally, on the produce of the soil. The methods of organising such production were diverse and, although we tend to think of medieval agriculture solely in terms of manorial organisation, where unfree villagers (villeins and serfs) cultivated their Lord's domain as the price of their serfdom, and of the use of a holding of land, we must remember that the agricultural actiVities of the great monasteries stamped their own pattern on the countryside.[5] There was in reality great variety in the forms of land tenure and cultivation. Whatever the form of the ownership, the organisation of the work

---

[3] This effort was not limited to traditional farming. Much disused land within city boundaries was brought into use as allotments to help augment the food supplies. By 1943 there were some 1.4 million allotments in use as compared with 0.8 million in 1939 — figures quoted by Angus Calder in *The People's War*.

[4] It was not for nothing that the outstanding practitioner Lancelot Brown achieved world renown under the sobriquet of 'Capability Brown'.

[5] Their dissolution by Henry VIII, and their break up into landed estates, caused further changes.

imposed a pattern on the field structure of the countryside, which can be seen in some places to this day. This is particularly true of the medieval open-field system which has left behind the ridge and furrow pattern, plainly visible in some of the Midland counties of England.

As the economic tide turned in favour of agriculture, and there was an increasing amount of money to be made, prosperous owners and farmers wished to add to their acreage, and they sought to do this by beginning to cultivate some of the waste lands, and more importantly, by encroaching on the common lands. The enclosure movement in England was well under way in the thirteenth century. The Statute of Merton, which was passed in the year 1235, provided that the lord could occupy wasteland, if he left enough for his free tenants. It made no mention, however, of the unfree tenants, i.e. the villeins and serfs, and they had no protection against these inroads into their only hope for self-sufficiency.[6]

The real pressure for enclosure took place in England in the seventeenth century. Growing markets and rising prices made yeomen and landlords alike take steps to maximise the profit from their land. They did this by consolidating scattered arable strips into compact fields and pressing ahead with enclosing the commons, wastes and woodlands to provide additional cultivateable acres and larger meadows or better pastures. It was this that led to the creation of the English landscape as we now know it, and accept as 'natural'.

The technology of agriculture increased the pressure for enclosures as the seventeenth century came to an end. The modern methods of farming that were first developed in Norfolk, based on the rotation of crops and the proper use of fertilisers, seeding and mechanical techniques, enormously improving the productivity of farmland, depended upon being able to protect the land so cultivated from outside influences.[7] It was impossible to think of major cultivation without a sufficient number of clearly defined, protected fields. This had to be done by planting hedgerows and clearing woodlands of anything else that happened to be in the way. For this reason the House of Lords in the eighteenth century found itself faced with enclosure bill after enclosure bill, and although local inhabitants protested, often very vociferously, that these bills were destroying their way of life, the procedure went on remorselessly.

There is little doubt that enclosure caused much human suffering, but it did bring about a major improvement in agricultural production and productivity throughout the country. It was not only a question of crops, but the new breeding techniques with improved strains of plants and animals, could also only be applied when enclosure took place.

The aim of the enclosure movement was strictly commercial and no

[6] The Statute of Merton was followed by the Statute of Westminster in 1285, under which Edward I gave the Lord of the Manor the right to enclose the commonland.
[7] The best known innovators were perhaps Jethro Tull and Viscount 'Turnip' Townshend.

attention was paid to the effect that it would have on the 'natural countryside'. But it created the patchwork of hedges and fields which we know so well and regard as being typical English countryside, and it introduced the regularity of fields, often split up by straight lines of hawthorn hedges with shelter belts of trees.

Thus, the landscape that we regard as being only natural, and the one that we are most accustomed to, is a highly artificial creation. It is the unintended result of the enclosure acts and the proposals of the Enclosure Commission, which, in turn, were dictated by the economic needs and necessities of the agricultural industry at that particular time. Although it does not seem likely that they envisaged the end result in terms of landscape, the Enclosure Commission certainly intended to introduce some uniformity into their actions. They laid down specific and regular rules to bring their enclosures into being and these inevitably led to a specific and regular pattern in the countryside. According to Heaton's *Economic History of Europe* some four thousand Enclosure Acts had been passed, affecting some six million acres (about a fifth of the country) by 1845.

To facilitate the enclosure movement, thousands of miles of ditches and hedges were dug and planted, and many of the remaining trees were chopped down to provide wood for the fences. However, with commendable thought for the future, the Commissioners planted new hedges with trees at regular intervals and endeavoured to make good some of the decrease in resources they were causing.

When this work was first carried out, the landscape must have appeared most unattractive and uninviting. The ditches that were dug must have looked like small scars across the countryside, as it would be many years before they were screened by hedges and trees, at this stage only insignificant seedlings.

In the initial stages, it would have been impossible for most people to envisage the end result as we know it. At the time that it was carried out, it was seen in many eyes as the destruction of the land as the people then knew it. The old countryside was seen as being killed off in the interest of the ruthless efficiency that had commercial advantage as its sole aim. A theme which has a remarkably modern ring to it.[8]

Much of the pleasure we get from looking at the landscape now is the result of actions which, at the time, were bitterly and strongly resisted by the traditionalists as an affront to the land they knew. It is true that it evolved over a considerable period of time and was not in any sense an 'instant landscape' but, nevertheless, it is man-made. For examples of instant landscape, a better impression is obtained by looking at North America in the nineteenth century, the move westward and the creation of new homesteads, farmlands, territories and, eventually, States. The artificial nature of some of these areas can be clearly appreciated by a close look at a political atlas of the United States,

---

[8] As Oliver Goldsmith acidly puts it in his *Deserted Village* — 'Where wealth accumulates and men decay.'

where many of the State lines in the West appear to have been derived from an assiduous application of the ruler and the pen on a blank sheet of paper. Much of the landscape gives the same impression — acre after acre, mile after mile, of plains, with few trees and fewer breaks in what can be a monotonous landscape.

Nan Fairbrother has argued that the American West shows the direct impact of an industrial society on the natural habitat, with no transition of man-made agricultural landscape. The contrast with the English experience is marked indeed.

I am not trying to make out an argument that if commercial advantage is followed, the effects on the environment will be beneficial. This would be foolish and a totally insupportable case to put forward. What I do want to establish is that much of what we take as the standard of present day excellence is not natural but has been created, whether by chance or design, by the activities or the interference of man, much of it as a by-product of his main activity. We should therefore look at carefully thought-out proposals for change through eyes as unbiased as possible.

Home sweet home

With the changing nature of industrial activity, man's needs for a roof over his head also changed. From living and working on the land, the pattern changed to industrialisation. Long before the industrial revolution, as we know it, towns were growing in size. They were based very much on their function as market centres where the produce could be bought and sold or bartered and where the agricultural workers could get the services and goods they could not produce themselves. Towns also had a strategic importance — they provided the necessary strongholds into which the population in the countryside could retreat when faced with foreign invaders.

The major influence on the environment of town living came with the full-scale development of the so-called industrial revolution in the late eighteenth and nineteenth centuries.

The industrial revolution brought with it the need to gather together large quantities of labour in a limited area. The new mills and factories found that, with their new mechanical techniques, they could work on a scale previously unimaginable.

The very size and scale of these operations brought with them a demand for a concentration of labour which previously could not have been contemplated. When you had a mill or a factory which needed hundred of workpeople to keep it going, you had the problem of finding them. They had to be attracted from the countryside (where many of them had in fact been displaced by the enclosure movement); they had to be brought together in one place and they had to be provided with some form of accommodation. Housing was put up near the mill or factory and it spread away from the centre buildings, in the all too familiar long, straight lines of close-backed houses, radiating out from the nucleus of the work place itself. That such developments had a profound effect on the environment cannot be doubted. Whether one's view of them is taken from the many parliamentary *Blue Books* of the period, describing the conditions and the habits of the labouring classes, or from the imaginative insights of the nineteenth century novelists, the result is the same — we are left with a feeling of the way in which the lives of the people were moulded and, in many cases, warped by the conditions in which they lived and worked.

It was this period which saw the birth of the industrial town as we know it. The greatest was Manchester, the centre of the cotton boom in the early part of the nineteenth century. The town grew six fold in a period of sixty years and aroused both admiration and horror. Visited by statesmen and scholars it was regarded as both the wonder and the curse of the modern world. It represented man's apparently unbounded power for good and for evil, at one and the same time, becoming a symbol of progress on the one hand and of squalor on the other. It provided Engels with much of his material for his seminal *The Condition of the Working Classes in England* published in 1845, which in turn deeply influenced Marx. The birthplace of new and alarming social relationships, it is perhaps not surprising that one of the few clashes between the military and the working population to occur in England in the nineteenth century took place on St Peter's Fields, Manchester in 1819. This confrontation culminated in eleven people being killed[9] and hundreds injured, when the Yeomanry charged the helpless crowd. The ironically named 'Battle of Peterloo' seemed to crystallise the hope and the promise, as well as the potential disaster, which this type of township was creating. This unplanned environment was one which could not be looked at with the same satisfaction as the changed environment of the English countryside.

It is easy to be superior about the failure of our forefathers in respect of housing and town planning. It is arguable that our efforts to solve the same types of problems have been conspicuous successes. The building of high-rise flats, while possibly a technological achievement on the part of the planners, architects and builders, has been far from a sociological success. Here is another example where decisions made by individual managers, whether operating in the field of planning, architecture or politics, have created an environment far different from the one that they intended. It is a significant commentary that, whereas people had to be compelled to leave their old overcrowded terrace housing, local authorities in some instances have been unable to keep the new high-rise flats occupied and some have been vandalised to an extent that has made them uninhabitable. In very few instances was sufficient thought given to the purely environmental effects that the proposals

---

[9] Strictly speaking, this occurred before the main expansion of the town but the concentration of workers in poor housing had already begun. There is a good account by Joyce Marlow in *The Peterloo Massacre*.

would have. It seems more likely that they saw the problem in the narrow terms of efficiently creating the maximum number of housing units in the shortest time. How much better it would have been if everybody involved had asked themselves more frequently what were the environmental effects of the decisions they were taking.

The whistle of a train

Ironically, the industrial revolution did not initially have a major effect on the landscape. The introduction of machinery into the textile industry called for running water to provide the power.[10] The first effect was therefore the building of mills by streams, which nowadays we would consider to be picturesque and traditional. The first major invention that was to have a profound impact on the landscape was that of the steam engine. This liberated the factory from dependence on running water. It could be built anywhere. Energy could be supplied in the form of coal, transported to the factory and turned into steam. It then became obvious that it would be sensible and convenient to group factories or mills together in one centre and to provide houses around them. Once this was realised, the industrial town and the industrial slum were well on their way to being born.

The development of the steam engine led eventually to the other invention which had a profound effect on the landscape of the country, the railway.

The railway caused what was probably the first outcry among what we would now term environmentalists.[11] In his book *The History of the English Railway*, published as long ago as 1851, a Mr Francis reports that

> 'The country gentleman was told that the smoke would kill the birds
> as they passed over the locomotive ... foxes and pheasants would
> cease in the neighbourhood of a railway. The race of horses would
> be extinguished ... cows, it was said, would cease to yield their milk,
> Vegetation would cease wherever the locomotive passed. The value
> of land would be lowered by it, the market gardener would be
> ruined by it ...'

Ridiculous as these fears now appear, their ghosts still walk on occasions, opposing some twentieth century form of development.

The visual effect of the railway was profound. It required bridges, tunnels, viaducts, stations, railway track itself, and the building of railway towns to service this new all-embracing monster. But, more than that, it affected the

---

[10] The first textile factory was built as early as 1719 at Derby for the manufacture of silk by a secret manufacturing process which was allegedly stolen from the Italians. It was powered by a large water wheel.

[11] The outcry against the destruction of the forests of England in the fifteenth and sixteenth centuries was more of a political than an environmental argument. The fear was that we would not have enough wood to build ships for the Navy.

landscape indirectly, by facilitating the creation of bigger towns and eventually suburbia. No longer was it necessary for people to live within walking distance of their work. They could now live a considerable distance away and still travel comfortably to and from their daily task.

The effect of the railway on the landscape can hardly be overestimated, and it aroused the utmost horror and indignation at the time. Nowadays, we regard the railways with nostalgia. We see the old viaducts and railway tracks as something to be preserved, something which we believe add to rather than detract from our landscape. Yet, at the time, there was furious opposition from the preservationists of the day that this desecration would destroy not only the character of the countryside, but also the character of the people. In *The Making of the English Landscape*, W.G. Hoskins quotes Wordsworth, who, writing to the *Morning Post*, decided,

> 'We have too much hurrying about in these islands, much for idle pleasure, and more from over activity in the pursuit of wealth without regard to the good or happiness of others'.

In fact, nothing of the kind happened — the railway blended into the landscape and became part of it. It became something we expected to see, and something we enjoyed seeing. The opposition to the early railway is so similar to that which has grown up against new motorways and freeways that I wonder whether over the next fifty years we shall come to regard our modern motorway network in the same benevolent light.

A car in every garage

This takes us on to one of the major changing forces in the environment of the present century, that of the internal combustion engine. Its development in the form of personal transport in particular, has totally changed our environment, both in terms of concept and achievement.

It has not been just a question of having to build roads or to maintain them to high standards or to endure the higher volume of traffic passing our doors. Traffic has in a real way caused our historic town centres to crumble and to be changed out of all recognition. The volume of traffic has done more to damage some of our ancient buildings in thirty years than the ravages of time have done in the previous three hundred. In some cases we didn't even bother to let the traffic do its worst, we simply pulled down the buildings in the name of improving the traffic flow and totally transformed town centres, ancient and modern.

Many a small town or village, which has found itself on one of the trunk routes to and from the Continent, has been made only too well aware of the havoc that can be caused by the traffic volume on our congested roads. But the classic example of the damage that the internal combustion engine can do to the atmosphere can be seen in cities like Los Angeles where the combination of air pollution from motor vehicles coupled with climatic conditions, has led to a crisis situation. In Sao Paulo, city legislation has been introduced to provide for three levels of emergency, when the second one is declared the movement of all road vehicles must cease. (The final stage calls for cessation of industry.) Traffic in that city can literally grind to a stop.

The development of public awareness to this kind of pollution, has led to the introduction of new regulations on the emission of fumes from vehicles and this, in turn, has had a considerable effect on the structure and economics of the car industry. This is a classic example of the way in which environmental matters, which it seemed that manufacturers could afford to ignore, have in the end become a major factor in limiting management decisions. With hindsight, they may well be wishing that they had taken different courses of action sooner and so avoided some of the present difficulties.

The car has led to a complete recasting of the roles of town and country. Whereas at one time the functions seemed to be quite distinct, they have now merged together for, at one time, people who needed to work in a town, lived there. The automobile changed all this and it is now increasingly common for people to live in the country and work in the town. They have begun to use villages as dormitories. Once this began to happen, started by the railways, aided by the motor car, villages grew far beyond their natural size, often without developing the facilities and amenities that a community of this new size required.

The problem is even greater because, understandably, the interests of the people who live and work in the villages do not necessarily coincide with the interests of the 'incomers', who want to live in a village because it is a pretty and a peaceful place to be in. For those who live and work in the village, their interest is in maintaining work there and they may well be prepared to sacrifice the picturesqueness of the village in order to maintain employment or to extend their own particular interest. However, the incomers are likely to resist strongly any proposals that would lead to the diminution in its attractiveness. It is therefore quite easy to get a conflict between the two groups of people because their objectives are different. This is frequently seen when industrial development which would affect amenities, but would also provide jobs, is proposed.

The situation is even worse where the 'city folk' are merely seeking a second, or a holiday home, in the village. In such situations, the conflicts can be strong. A classic example of this in Britain, was in a battle that took place over the proposal by RTZ to prospect for copper in the Snowdonia National Park in North Wales. The proposal was finally withdrawn by the company but, before this happened, it was interesting to see that, although there was much local opposition to the proposal, a lot of it came from people who did not live in the area, but merely enjoyed going there for a holiday, or had holiday homes or caravan sites there. Some of the local residents who lived in the area the whole year round, supported by the Welsh Nationalist Party (Plaid Cymru), argued in favour of such a development in the light of the work it could bring to a severely depressed area with high rates of unemployment.

I am at the moment, of course, making out the advocate's case against the internal combustion engine, but I am fully aware of the tremendous advantages that it has bestowed on the community at large. The point I am trying to make is that whether for good or for evil, the car has had a profound effect on our environment in more ways than the obvious ones.

I have developed the example of the automobile at some length because to each of us as individuals, the car is a matter of convenience and we rarely stop to think of the environmental changes that have been, or are being brought about, by its use. We tend to think of damage to the environment as only coming from activities which we regard as in some way undesirable in themselves. This is far from the truth. Take, for example, something as desirable and necessary as water. Everyone will agree we must take adequate steps to provide proper water supplies which will meet our needs. Unfortunately, such actions often cut across other people's environmental interests in a very severe way. To provide additional reservoirs usually means flooding valleys and this in turn means, in heavily populated countries, physically moving families and communities out of valleys in which they have lived their whole lives, into some other area. Almost inevitably, reservoir sites tend to be in the most beautiful parts of the country and this immediately sets up an environmental argument. The interests of those who will benefit from the new reservoir and those who will suffer from it, are diametrically opposed and there is usually little point of contact. People in the area where the reservoir is to be created are seldom in need of additional water supplies. They very often see their overriding need as being to maintain the *status quo*.

When we move on to the development of new industries, new technologies and new techniques, then the problems are more obvious. We have to face up to the fact that each new industrial activity in the last two hundred years had tended to bring some type of pollution in its wake. In time, if public opinion demands it, we catch up with such environmental effects by means of laws and regulations, but unless such action arises from a disaster, the time lag tends to be a long one.

We are all aware of the pollution caused by the older industries of the industrial revolution — coal, iron, steel. In fact, a great deal of time has been spent in the last twenty-five years trying to remedy the effects of the environmental damage caused by these industries over the last century.[12]

The first moves towards clean air were in relation to taking the smoke caused by the inefficient burning of coal out of the atmosphere. But this only dealt with visible pollution and the greatest dangers now appear to be from pollution which cannot be seen by the naked eye. While it is often thought that

[12] See, for example, the *Annual Reports* of the National Coal Board.

pollution is something that arises from the older technologies, this is a misunderstanding. The visible pollution of the older technologies is there for all to see and so are the efforts which have been made successfully by these industries to prevent pollution in their current activities. We now find that we have to worry more about many of the latest technologies simply because they are new and their effects may not have been anticipated. The newer technologies, such as the chemical industries and nuclear power, are areas in which increasing concern has been shown about environmental aspects, arising out of all the damage which has been caused when accidents have occurred.

So far we have looked at a number of ways in which we have modified our own environment. Many of them are not self apparent and are best seen if we list the main areas of activity which have produced a profound effect on the environments in which we live. These are: farming; industrialisation; development of transport; new technologies, such as nuclear power, the chemical industry, etc.

In this context it will be seen, if we think about it for a moment, that our present environment is the direct product of a multiplicity of managerial decisions taken over the last two hundred years, by managers like ourselves. The frightening thing about the individual decisions is that, in all probability, they were taken without a moment's thought about their environmental repercussions.

The farmer, concerned with improving his productivity and the yield from the land, pressed ahead with enclosures and the clearance of woodland. His counterpart today is concerned with productivity when he pulls up the hedgerows, some of which have taken centuries to grow, in order to get larger and more productive fields.

The industrialist or the factory owner was concerned to maximise his profitability and his efficiency, when he developed housing around his place of employment, in order to gather his work force in one spot. The continuing transport revolution by way of canals, railways, roads to airports, has promoted the convenience of man, but has also undoubtedly brought severe environmental change in its wake. The attempts to harness the forces of nature in the form of nuclear power, have themselves brought the possibility of nuclear damage.

Ironically, even the pursuit of desirable ends can produce major detrimental environmental effects. It can be argued, for example, that the tremendous effect of modern medicine in destroying many of the diseases which have been the scourge of mankind since time began, has sustained the massive population increase which, it could also be argued, forms the basis of most of our environmental concerns.

It is all too apparent that our environment is, and always will be, the result of millions of managerial decisions, most of them taken with little attention to their environmental importance or implications. Most of the individual decisions are not particularly significant in themselves, but they are as a part of the totality, and therefore managers should be aware of the environmental implications of all their actions.

Decisions of managers in relation to environmental matters have, in most cases up till now, only been modified by the legal restraints operating at the time the decisions were taken. Because the law inevitably tends to be the ossification of a particular viewpoint in time, the legal restrictions are often behind the technology they attempt to control. This leads to pressures, once the law is invoked, to provide in statute for future changes and development which have not yet materialised. This can be unnecessarily restrictive.

If managers want to avoid unnecessary heavy handed legal interference in their affairs, then they have to be prepared to see that their activities take full account of the environmental aspects which are susceptible to criticism and complaint. If we managers are making the future, let us try to make it one we can be proud of. The world our children, and our children's children, will live in depends in environmental terms, on the decisions of today's managers.

How did we get here anyway?

Because of the decisions of people like you and me.

4   We never used to have an environment

Where did it come from?

Environment is an impressive sounding word, but a relative newcomer to our political and social vocabulary.[1] Its very use seems to add significance and moment to any comment. But it is not a word with which we were familiar, even a dozen years ago. Why has it suddenly appeared and why is it so suddenly significant? To some extent we are in the position of the man who found he had been speaking 'prose' all his life, without knowing it. We have to be careful not to be over impressed by the mere fact of a new nomenclature. We should not allow ourselves to get too excited merely because we have learnt a new name for something that has been there all the time. Is that the present case? Have we simply developed a different way of analysing our human predicament, which merely adds perspective to a fundamentally unchanging view? I am suggesting that this is not the case. We have broadened our understanding of the interaction between man and the environment, and at a time when this interdependence is alleged to be reaching breaking strain.

Will it go away?

If it is true that environmental issues have only come to be generally recognised as matters of public concern in the last decade or so,[2] the obvious question is, why should this be? What has happened to arouse this feeling and, is it likely that it will fade with equal rapidity?

In the same way that we are only conscious of the blessing of good health when we fall ill, we have become aware of the importance of the environment only as some of the implications of neglect have become apparent.

---

[1] A dictionary definition is worth recalling: 'a surrounding; conditions influencing development of growth'.

[2] The relative novelty of the concept can be seen by referring to the index of any modern history of Britain published before 1960. You are unlikely to find 'environment' or 'environmentalists' mentioned there.

We can press the analogy further. Those who have experienced a few bouts of illness are more likely to be on the look out for symptoms of future maladies (whether real or imaginary). There are all too many environmental hypochondriacs at large — the difficulty is in recognising genuine symptoms when they occur.

There have been a number of genuine environmental illnesses in recent decades, occurrences that created real cause for concern. This has meant that the monitoring of symptoms has become much more widespread, but not necessarily more perceptive. Even if the symptoms decline, it is unlikely that this situation will be reversed. Unfortunately it is much more likely that the pains will get worse. This is because of three basic factors:

1. The increasing complexity of the relationship between man and nature.
2. The world population explosion.
3. The demand for continuing improvements in living standards which, once having been awakened, is not likely to slumber again.

'Please sir, I want some more'

Young Oliver Twist's request was modest indeed but it has continued to be echoed in much less deserving circumstances and in less polite forms, it assails the ears of politicians the world over.

Whatever the attitude taken by ecologists or economists, I believe that the pressure of individuals, expressed through the selfish medium of the nation state (which has long outlived its usefulness), will increase the demands on world resources rather than reduce them. There is no sign that the cult of the nation state is on the wane. There are far more so called 'nations' today than there were at the end of the Second World War. We could do with more like Shakespeare's Captain MacMorris, in *Henry V*, who responding to Fluellen's comment that there were 'not many of your nation ....' demanded to know 'Of my nation? What is my nation? Is a villain and a bastard and a knave and a rascal. What is my nation? Who talks of my nation.' (*Act 3 Scene 2.*) But while we must work towards recognition of the underlying resource problems of the world and derive more rational means of arriving at fair and equitable solutions, it would be foolish to assume that we shall be able to achieve the millennium overnight.

There is, however, a much stronger reason than the crude selfishness of individuals and of nations for believing that increasing demands on resources will be the pattern of the future.

The population explosion alone is of such frightening proportions that it seems destined to ensure that the demands of the human race on the resources of the earth will continue to grow at an alarming rate. The vast majority of us will continue to demand more and more of the world's limited resources in the shape of increased living standards. It would appear that this is true whatever the standard of living of a particular country. The facility for rapid adjustment to ever increasing living standards is not narrowly confined.

It has been estimated that, at the beginning of the Christian era, there was a world population of around 250 million people. This took some 1600 years to double. By 1750, it is thought that there were 725 million people in the world. By then, the rapid growth had commenced and by 1800 the world population had risen to 900 million, and by 1900 to 1600 million; but between 1900 and 1970, the population had more than doubled to 3600 million people. Even with the recent relative slowing down in the birth rate, it seems more than likely that it will reach a figure of between 6000 million and 7000 million by the year 2000.

To put these figures into context, if the demands on the world resources are not to increase above present levels then, on average, each individual's demands on natural resources will have to halve in the next twenty-five years.

I must stress that this is not the task we are setting ourselves. It merely indicates the size of the problem to which we have to seek solutions. There will certainly be a shift from one resource to another over the next twenty years and substitutes may, in fact must, be found for scarce materials. The opponents of the *Limits to Growth* approach have rightly pointed out that with increasing shortfalls in supply the pricing mechanism will ensue that demand for those resources will fall; but many of them seem to have missed the point that in many cases we are talking about non-substitutable goods for which the demand will remain, in economists' terms, 'inelastic', and thus standards of living will fall unless some counterbalancing improvement can be found. But, even if we do not improve living standards one iota, somehow we have to find the equivalent of a doubling of world resources in one form or another in this period.

The problem is intrinsically difficult enough but we have superimposed upon it the complexities of our political systems whether they be democracies or dictatorships. One effect of democratic elections has been to raise the expectations of the electorate to ever improving standards. It is hardly conceivable a party would seek election on a platform that living standards should not only inevitably fall for the foreseeable future, but that action should be taken to ensure this decline. It is a great temptation to opposition parties, of whatever creed, to argue that such a fall in living standards would occur only as the result of the ineptitude and inefficiency of the ruling party.

We are some way from an electorate that will accept the sophisticated argument that we are beginning to scrape the bottoms of numerous barrels and that the scope for overall material advancement is becoming severely restricted. There may be some slight grounds for hope in the growth of cynicism in electorates in recent years about the intentions and the capabilities of their politicians to deliver the promised goods. This in turn is leading some politicians to wonder whether honesty is perhaps the best policy after all! It is doubtful whether the situation is much better for dictatorships either. Dictators equally wish to promise the delivery of the goods and, although they are probably in a better position to overcome any scruples that might be imposed by environmental effects, these can be outweighed by the inherent inefficiences of their particular economic systems.

Communications within the world are now such that people in deprived countries soon become aware of the incredible difference between their standards of living and those of more developed countries. This awareness is used by politicians as a stepping stone to power. The pressure placed on Governments to redeem their promises to bring about improvements is heavy indeed. It is true that with the hoary old weapons of fear, repression and nationalism, time can be bought by the more unscrupulous leader, but eventually some attempt to pay the bill has to be made.

More of what?

What do we mean by increased living standards? If we were on the bread line the first priority for most of us would be more and better food; then would come better shelter. Having got these, we might move on to wanting more satisfying work, better education or services of any description. Many of us would want the opportunity to travel more widely and to enjoy greater leisure. All these praiseworthy objectives have one thing in common — they increase the demand on natural resources.

More and better food requires more land to be taken into cultivation and existing agricultural land to be made more productive.[3] This, in turn, requires a greater supply of fertilisers. Once the pressure grows for increasing agricultural production, then there is a need to eliminate natural pests. But, as we now know, removing such pests can have totally unexpected and undesirable ecological consequences. It is hard to be selective and simply eliminate those insects that are damaging your crops without destroying other species which are the natural enemies of pests. Pesticides can result in merely replacing one pest with another.

If work is to be provided, this may mean bringing alien industry into attractive localities. People may have to work in a fashion and in conditions to which they are totally unaccustomed. While this is essentially a sociological point, it does have some bearing on the attitude of people to their environment, insofar as the end results of the operation, i.e. the goods and services produced, are seen as alien elements which have destroyed a preferred lifestyle. People can be very adept at forgetting the benefits they obtain from change, and simply looking at the detrimental effects. The recent leap in the wealth of the

---

[3] Although agricultural resources are renewable if treated properly and there is still much land that could be brought into use, the total estimated area of the world's land mass that is thought capable of sustaining productive agriculture is only some twenty-five per cent.

oil-rich states of the Middle East has resulted in their wishing to maximise the building up of their domestic economic superstructure. However, they do not have large or skilled enough populations to carry out the necessary work and this has resulted in their having to accept massive inflows of migrant labour. This is likely to have the most profound long-term effects on the societies concerned.

The call for better services, including communications, has clear cut effects on the environment. Initially, faster communications result in advantages to everybody. But once we are gripped by the apparently obsessional need to travel, the demands for transport fuel, for either roads or airports, the effect of the emission of the waste products from the fuel into the atmosphere and, as the means of transport have got bigger and more intense, the effect of the resultant noise render the benefits of such activities debatable. Robert Louis Stevenson's axiom that 'it is better to travel than to arrive' appears to have become the maxim for the last half of the twentieth century.

There seems to be little doubt that rising expectations will persist for many years yet. The irony is not only that these expectations are becoming increasingly less capable of fulfilment, but that it is in the developed countries where the concern with environmental problems has its greatest support — those very countries where the pressures for a continued increase in material living standards are still the greatest. Perhaps this is not surprising. You would hardly expect to find people on a subsistence diet overmuch concerned with relatively remote pollution hazards.

The finite natural resources of the world form the foundation of our living standards. Some of them are abundant, others scarce; some are replenishable, others literally irreplaceable.[4] In such cases, we are going to have to find

Table 2 Reserves and ultimate abundance of metals, 1973

(tonnes)

	Life of reserves at current consumption rates* (years)	Life of reserves allowing for trend growth-rate in consumption* (years)
Aluminium	100	31
Copper	36	21
Iron	240	93
Lead	26	21
Mercury	13	13
Nickel	150	53
Tin	17	15
Zinc	23	18

*Taken from D.H. Meadows, et al., *The Limits to Growth*.
Sources: US Bureau of Mines, *Commodity Statements* 1973: J.L. Mero, Oceanic Mineral Resources, in *Futures* 1, 2, 1968; crustal abundance derived from *Encyclopaedia Britannica*, 1973, article 'Geochemistry'.

[4] If we look at the world's resources of vital metals we see that, in terms of the life time of a civilisation, time is not on our side.

alternative resources which can be used in their place. It is sensible in the meantime to make sure we use such crucial resources with the utmost circumspection. We must use them to buy time in which we will either develop substitutes, or learn to live without them. But, whatever we do, the demand for improved living standards will inevitably be reflected in increased pressure on the world's natural resources. Our present levels of activity are already causing considerable environmental objections, justified or not, but the situation is going to become much more difficult in the future.

Share and share alike

The desire to sustain rising expectations is the fundamental reason why environmental issues appear with increasing frequency on the manager's desk. Managers are having to think more and more about the nature of environmental problems because they are an inevitable outcome of normal day to day management decisions aimed at improving production and efficiency to the levels demanded by society.

It is this concern with maximising production that has resulted in many ecologists (but fewer economists) arguing that the world community should make a conscious decision to move away from the growth economics of the last two hundred years and try to evolve economic systems based on a more rational approach, which would restrict the demand on natural resources. This view, often termed the 'no growth' approach, is a logical response to the dilemma I have outlined. However great the intrinsic merits of such a philosophy, the possibility of its gaining widespread acceptance in the near future does not seem high.

In recent years it has been argued with increasing vigour that we must find ways of getting fairer shares of limited resources; that the developed countries should adopt 'no growth' policies and, by so doing, cut back on their demands for world resources. While the morality is impeccable, the argument confuses the general with the particular. Because the standard of living in a particular country is higher than the average, it does not follow that the standards of all people within that country are higher than the world average. We are all aware that within the richest countries of the earth there are stubborn pockets of poverty and deprivation. While these persist, it is hard to see how the acceptance of a philosophy of restricted growth is likely to command wide acceptance. 'No growth' economics may well be forced on countries by circumstance, but there is little chance that they will be accepted with acclaim.

The problem is complicated by the fact that many of the raw materials and resources required by the world in general are under the control of the so called 'under-developed countries'. They are suspicious of any move to curtail economic growth, which they see as being inspired by self-interest rather than a genuine altruistic desire to treat the world's problems in a rational way. It is therefore doubtful whether such an appeal would fall on any but those ears which are at least partially deaf.

However persuasive the reasons put forward, both the developing countries, and the underprivileged in the developed countries, see such a philosophy in terms of stopping the poker game when your pile of chips is twice the size of anybody else's. After they have had many a hand not worth playing, they naturally want a chance to enjoy a winning streak, and do not want you to stop dealing the cards just when they think their luck is bound to change.

This is one of the fundamental dilemmas of the manager's attitude. Many of them have doubted the motives of those who argue in favour of change. It is only with increasing awareness of the genuine nature of the problem that people can become actively concerned. As yet, many managers still question whether there are any fundamental problems to be tackled and the excesses of the 'doomsday' type of analysts have done little to convince them otherwise.

No concern of mine

We should not confuse lack of action with lack of interest or concern. It is a widespread human characteristic to ignore problems until they become in some way personal, affecting us directly. This approach, in relation to metals and minerals and in particular energy, is the road over the cliff edge, because of the long lead times involved in finding, proving and developing new sources. This is graphically shown in the following table:

Table 3 Estimated facility leadtimes
Estimated facility leadtimes
(Years from decision to start up)

Type of facility	Years leadtime
Nuclear electric plants	8–9
Coal electric plants	5
Oil electric plants	5
Synthetic plants	
Low btu gas	5
Pipeline gas	5
Liquification	5
Shale oil plants	6
New mines	
Surface	
Private lands	3
Federal lands	5
Underground	
Private lands	5
Federal lands	5–6
New OCS oil fields	2–4
New onshore oil fields	1–3
Geothermal electric	5
Hydro–electric	20

It will be seen from Table 3 that time is not on our side. Unless difficult decisions are taken know, the problem will multiply.

In the more developed countries, it is not just in recent years that many people have been aware of the environmental problems to confronting them everyday. What has changed, is that until recently what we might loosely term the opinion-forming classes could 'buy their way out' of most environmental problems. We can see this most clearly in their living environment. As the centres of towns became more crowded, dirty, or fog-bound, then the move of professional and managerial people towards the outskirts became marked. They were voting with their feet, because they could afford to.

Management down to quite a low level bought their way out of the environmental problems derived from their own activities. Not for them the sight, and often the smell, of the factory, morning, noon and night. Once they were away from these environmental problems, it is not surprising they soon began to ignore their existence.

As general living standards improved, the management classes were followed by the draughtsmen and the clerks, and suburbia was born. For much of this century this movement has become increasingly pronounced. We have now reached the situation where some of the services which were previously the monopoly of the town, such as major shopping centres, have tended to follow and establish themselves in the suburbs.

It is interesting to note that the growth of new environmental problems has begun to have some effect on reversing this movement. Originally the advantages offered by suburbia were those of living in, or almost in, the country, with cheap and rapid public transport systems into work in the city centre. The Metropolitan Underground Railway in London ran advertising campaigns to persuade people to go to live in 'Metroland' — those areas of Middlesex which were brought into easy travelling distance. With the growth in ownership of private cars and the overloading of both the roads and the public transport systems, journeys from out of town into the city centres have become longer, increasingly unreliable and unpleasant, and expensive. Suburbia has become almost totally built up and the green fields have vanished under even more bricks and mortar. Neither town nor country, it is no longer even convenient. As this tendency has developed, the reasons for living in suburbia become fewer and the suburban environment develops new problems of its own. What was once relatively peaceful suburbia may now be on the fringes of either a motorway or a flight path to a local airport and there may be the feeling of suffering the worst of both worlds. Transport to the town is now neither cheap nor easy and shopping may be expensive. Suburbia has now become such a word of abuse that it takes some effort to recall that originally it had many attractions. As well as providing an acceptable half-way house to 'living in the country', suburbia had the negative attraction that, in the beginning at any rate, it removed the residents from the proximity of factories and industry and all the environmental problems associated with them.

Environmental pressures can be seen as both a pushing and a pulling force in determining where people should live. However, one thing is quite clear and that is that there is no prospect of attracting people back to the town centres unless the environmental problems which eventually drove them away can be overcome.

The demands on the natural resources of the world include those on living space, on the air, the water and the land which surround us. Even if we are able to meet the current resource needs of the world in new ways, through man-made materials etc., these in turn will produce different pressures on the environment. Synthetic materials are dependent on natural resources at some point in the chain while all too often, developments which appear to be offering mankind a way out of a particular dilemma bring new problems in their wake. So-called 'plastics', which in many ways are one of the hallmarks of our civilisation, depend largely on crude oil as a basic feedstock.

The gypsy's warning

It may seem a short step from here to the disasters that we are constantly being warned about by the 'doomsday' prophets. But this is not the case. We do need to be aware of the full extent to which we could damage irretrievably the environment in which we live and equally to take steps to avoid so doing.

It is not very helpful to terrify ourselves into believing there is little or nothing we can do about it, other than to adopt a philosophy and way of life which manifestly the vast majority of the world's population would be unwilling to accept.

However, we must not go to the other extreme and assume 'God is in his heaven and all is right with the [environmental] world'. In order to appreciate the seriousness of our potential problems, it is worthwhile taking a brief look at certain aspects of our environment to see what could be in store for us, unless we heed the warning signs.

Don't touch anything

Let us start by looking at the human eco-system, that is, the system in which we all live and have to operate. In this context, the basic fact is that all life on this planet depends upon the transformation of radiant energy from the sun into the energy which we, as humans, can use to maintain our life. This energy may be consumed in the form of food, of heat, or of physical energy, but the net result is the same: it enables us to carry on our lives. The transformation of energy from the sun into the chemical energy of hydrocarbons, is carried out through the process of photosynthesis. This process is based on the substance chlorophyll and the chlorophyll-bearing organisms that carry out this photosynthesis are usually termed the 'producers' by ecologists. The animals, including man, that live off them directly or indirectly, are the consumers. In any eco-system it has to be accepted that each organism is affected by the conditions in the micro-world in which it lives and every organism also has some effect however trivial, on those very conditions.

Man is perhaps unique in actively trying to modify those conditions, if not always knowingly. In many respects, the action of man on his own eco-system is an attempt to simplify it and therefore meet his needs more easily. Let me give an example. In clearing waste lands for cultivation for food, rather than face up to a multiplicity of species of plants, he tends to replace the plant life with a single product, such as wheat, maize or rice. This single plant may extend over a wide area and man may further narrow the concept of plant culture by reducing it to a particular variety of rice or maize which gives a high yield. In many respects this was the basis of the so-called 'green revolution', which offers spectacular ways of increasing the world's ability to supply its food needs. This is all very well, while the species is healthy and producing in quantity, but the very action of refining its productive capacity, or leaving it as a single model culture, makes the whole operation far more susceptible to disease. If this happens, then the effects can be catastrophic. Instead of just certain varieties being affected, the whole crop is at risk.

The most dramatic example of such a catastrophe is probably the Irish potato blight of 1846, 'the Great Hunger'.[5] The potato disease destroyed three out of every four acres and hundreds of thousands died; the famine sparked off one of the biggest migrations in history and an exodus of politically conscious emigrants to the United States, to probably shape its political structure for the next 100 years.

Coming to our own times, the spread of Dutch Elm disease from the Continent to Britain in the early 1970s has had major effects which any visitor to the British countryside can see, but imagine how much greater the impact would have been, if say, for example, ninety-five per cent of all the trees in Britain had been elms. The disaster was mitigated by the fact that only a proportion of the trees were susceptible. The catastrophe was avoided because we did not have all our eggs in one basket.

Interference with the eco-system certainly can bring problems. Unfortunately, all too often people move from this starting point to the assumption that any attempted change is always for the worse. This is not a defensible position. The intervention into the eco-system of viruses that have worked to eliminate typhus and cholera and many of the other diseases of mankind, has certainly been of incalculable benefit.

In this connection, it is quite interesting that the case of the smallpox bacilli has raised considerable argument among conservationists and ecologists. For countless centuries, smallpox has been one of the major scourges of mankind

---

[5] For a heart rending and meticulous account of these events and their consequences, see Cecil Woodham Smith's classic of this name.

but, as the result of a magnificent piece of organisation, the scientific work carried out by the World Health Organisation has practically eliminated smallpox as a major disease. Because it has been eliminated, the need to maintain stocks of the smallpox vaccine has also decreased and many of the health centres holding supplies have been asking whether such vaccine should be destroyed. This raises the fundamental question, should the whole of the bacilli in the world be destroyed? If it is, then mankind will certainly be eliminating one of its most virulent enemies, but also a natural strain, which has taken many thousands of years to develop. It has been argued that, at some time in the future, mankind might want such a strain in order to counteract other diseases and that the destruction of the bacilli might be regarded as a major crime. If mankind takes this opportunity to eliminate from the face of the earth one type of living creature, no matter how apparently obnoxious, where does the line stop? On the other hand, if the vaccine is not destroyed, then it is easy to imagine that in a world in which smallpox has been eliminated, the natural resistance of mankind to the disease will quickly evaporate. And if in the future, by accident or design, the bacilli should get into general circulation, then the scourge could be far greater and more effective than was ever experienced before. It is when problems of this kind are raised, that the complexity of the issues that are being dealt with can be appreciated.

Ecology is relatively a new science. The British Institute of Ecology was founded as late as 1912 and it seems that ecology as a science does not carry the weight it deserves. This is perhaps because of the feeling that a number of the practitioners on the world stage have tended to be either excessively devoted to one particular aspect of ecology, or have appeared, whatever the problems, to have been pursuing a policy of no change.

It may be that they have not fully appreciated the nature of the world's dilemma. It is no use saying that the traffic lights should remain at red, if the aim is to keep vehicles moving. We therefore want advice from ecologists as to what the effect will be of proposed actions, since we have to learn to manage our environment, not just to accept it.

The ecologists' argument is that you cannot take one aspect of man's activity on its own. Attempting to interfere with nature in any of its aspects will inevitably initiate unexpected repercussions and chain reactions. Again, the example of DDT comes to mind, and we are now in a situation where, because of some pretty calamitous happenings over the years, we are far more inclined to pay attention to people who issue words of warning about the likely effects of certain courses of action, than we were in the past. We need positive help rather than pure negativism. However, there are danger signals and it is time that we looked at some of them.

Will it rain tomorrow?

We tend to believe that we can do nothing about the weather; that of all the aspects of the environment, this is one over which we have no influence or effect — not an argument that would be accepted by the 'rainmakers'.

There is now some evidence that the climate is changing and that it has changed relatively rapidly over recent periods. If we look at the facts, we find that average temperatures in higher latitudes began to rise in the early 1900s and Indian monsoons became more reliable. Throughout the first half of this century, European winters became less severe and the summer frosts in the northern States of America ceased. In the last quarter of a century, these changes began to reverse. Since then, average temperatures in the Northern Hemisphere have fallen. The growing season in England is now said to be shorter by some two weeks a year, the frequency of drought in north-west India has increased, the monsoon has gradually retreated towards the Equator in West Africa, culminating in seven years of famine, and midsummer frosts have returned to the upper mid-western United States.

There is much argument among the climatologists as to whether the actions of mankind have affected these changes and it has been claimed that the heat balance of the whole of the earth's atmosphere can be affected by a variety of human activities, ranging from widespread forest clearance to flights in the stratosphere. Some climatologists have claimed that climatic changes are likely to lead to major crop failures within a decade.

I have no wish to get involved in the argument as to whether the amount of carbon dioxide that the human race is now pumping into the atmosphere is a force for raising or lowering the world's temperature. That it could have some effect is the only point that seems to be generally accepted. The basic argument here is whether the atmospheric content of carbon dioxide, which has increased by between five per cent and ten per cent since 1960, will have a beneficial effect on plant photosynthesis, or whether the greenhouse effect of reducing the re-radiation into the upper atmosphere of the heat energy required from the sun by the earth's surface, will tend to increase the temperature of the earth's surface. If this happens, then the effect of continuing to build up the carbon dioxide in the atmosphere through the burning of petroleum and fossil fuels could lead to the melting of the ice caps and the consequential raising of oceans by up to fifty metres. This would be an eco-disaster of almost unimaginable proportions. Think how many ports and how much land would be flooded by such a change. If it could be shown that this was a real possibility, then industrial man would have to change his habits quickly.

I am looking for some good farming land

Of the world's area of ice-free land, only about a quarter is potential arable farmland and, of that quarter, only a third is currently being actively cultivated. Because of increased population, the cultivation of these areas is becoming more intense.

In parts of the world, soil is being over-worked at a terrifying rate. We are all aware of the tragic effect of over-intensive farming in the Mid-west of the United States which resulted in the dust storms of the 1930s and left massive dust bowls throughout these areas.

Despite the heroic attempts of the US Soil Conservation Service to counteract these effects, they have caused lasting damage. If current trends continue, much of the world's arable land could be turned into non-productive deserts over the next two to three centuries. There is a connection here with our possible effects on the climate. The deforestation that has taken place has led to stronger (or more uninterrupted) winds and has frequently been followed by soil erosion.

In relation to soil quality we are moving into a new area. The difficulty is that the most widely recognised way of preventing the destruction of the quality of the soil is to carry out major programmes of fertilisation. Unfortunately, some of the major fertilisers used, i.e. phosphates, are in increasingly short supply and the world's resources in this field will be exhausted relatively soon. When this happens, we shall have no obvious way of returning the energy to the soil.

It is not only over-cultivation that is affecting the soil situation. As well as deforestation, there are methods of cultivation, leading to the erosion of soil from slopes, and the irrigation of flat areas without proper drainage, which can lead to the salinisation of soils beyond the point where any crop can be produced.

Even the use of fertilisers can lead to dangers. The excessive use of fertilisers can pollute adjacent fresh waters. The over-enrichment of river waters seems to be the inevitable consequence of the so-called green revolution which was meant to increase the world's food supply by raising the yield from soil by massive use of fertilisers coupled with special strains of plants.

Against this background, we should not be surprised if our proposals for carrying out industrial development on good farming land is opposed. Where such use is necessary the case must be fully argued.

Can you eat the fish?

Less than one twentieth of all the water on the earth is fresh water and we need to treat this with care and respect. This is perhaps the most obvious area in which industry directly affects the environment in which we all live. Industry creates a tremendous demand for water for its processes and all too often it pollutes good supplies with its effluent. The pollution in the Rhine is well known, the Dutch at the receiving end of what has become almost an open sewer for Europe, collecting the unwanted effluent and by-products of man and industry from every point on its banks from Switzerland to the North Sea. It is hard to get a proper concept of the number and variety of pollutants now in the world. One estimate suggested that there are half a million substances which are known to pollute water which have to be guarded against, and there is little doubt that this number is being added to substantially each year.

It is not only in fresh water that the problems occur. There has been a substantial degradation of marine life in salt waters. The most obvious pollution in these areas has been oil spillages from tankers and from sewage, but the more potent and fundamental danger comes from nuclear waste which, theoretically, might some day begin to build up through the fish into food chains with catastrophic consequences.

Leaving nuclear energy aside for the moment, there is the classic case of the Minamata disease caused by the discharge of mercury compounds into Minamata Bay in Japan. Contaminated fish were eaten by the local inhabitants who subsequently suffered from mercury poisoning, with all the horror that that entails. And it was not only a question of poisoning individuals. Once the poisoning was discovered, people naturally no longer had the same desire to see fish on the menu with the result that the fishermen lost their livelihood. Here is a clear example of where the industrial effluent of one part of the population deprived another part of the population of its normal and customary livelihood.

The very packaging of food itself can present a health hazard, since the packaging material can contain toxic substances. In itself, the packaging substance may be harmless, but in combination with the food, it produces harmful by-products. If the food processor fails to select the most suitable package from the 1500 different chemical compounds, then a health hazard could be created and food poisoning result.

The World Health Organisation is aiming to develop international food standards and, in so doing, will attempt to co-ordinate all the food standards of existing organisations and convert them into a unified food code.

There is an area of major concern and danger here, and one which should be in the forefront of the minds of everybody managing industries or organisations connected with the sale or distribution of foodstuffs.

We've got problems

The basic problem is, as the American National Academy of Sciences Research Council put it, that 'Man is not only part of his eco-system, he is the most powerful influence in it. He is simultaneously its potentially most precious resource and its most serious threat.'

The 'quality of life' is threatened by the demands of expanding populations and growing economies. These threats derive from the restrictive and harmful effects of pollution, the increasing complexity of human society and the inevitable growth on restrictions on what individuals are able or allowed to do. Although these restrictions may be necessary in order to protect the wider interests of society, they can create insoluble problems if they are overlooked at a time of severe competition for increasingly scarce resources such as space, foodstuffs, housing, etc.

One of the basic difficulties is that although for every substance found in nature there is another substance occurring naturally which can break it down, this is not true of man-made wastes. Initially, every bit of man-made fibre has either had to be burnt, thereby creating some air pollution, or left lying around as litter. It cannot be broken down naturally by the types of organisms which would break down, say, pure woollen fibre or any other natural raw material. But we must appreciate also that the man-made materials may offer certain distinct advantages over the natural ones. These may be intrinsic or economic, but we should not fall into the trap of believing that the natural alternatives are always self-evidently better for all purposes.

It is easy to mistake the symptoms of man's problem, the pollution that you can see, smell or feel — noise, dirt, dust — for the disease itself, the old familiar one of wanting to have your cake and eat it. Mankind has either to adopt a totally changed lifestyle or to find ways of compromising and living with the particular environmental problems being created around it.

So far, not a great deal of attention has been paid to ways in which such environmental problems can be overcome. The amount of money spent on tackling these issues at their core is almost derisory. It is not always appreciated that our consumption of non-renewable materials is equivalent to living on capital. With an increase in population, the world requires more 'capital' in the form of resources, and not less. The present situation in which the world's reserves of natural resources are being reduced at an ever growing rate, is one which promises catastrophe. To put the issue into perspective, at the current rate of increase in oil consumption, within fifteen year's time we shall need, every year, a new oil field producing more than Saudi Arabia produces now, just to cover the increase in demand.

Similar arguments apply to copper reserves. We are already reduced to mining the relatively poor ores, with the result that we have to process and discard a tremendous amount of material in order to produce each ton of copper and at the present rate of consumption it is hard to see copper reserves lasting fifty years. This is a crucial situation, because industrial society as we know it cannot work without ample supplies of copper. We ought, therefore, to be using the time that these reserves allow us (i.e. our copper capital) to discovering alternatives for copper or to reducing the demand for the products which currently consume copper. There is also an obvious need to recycle copper in our industrial activities. At present, most copper, once used, is thrown away as waste. In any examination of the problems facing the world, the most glaring fact is that we fail to draw a distinction between the natural resources which are non-renewable, such as oil, coal, iron, copper, and those animal and vegetable resources which, given a reasonable timespan and proper management, can be replaced in an orderly way.

This distinction can be further broken down into those non-renewable minerals which can be reduced to a greater or lesser extent — most metals — and those which we destroy in the process of consumption — fuel such as coal and oil.

It is because of concern about the reserves of non-renewable resources, that groups like the Club of Rome take such a pessimistic view of mankind's future. In many ways, they have reverted to the Malthusian approach of the early nineteenth century. Thomas Malthus was an English clergyman who decided that man's nature was such that the population would increase until it reached the limits of subsistence and then would be driven down by the natural consequences of starvation and disease. Throughout the nineteenth century it was argued that his gloomy prophesy had been shown to be ill-founded. But this opposing view was the result of the opening up of North America which provided the world with a new larder, and with better methods and growing popular understanding of birth control. The population explosion in developed countries was not as severe as he would have anticipated. However, it is hard to maintain that the Malthusian doctrine has not shown its essential validity in many of the underdeveloped areas of the world, where population increases have exerted such pressure on local food resources that millions have and are starving.

Whatever the argument about the extrapolation of figures used by bodies such as the Club of Rome, the fundamental question to be asked is whether the underlying basis of the world economy is moving in the direction of increasing shortages. Shortages which will turn out not to be temporary bottlenecks, but an eventual drying up of the total supply.

These are the kind of issues which have an undeniable importance for the future of mankind and must be taken seriously by all who claim to have a professional interest in the management of affairs and resources. We all know the story of the manager who had on his desk a notice that said 'Are you part of the answer or part of the problem?' It should be the task of professional managers to contribute to the solution of such problems rather than to help create them.

The underlying environmental problems are very real. That is why, although we never used to have an environment, we have one now.

5 The way we live now

What are we trying to do?

Having looked at the history of the environmental issues, and seen how they have developed, this is a good point at which to take stock and examine the way in which they have come to a head at the present time. It would be useful to assess our current attitudes before going on to consider possible ways of tackling the problems facing us.

Managers are faced currently with a hotchpotch of legislation, restrictions, Government edicts and pressure groups of all kinds, each one aiming to influence and modify their decisions. It is not surprising, therefore, that their reaction, when confronted with environmental considerations, tends to be defensive. It is defensive because they feel, all too often, that the proponents of a particular environmental point of view have seized on one aspect of the problem and have failed to consider the practical implications of the proposed sanctions they are putting forward. Management has become used to being misrepresented and pilloried on most environmental issues. The assumption, always implicit and sometimes explicit, is that managers do not pay proper heed or attention to the basic environmental problems and resort to evasion, if not downright deception, in their dealings with the environmentalists' arguments. Like most generalisations, there is a germ of truth in the proposition and it is quite possible to find examples where this attitude is justified by the facts. But again, like most generalisations, it totally ignores all the evidence to the contrary. It also makes certain assumptions about the nature of the society in which we live, which are questionable, to say the least.

The anti-management argument can be put in simple terms. The industrial environment in which we find ourselves can be regarded as the result of decisions taken by industrial managers and boards of directors over the last two hundred years. Insofar as the end result is unsatisfactory, then the people who initiated the changes for their own ends must bear the responsibility. If it is accepted that the present environment is unsatisfactory, then it follows that we should have had more 'protection' against these 'bad' environmental decision makers. There has not been sufficient evidence that managers have changed their spots, therefore the conclusion that the environment needs protecting from them is inescapable. It is sometimes hard to be sure whether managers are being painted as ignoramuses who just don't know any better, or satanic figures hell bent on destroying 'all things bright and beautiful', not to mention 'all creatures great and small'. Whatever the view, there is an expectation that, left to their own devices, the managers will continue somehow to wreck the environment which all right thinking people desire to preserve, and therefore they must be brought under stricter control.

Ironically, the approach of some managers gives credence to this view, as they take the line that they are in business to make the maximum profits possible within the law without reference to any other criteria. If the law allows them to carry out certain actions, even if the probable results will be unacceptable to the community, then they believe they are entitled to so act in the pursuit of their own objectives. Such managers would argue that any resulting deterioration of the environment is the consequence, and therefore the responsibility, of the law makers for not laying down efficiently enough the permitted conditions of operation. They would maintain that they are prepared to obey the law but need do no more, since their competitors certainly do not, and to take any other attitude would eventually result in their not being able to continue with their activities.

The logic of this approach is that if society wants to protect its environment, it is going to have to do so almost entirely through the due process of law. It is in fact a demand for stricter legislation and controls over the activities of management; surely an odd paradox when those who are arguing for the maximum freedom of management are indirectly promoting the introduction of tighter controls over themselves!

Mind your own business

The introduction of even tighter controls over management goes against the historical grain. Traditionally, the decision makers in industry and commerce in the western world have seen any increase in control over their activities not only as totally unwarranted interference, but also as opposed to the interests of the society in which we live. The approach has been that the benefits of free enterprise stem from the relatively unfettered operation of individual firms and concerns, all aiming at satisfying the wants of individuals. There has been a tendency to argue that any restriction on such activity can only result (as a logical consequence) in a decreased ability to supply the wants and needs of the community. Such interference is therefore seen as diminishing the general well-being of the community. Professor F.A. Hayek in his *Road to Serfdom* and subsequent works, is perhaps the most eloquent advocate of this point of view.[1]

The weakness of this argument is that it totally ignores the social costs that could be involved in meeting the desires of particular individuals. The right of an individual to buy armaments, addictive drugs or pornography, is affected by the controls placed on such activities by governments. It is difficult to argue, however, that the well-being of the community is thereby necessarily diminished. If we allow that some controls are necessary, then we are back to the familiar problem of where do you draw the line? In any event, it is a line that is not static and it can move over time in either direction.

Nevertheless, decision takers in industry and commerce have always resisted interference in their affairs. The assumption has been that management has the right to be master in its own house. Any lessening of this precept has been seen in certain quarters as always politically motivated. Social controls have been called everything from bureaucratic to communistic.

The problem about assuming that such controls are necessarily politically motivated is that it inevitably promotes an emotional, rather than a rational response. There is little point in denying that the attitude of private industry and commerce to proposed legislation to improve environmental control, has tended to be in this category. In the same way much of the opposition to the interests of 'Big Business' has been based primarily on political considerations rather than on objective appraisal.

The danger is that once emotion is allowed to rule reason, somewhat illogical and indefensible arguments tend to be put forward. Reaction to criticism, or even questions, then tends to be instinctive and stereotyped, rather than constructive. denial that there is a problem!

What do the newspapers say?

Unfortunately, there is considerable justification for this type of response. As concern with the environment has grown, the media have quite properly reflected this growing interest in the amount of coverage that they have given to environmental issues. This has, however, been based on what is apparently the first commandment of all news promoters, not that 'no news is good news' but that 'no *good* news, is news!'. While many newsmen deplore this attitude, it seems to be a fact of media life. People, we are told, are not interested in 'good news' stories. Murder and mayhem, peril and poison, are far better magnets to public attention. We should therefore not be surprised when we find that environmental triumphs are skimmed over in, at most, a paragraph or, more likely, a sentence or two, whereas potential problems, however

---

[1] See also the classic work by Joseph Schumpeter, *Capitalism, Socialism and Democracy*. He emphasised the changing nature of the free enterprise economies and predicted a growth of monopoly capitalism. Under this system, he thought that firms would place less emphasis on price and would increasingly compete in other ways.

remote, (particularly if they can be portrayed as possible 'doomsday disasters'), get the headlines and the full treatment. Management must expect that any mistakes that it has made, or chances which it has taken for good reasons which have not come off, and which some way have affected the environment, will receive full-scale publicity. They must also expect that the stories will be presented in such a way that will damn the particular project or activity, and the management concerned. A scapegoat must be found. Even when the reporter sticks strictly to the facts of the situation, it is asking a lot to expect him to ignore a flight of fancy into the possible dire consequences of the activities under scrutiny. While the accent may be fairly placed on the *possibilities* and not the *probabilities*, how many of the readers or listeners will appreciate the crucial nature of this distinction?

This approach by the media should not be much of a surprise. Insofar as it reflects what people are prepared to pay for, we all bear some responsibility, but it is an approach that should not be defended. Such irresponsible comment must always be attacked. It is particularly prevalent at times, or in places, where authority is coming under criticism. In a democracy, criticism of those with positions of power and authority is an essential part of the game; we need to maintain an atmosphere of vigilance and critical assessment, in order that we can exercise our democratic rights. Unfortunately, when this attitude is linked with a desire for 'sensation', the inevitable result is that an atmosphere is created in which negative criticism not only flourishes, but also provides a positive road to prosperity for some.

It is sad, but true, that much of the criticism in the environmental field, as in so many others, gives no guide to future action. The analysis, if there is any, is usually of the 'this must not be allowed to happen again' variety. Seldom, if ever, are the choices facing society honestly examined. Neither is any indication given that the author realises that there are choices to be made and that most of them have some undesirable repercussions. The euphony of an eye-catching heading, or the prospect of a television enquiry programme that will get into the ratings is all too attractive.

People, in choosing one course of action, are condemning themselves to consequences which they may find unacceptable. For example, criticisms of new industrial development proposals are seldom made in terms of questioning the need for the activity. They are usually made in terms of the disruption that it will cause the local community and in arguing that the development should take place somewhere else. This kind of criticism does not require very much thought. It is obvious that any new development which permanently brings something into an environment that was not there before, whether a factory, a housing estate or a motorway, will undoubtedly have a major effect, usually for the worse, on the environment of people living locally. The argument should be not whether the environment might or might not be made worse, but whether or not this effect is inevitable, and whether it is in the wider interests of the community.

On the one hand, communities will profess profound concern about the level of unemployment in their area, while opposing and rejecting developments which would often help the situation. On the other hand, the real consequences of development are seldom thought through. It is interesting to speculate how much the employment rate has been adversely affected in certain areas by the attitudes of planners and local environmental pressure groups, and whether the balance of maintaining the best 'quality of life' for everybody has been reasonably achieved.

To be valid, criticisms of proposals should be based in the first place on the overall need for the activity. If it can be shown it is needed, then the next question is whether or not it is proposed to site the activity in the place that will cause the least environmental damage. In such circumstances, it is not an adequate response to agree that the facility is necessary, but to argue that somebody else should do the suffering. Unfortunately, much of the comment on environmental matters, on radio, television and in the press, falls into this category. We hear heartrending stories as to how a new development will affect a particular individual, or a particular locality, but we are not asked to consider alternatives. In reality, the public is faced with choosing between alternatives, all of which have *some* disadvantages. They are asked to judge in absolute and not relative terms. The old and well tried maxim that hard cases make bad law is conveniently ignored. There is a tendency to assume that, if it can be established that some people will be put to inconvenience and occasionally hardship, then that is sufficient to justify the prevention of that activity, irrespective of any offsetting benefits to the community at large.

Trial of strength

I do not regard this as a healthy attitude in a democracy because, logically, it must mean that proposals will only be able to go ahead where the opposition, for one reason or another, is weakest. If all opponents were equally able and had the same resources at their disposal, then this would be a satisfactory solution, because it would indicate that if the proposals were going to be carried out, then they would take place in those areas with the weakest case for opposing them. In practice, we all know that this is not the case. The best organised pressure groups are all too often those with the greatest financial resources at their disposal; these are more likely to be able to carry the day than more impoverished areas with perhaps a greater feeling of resignation towards the impending developments. For this reason, in many instances, the arguments and interests of the middle classes carry more weight than their intrinsic merit deserves. This tendency is reinforced if much of the argument takes place on the basis of the law. This automatically puts certain groups at a major disadvantage compared with others.

This type of argument is exemplified in those cases where it is maintained that the development should not take place in such and such an area as it would be contrary to the character of the district, but that it is all right for it to take place somewhere else because it already has a high proportion of industrial activity within its boundaries. Are we in other words saying that if an area is suffering already, it might as well suffer more?

There will be occasions when this is a sensible policy, if, for example, it is decided to devote an area to particularly unpleasant industries and to separate living and working environments, thus ensuring that the poeple who have to work in such an area do not have to live in it. Unfortunately, this is not the usual outcome.

The reality of this type of approach to varying degrees of opposition, irrespective of practical realities, inevitably affects management. There is a tendency to go for the 'soft option' and to carry out developments in those areas where the opposition is expected to be weakest, irrespective of whether that is the ideal situation from an environmental point of view. This is a danger which I believe management should endeavour to avoid, if it is to live up to its wider social obligations.

What would you do?

This inability to get critics to put forward constructive alternative proposals or workable solutions to environmental problems, is another factor which has tended to put management on the defensive. There is all the difference in the world between a joint approach to try to reach mutually acceptable solutions to problems which both sides agree are there, and an outright war between two sides, both of which are convinced that they can get something nearer to unconditional surrender from the other. Environmentalists should therefore not be surprised if sometimes their requests for information fall on deaf ears. It is not usual to hand over voluntarily your ammunition to a sworn enemy. If information supplied indicating the parameters of the problem is used in an attempt to suggest that the problem is insoluble, and therefore necessitates preventative action, management is unlikely to be so forthcoming on future occasions.

If environmental problems are to be tackled sensibly, with due regard for the overall needs of society, then they will require the combined applied intelligence of both sides to reach satisfactory solutions. All too often today, we have the position in which, on the one hand, the proposers of the development are determined to push it through with scant regard for genuine environmental considerations, while on the other, the opponents refuse to see any reason for the proposal and devote no time at all to considering ways in which it can be made more acceptable and palatable. Their aim is purely negative: to prevent the development. The prevailing attitude is one of conflict and non co-operation. Management should not be surprised at this, because amenity and environmental pressure groups very often arise in response to proposals to change the local environment. Their whole purpose is protective and restrictive and perhaps it is asking too much to expect them to be constructive and creative. However, unless such bodies are given the opportunity, this would not be a reasonable view to take. Joint approaches must be developed if progress is to be made and it is difficult to develop a worthwhile dialogue from behind opposing dugouts!

The dangers of the existing situation are very obvious. The main one is that of polarisation of attitudes. People are put into black and white situations; or sometimes the argument is in terms of the opposition between the civilised man and the Philistine. However, I think I have said enough to indicate that this is seldom the case. Very often the reason for a great bulk of the opposition is materialism of a particularly self-centred kind (however understandable), which rides on the back of genuine fundamental environmental concern, in an attempt to prevent change and so preserve the *status quo*. Similarly, it is astonishing what the materialists are able to do to lessen the environmental impact if they feel that, in order to go ahead with their developments, they have no alternative course.

The tragedy of this polarisation of opponents is that often more resources and effort are spent on the battle than on seeking solutions. This approach is based on the frequently false assumption that there can be a final winner. The fact is that the problems are usually difficult but rarely intractable. We have, however, to put more effort into building up an understanding of the other man's point of view and so attempt to meet reasonable objections by reasoned arguments rather than polemics.

Although we all have our own individual ideas on every subject under the sun, it has become conventional to ascribe certain attitudes or approaches to society in general. We speak of society's view about this or that, although, when we come to analyse this concept, all we really mean is that this seems to be a broadly acceptable view to the majority of people. We therefore have to be somewhat suspicious when we hear or use expressions like 'the view of society', or ascribe feelings to society as a whole; terms which may make sense when applied to an individual sometimes acquire a more dubious value when applied to people *en masse*. Nevertheless, the concept does have its usefulness and, in relation to environmental matters, it would appear that society is extremely schizophrenic. Society seems to wish to follow two diverging roads at one and the same time. It wants continued material progress on the one hand, and the elimination of *all* conceivable environmental risks, on the other.

It is remarkable how often we wish governments to try to do something which we all know is an impossibility. The elimination of risk would totally transform society as we know it and would not be accepted. In fact we implicitly accept that certain risks are ever present and cannot be avoided. We pay lip service to avoiding the dangers that these activities bring in their wake, but we are seldom anxious to follow the logic of the argument to the extent of eliminating the activity.

Don't take any risks

A few moment's thought will show that there are certain risks which society accepts or, perhaps it would be truer to say, prefers to ignore, because it likes the end result. The most obvious example of this is the attitude of society to the automobile. When the facts are put in front of us, none of us can deny that driving a car multiplies the risk of injury or death by a frightening degree. In absolute terms, the annual carnage on the roads of any civilised country is appalling. In a relatively small country like the United Kingdom, some 7000 people are killed each year, and over 77000 injured. If all injuries are taken into account, then no less than a third of a million people can expect to be killed or injured on the roads of the United Kingdom each year. When the French take off for their yearly August holiday, it can be guaranteed that over 200 of them will die on the way to their holiday resort on the first day of the holiday. More people have been killed on the world's roads than perished in the whole of the Second World War. We are all aware of these facts, yet we prefer not to think about them. It is possible, for example, to have a prolonged debate in Great Britain on whether the compulsory use of seat belts to reduce injury is an infringement of the fundamental liberties of the subject without much attention being paid to the human suffering that is the price paid for ideological purity.

Such matters are a very real aspect of the environment in which we live and, if we were genuinely concerned to remove all environmental risks, then we would have to do something to break our invidious habit of almost constant travel on the highways and byways of the world.

Suppose that at this time, somebody came forward and said that they had a new invention, the application of which would enormously enhance the horizons of mankind, in that it would make possible a revolution in personal mobility. Moreover the invention would bring work for millions of people, and would create much happiness. We would, of course, want to know more. But if our benefactor were then to go on to say that the invention had one serious drawback, it carried a certain degree of danger. Although millions of people would benefit each year, about a million people would inevitably suffer and more than ten per cent of these would die. I submit that we might have second, third or fourth thoughts about the advisability of going ahead with such an invention. It is only because we never knew what the result would be that we have found ourselves uncritically accepting the motor car, and have subsequently found the price one we are prepared to pay.

All human life should be considered sacred. One of the tragedies of the twentieth century is that we seem to have lost this overwhelming regard for the sanctity of life. It is intolerable to contemplate the deliberate sacrifice of anybody for material benefits of whatever kind. Yet, in practice, when we think about it, we are all aware that this is what we do. The difference is that we do not know which individuals will suffer, or at what time they will be sacrificed. It is this randomness, coupled with a belief that it will not happen to us, that makes the situation tolerable, as we concentrate on the benefits we are getting.

It is this aspect of what people demand in the form of goods and services that we need to bear in mind when looking at industry. We have a duty to do everything possible to produce fail-safe systems for each industrial operation and never to give up the struggle to eliminate all risks of serious injury or death. But does this mean that we must cease all activities in which there still remains a risk? It would appear not. We accept that some degree of risk is an inevitable factor of life on this earth and in fact, many people go out of their way to experience risk in their leisure activities. Our concern is that the risk should not be unnecessary or unreasonable. We want safe processes and safe activities, but we inevitably have to put these into perspective. Would you challenge the automobile manufacturer about the accidents caused by his products? He is likely to reply that there are far more serious accidents in people's homes than there are on the roads. It is impossible to provide accurate figures, as statistics on serious injuries in the home are not as reliable as those on motor vehicle accidents. The number of deaths from accidents in the home in 1974 was approximately 6000, about 1000 lower than road deaths. Here we have the paradox; while we must strive all the time to remove and reduce risk, we have to accept that complete success is unlikely. We are always striking an invisible balance which only causes us concern periodically when disaster makes the reality apparent.

Certain activities are, at certain times, more risky than others. The statistics are there to tell us of the relative danger of being a fisherman or working down a mine. All disasters are, by definition, newsworthy, and five people killed in a mine or in an explosion at a chemical plant will rate a headline in the newspaper, whereas the same number killed in separate incidents on the same day, driving their long distance trucks, will not rate a mention.

Here we tread on extremely difficult ground. So long as we require the products of industries and activities which would involve risk, then we, as a society, have to be prepared to accept the accidents. It is essential that, when disaster strikes, industry must do all it can to learn lessons and to ensure that similar accidents cannot occur in the future. But it is not a sensible approach to assume that disasters, in themselves, should be regarded as a reason for trying to prevent that activity taking place in the future. Society has to draw up its own balance sheet. How much are we prepared and able to pay to eliminate the risks involved? If we require the products and the services of the activities, then we have to accept the dangers involved. To make such judgements we need to be in full possession of the facts and we should not make them in the upsurge of the right and proper emotion that emerges at times of disaster. If it is decided that it is too risky to carry on sending people deep sea fishing, following the disappearance of a modern trawler without apparent cause, then society has got to accept the consequence for the diet and standard of living of its people. Demands that we should stop fishing in dangerous waters are real enough although in fact, we often have the spectacle of both the owners and the seamen agitating for financial support to enable them to continue to operate in such conditions.

As a society, our collective split personality becomes more and more apparent. Certain activities are condemned because of possible or even potential danger, whereas we are prepared to go on accepting others which involve far greater risks. If there is any danger that a raw material may be carcinogenous, there is understandable concern and pressure to limit its use, yet at the same time we are ambivalent to the use of tobacco in our society. The fact that this is a hackneyed example does not make it any less relevant. If you compare the concern shown and the actions taken if there is any evidence that certain substances may be carcinogenous with our continued toleration of massive promotion (either overt or covert) of cigarette smoking, where there is probably more detailed evidence of a direct connection between the activity and the feared result, then you cannot help being amazed at our double standards. While it is asking too much of society to expect it to cease tolerating double standards, we should at least make sure that their existence is recognised and act accordingly.

This is where emotionalism is such a dangerous factor. It is this ability of the media to whip up what amounts to hysteria against a particular activity, which is potentially so serious. If additional safety measures are introduced in any industry causing a substantial price increase, the complaints of the people who genuinely cannot afford to pay will not be any the less. Everybody praises the work of the miner and his acceptance of risk, but it does not stop people grumbling about the price of coal.

The media have an exceptionally important role to play in this area if they would only seize it in a socially responsible way.[2] Of course the newspaper or television reporter will not see an explosion or a disaster in the same context as the industrialist responsible for the process or the continued employment of the labour force. This is not the crucial issue. It is a matter of the utmost concern that the genuine suffering and distress caused by avoidable accidents, is brought fully home to the people at large, and that they are made aware of the real costs involved in the production of certain goods and services. In this the media have a vital service to perform. What is reprehensible and, in fact, counter-productive, is to give the impression that there are easy answers and that risks can be eliminated . All too often the suggestion is that the activity should cease, regardless of the consequences. By all means put the choice fairly and squarely before society and say, for example, that fishing disasters can be avoided by not fishing in certain areas, and by insisting on far higher standards for fishing vessels. But, the argument must be carried a stage further and the

---

[2] The danger is that the media will continue to do precisely the opposite and build up people's fears by publishing rumour and speculation on highly emotive issues before the true facts can be known.

public told that, to follow that course of action will mean a real increase in the cost of living, which cannot be passed on in terms of inflationary wage increases. The important issue is to ensure that all the facts are put before society when it is trying to judge the issue. This means drawing up both sides of the balance sheet, the credits as well as the debits — something we are often reluctant to do.

Similar arguments arise in relation to measures to protect the environment. Where the concern is to find ways in which the impact of industry or commerce on the environment can be lessened, and the argument is that money should be spent to lessen the impact, then there can be a reasoned debate. All too often, however, the argument starts from closed positions, with the proposers unwilling to make major modifications to their scheme, and their opponents having no wish to see the activity take place on any conditions, or in any circumstances. It would be a more honest procedure in such cases to come out flatly against a particular development for the real grounds of the opposition, and not to cloak it in some quasi-environmental fog. All of us, at some time or another, are likely to have a vested interest in ensuring that a particular development does or does not take place, depending upon whether we are on the receiving end or not. It should be the aim of a responsible society to have these arguments out in the open, rather than have them carried out behind various forms of disguise. Society can then try to tackle the real problems created by the proposals and not the alleged ones.

There are many activities in our present day society, which cause inconvenience and suffering to individuals, and for which they get no real recompense. They have to put up with a deterioration in their conditions of life in order that the majority of us may reap some benefit. Few people want to live next to a rubbish tip, yet most people want their rubbish collected and disposed of without any inconvenience to themselves. Sewage has to be disposed of somewhere. We all want to use energy whether produced from coal, nuclear power or oil. None of us seems to want a coal mine, a deep or open pit, a power station (particularly if nuclear powered), or even an oil refinery, on our doorstop. In the words of the old proverb 'we want both the toffee and the halfpenny'. Reluctant to accept that the choice of some of the good things in life means accepting some of the bad, we will support the need for rubbish tips, but insist they must be in front of somebody else's window!

We tend to ignore the logic of much of our protesting activities. If we oppose the creation of a rubbish tip near our own house, this may be on the grounds that there are demonstrably better places which will cause less inconvenience. But, all too often, it simply means that we want to wish our troubles on to somebody else. This is all very well if there is somebody else who is prepared to accept these troubles without kicking up a fuss. However, one of the effects of the success of the campaign to make people more aware of their environment and of their own place in society is that quite rightly the number of 'somebody else's' is diminishing all the time. We therefore have to reach a situation where we can learn to separate the wheat from the chaff; to act on the overall facts of the situation and not on the basis of the biased view of one side or the other. Until recent years, the bias was very much on the side of the industrialist or the developer, although now it is arguable that in certain respects it has already gone too far in the other direction.

I have already indicated that I think that the media have a tremendous responsibility to ensure that they place the full facts of the situation, and the alternatives, before the public. I will go further, and argue that a responsible communications industry could help to generate acceptable alternatives and not assume that they automatically come from either of the interested parties. This is perhaps asking for too much, but it is, as we all know, far easier to give the impression that you know all the answers, rather than actually to try to produce some of them.

Management for their part have so far not always measured up to environmental responsibilities. Far too much of the reaction to the recent growth of environmental pressures has been defensive and management has given the impression that it has something to hide. Only one or two examples needed to come out — instances when it was clear that management did have something it did not want in the open — to cast a question mark on the whole of its approach. At the moment, there is a great lack of confidence in environmental matters between the protagonists. Neither side believes that the other has got a genuine point of view and each seems to measure up for a battle before trying to see whether it can be avoided.

One of the problems of management is that, all too often, it has not got the facts itself, but feels that it cannot admit this because it looks somehow incompetent. Why it should be regarded as incompetent not to know the minute detail of every activity going on in any one of our major industrial concerns, is beyond me. The manager is paid to carry out his specific tasks, not to know the detailed facts of every activity under his control. If this were not the case, why have we heard so much about the famous failure of management to delegate properly? Delegation implies that there will be considerable lack of detailed knowledge on the part of any individual manager about many activities for which he or she is responsible. This does not remove the responsibility, but it should remove the embarrassment of saying 'I don't know, but I will find out and then I'll make a statement'.

The manager is now faced with the additional problem of what I would describe as involvement in the democratic process. Gone are the days when he could be aloof from the general climate of opinion, or the attitude of the workers in his own particular firm. We have reached the situation where, for better or for worse, there is a growing demand for participation in the decision-making process on the part of both employees and outside interests, such as consumer groups, etc. This does not make the manager's task any easier, but a problem will not be solved by pretending it is not there.

There are times when the general impression that the golden age of management was when it had only the clear-cut objective of the maximisation of profit, irrespective of any other consideration. In fact, there are many thousands of practising businessmen who follow this precept to this day and would be horrified if told that they ought to follow any other, while many others would like to turn the clock back. The problem is that as firms grow in size, the pressures to move from single-aim to multi-aim objectives, are becoming irresistible.

Most managers who have had a reasonable amount of experience will have been faced changing fashions in their objectives. At first it may have been maximisation of profit or production. In some industries, it appears to be becoming the elimination of all environmental risks, at whatever cost. Governments try to influence industry on occasions to maximise employment levels, by paying it large sums of money for this purpose. Then we have had the problem of developing maximum co-operation with all the employees. This has moved into demands in some countries for greater worker participation. The function of the manager is somehow to reconcile these various objectives and still keep his job!

The environmental issue has to be fitted in with all these other objectives and, what is more, somehow the manager has to convince society at large that it cannot pursue competing objectives; that the reconciliation of differing objectives has to be sought. We need to understand that the pursuit of a single one of these objectives to the exclusion of all others, will not provide society with what it wants. The manager has to be prepared to reconcile, but not to retreat unnecessarily. Other objectives are at times as important or more important than environmental ones. The judgement as to when this is so, is one which has to be made on the facts in each case.

It is much easier to pursue a single objective than to try to keep a number of balls in the air at one time but someone has to undertake the latter task, otherwise society will collapse. The role of a manager is a difficult one, but one which is an essential lynchpin to civilisation as we know it, irrespective of types of government.

Where have we got to?

So far, we have concerned ourselves with analysis. We have examined what is meant by 'environmental impact' and I hope that we have established that the cry of 'it will affect the environment' should not be taken as a stop signal, but only as a cautionary one as an amber, not a red traffic light.

However, we have also seen that, with fantastically rapid increases in world population and the growing demand for an ever rising standard of living, even in the developed countries, the demand for the exploitation of the world's natural resources will place ever increasing strain on the environment as we know it.

We have looked at how the environment has changed over the years and the way in which concern with environmental issues has become manifest. In the course of this, we have examined the reasons for such changes and have tried to distinguish between the different categories of environmental problems. This is not easy and, to some extent, will always be subjective. There is little doubt that each environmental problem is seen as a major problem by the people whom it affects, but this is not the same thing as saying that all environmental problems are of equal concern or seriousness to the community, or to the world in general. This gives us a starting point. I have tried to show that we have to analyse the various components of so-called environmental problems, to see which of them are genuine and which are in some sense or other a form of disguised self-interest masquerading as a matter of fundamental importance. Am I really objecting to the factory being built solely on the grounds that it will affect the ecology of the area, or in truth because it spoils my view or personal amenities? This is not always an easy question to answer.

It should be clear by now that the 'environmental problem' is one we cannot avoid. We may choose to ignore it, but that is a risky business and may be as helpful as trying to ignore the traffic on Fifth Avenue. Given this we are still left with a wide range of options as to how to respond.

Management was always a lonely job anyway!

It is unfortunate, but true, that no consideration by management of the approach to any problem, can be properly understood outside the context of the social and political system in which it operates. However, far too much can be made of this distinction and any attempts to distinguish between the approach of management to environmental problems in, say, capitalist and communist societies, is not very helpful. There is little evidence that either system has produced a clear distinction in its approach to environmental matters. The main difference lies in the terms of the objectives given to management in these societies. On the face of it, one would expect that in capitalist societies where the overwhelming accent is on the maximisation of profit, concern with the environment would have received the least attention. In practice, it is doubtful whether this argument can be sustained. Problems of environmental pollution have to be tackled in all countries, but each country may differ in its evaluation of the seriousness of particular environmental issues.

From the point of view of the individual manager, the differences between the two types of society are not, I would suggest, as marked as might be generally believed. In all societies and in all countries a manager is faced with the problem of maximising his output from given inputs of resources. The difference is that in a capitalist society, the effectiveness by which he achieves this still tends to be measured solely by the criterion of profit, whereas, in the communist society a different criterion is used, the achievement of the production targets under whatever aspects of whatever Five Year Plan the manager is operating.

It is certainly open to doubt as to whether a manager in a communist society would feel less inhibited than a manager in a capitalist society in not achieving his objectives, whether they be maximisation of profit or the achievement of production targets, in order to meet an environmental problem. The penalties of failure could be severe in either case. The cost of overcoming the conflict of interest between the preservation or conservation of the environment and the maximisation of the use of resources, has to be met in both types of society, and therefore there is little to be gained by an argument that one form of organisation is inherently more effective in dealing with environmental issues than the other.

If in practice, some communist countries have a better record than some non-communist countries, I would suggest that this is the result of the adjustment of the manager's objectives, whether in terms of profit or reaching his production plan, rather than the merit or otherwise of the system itself.

Historically, management has worked on the assumption that it has a basic right to run its own affairs. In the non-communist world, this was alleged to be based on the fact that the investment in the company, and therefore the risk in running the company, was taken by the shareholders, who originally were the managers of the enterprise. Although this relationship has now changed, and these days very few managers have an appreciable stake in the equity of the enterprise they are managing, the old attitudes die hard and the feeling still persists that management should have a right to govern its own affairs, as totally as possible. Certainly, in the non-communist world, any legislation or regulation that placed constraints on management in carrying out its duties was seen as being an unwarranted interference in a company's affairs, and one to be avoided. From Calvin Coolidge's immortal aphorism that 'the business of America is business', to present day concern as to whether or not too great a share of the gross national product is now being directly controlled by the public sector, the message has been the same. The advocates of the free enterprise system have consistently resisted what they term as interference in the internal running of their operations, on the grounds that, if you interfere with the mechanism of the clock, you can't expect it to keep on giving you the right time.

This attitude, that all outside interference should be resisted, has in some quarters been carried over into wholesale resistance to the pressures of environmental lobbies. It is all too easy to assume that, because the lobbies are adopting exaggerated and often self-interested postures, there is no merit in their arguments. It is this attitude which forms the Achilles heel of much of the business community. Where genuine public concern exists, to attempt to resist pressure for action, solely because such action would be against the short term interest of the companies involved, is a weak position to adopt. Its weakness is such that in the long run it will turn out to be indefensible. This is especially true where it can be shown that the dangers are being exaggerated, or the difficulties of implementation are being understated, by management. A classic case of this has been in relation to strip mining in the United States.[3]

The problem of adopting a purely negative attitude is that it makes any subsequent positive action on the part of such companies, appear a concession squeezed out by the environmentalists. This in turn casts doubt on the credibility of the company and can provoke further pressure. Once industry gets into a position of being on the defensive in relation to these matters, then the end result is likely to be greater, rather than less, government intervention. The record of industry historically (with a few notable exceptions) is not one to inspire confidence. This is an unpalatable truth that has to be recognised if progress is to be made.

The danger of a continuation of this approach is that attitudes will polarise. On the one hand, the environmentalists will claim that the apparent reluctance of companies and managements to face up to their own environmental problems is yet a further manifestation of the inability or ineffectiveness of the present systems of control to deliver the goods. On the other hand, management would see such opposition as being idealistic and totally ignoring the problems of the real world in getting goods and services to people when and where they want them. We are back again to the difficulty of competing objectives and each side assuming that the righteousness of its own case is so self-evident that it should be allowed to override the opposite views put forward. We want to throw out each other's babies with our own bathwater.

Management cowboys

If management continues to adopt the stance of resistance to criticism on environmental matters, on the grounds that this is outside interference in an activity which is no concern of the protestors, then there seems little hope of a practical solution. This essentially dogmatic approach results all too often in indefensible attitudes and arguments emerging. Take the example of environmental pollution. When faced with a complaint that a company or industry is causing pollution in this or that way, adherents to the 'non-interference' philosophy tend to respond by denying that there is any problem or, if there manifestly is a problem, to deny that the activities of the organisation make any contribution to it and that it exists independently of their company. Perhaps this has the virtue of making management feel good, but it has nothing else to commend it.

The difficulty with this approach is that if the existence of the problem is accepted (and more often than not it is impossible to deny that there is a

---

[3] See Chapter 8

problem) then people will continue to seek to find causes. In such circumstances, management needs to be absolutely sure of its ground in putting forward a categorical denial that they are not connected with the problem in any way. As, all too frequently, the problem has not been properly analysed, this approach can be foolhardy. If it is subsequently established that the company is implicated, then the loss of credibility to the concern in question is devastating.

Although we are all inclined to take the view that we would not be so foolish as to come out with an outright denial when we may have some connection with the causes, this is too facile a view to take. Very often, the honest view of management is that it cannot conceivably have any connection with the problem. The company may not have changed its working methods for many years and, as far as management is concerned, is continuing to work in traditional and accepted ways. There is then a strong tendency to assume that complaints about the activity are based on antagonism rather than fact. The difficulty here is that knowledge of processes and their effects is being obtained all the time, and some processes which were once considered totally acceptable, are now widely regarded as dangerous. It was many years, for example, before the dangers of working with asbestos were discovered and, I am afraid, even more years before there was general acceptance by parts of the industry that these dangers were as real and as potent as was being suggested. Even after the dangers of working in factories producing asbestos had been accepted, a further period of time elapsed before the dangers of using a particular type of asbestos in buildings were appreciated and action taken to remove this hazard.

So it follows that management has a considerable interest in establishing the truth of any environmental problems or difficulties that emerge, if only to establish the innocence of their own processes or activities.

Environmental Indians

However altruistic in intention, the attitude of the environmentalists often contributes to a hardening of management's attitudes. When a genuine problem is highlighted and management feels that it can work together with all the interested parties in trying to find ways of removing or mitigating the problem, then it is more likely to be forthcoming in its approach and to seek a mutually acceptable solution or compromise. But if the attitude, as is all too often the case, is to 'brand' management with accusations of lack of concern or interest, then little co-operation is likely and management's reaction of a blank denial of responsibility is likely to continue. Management has various responsibilities and it cannot, and should not, sacrifice any of them without a meticulous examination of the consequences for the community of the alternative courses of action.

We need to develop a mutual trust which will enable both sides to join together to establish the facts of any situation and, having established them, to see whether a problem exists. If it does, then it has to be decided whether this is a temporary or a permanent problem, and whether it can be tackled without other adverse effects, which may not be acceptable to the community, either locally or at large. It may well be that local residents would like to see a factory shut down in order to prevent the emission of an unpleasant smell (which may or may not have some element of danger in it). But there may be another part of the community who would be highly incensed at any such move and see it as action being taken by people, whom they may well see as already being privileged, which will result in increased unemployment, or the general decline of the economic prosperity of the district. It is no solution to transfer the problem to some other area where similar considerations obtain. Developed countries often export pollution without realising it. The consequence of not carrying out copper mining, for example, in North Wales, is to increase the need to extract copper from underdeveloped countries as yet unable to afford an 'environmental problem'.

There is a familiar pattern in which the argument is polarised into jobs versus environment. In itself this is dangerous, because often it can be shown that this is not the choice facing the community. If safeguards can be introduced which will provide the necessary protection to the environment, and such costs can then be passed on to the consumer, then a false alternative is being presented.

A defensive reaction on the part of management, the type of reaction which seeks to find a justification for carrying on its old ways, is likely to promote increasing control and restriction from outside; whether done by national or local government, the effect will be the same. Protestors, whether they have a good case or not, will use political methods to try and obtain tighter control over the operation of the industry. This in itself should be a strong incentive to management to establish ways in which particular problems can be tackled at source in relation to specific problems, rather than to escalate the argument and risk further strait-jackets of law and regulation being imposed.

6   The policeman at the gate

Something ought to be done

So far we have considered in some detail how interest in the environment has been brought to the forefront of public attention. This increasing concern has produced a reaction on the part of individuals and governments which, although it has varied in intensity and motivation, has generally been aimed at ameliorating the worst of the obvious environmental problems.

The rapid growth in population (which cannot be contained in the short term) and the arrival of instant communications, the television set in the shanty town (which means all the world knows how well developed nations live), is producing an ever increasing demand on the earth's limited natural resources.

As these pressures have increased, there have been areas where they have reached breaking point and where government action has been taken. Such actions have by no means always been either well judged, justified or sensible. Nevertheless, it is clear that there comes a time when governments, of whatever political persuasion, feel that they have no alternative but to take some action to demonstrate to their electorate that they are in 'control'.

I want, in this chapter, to take a brief look at some of the ways in which governments have responded to such pressures and to analyse the types of action they have pursued. This is particularly important for management, because it is the type of government response which can have such a tremendous impact on the future of individual companies. The ways in which governments have tried to control environmental matters have affected precisely those areas in which managers believe that they are merely trying to carry out their normal responsibilities and day-to-day tasks.

This control has been exercised through
a)   recommendation and exhortation
b)   financial encouragement to follow the required course of action
c)   legislative regulations
d)   prohibition or restriction of certain activities

In all this, governments have seldom been entirely self-motivated. The initial reaction often has come from the activities of a pressure group and the government has responded to such pressure.

Pressure groups operate at local, as well as national levels. The local level has sometimes been ignored as being relatively unimportant, but it must be remembered that a considerable degree of control can be exercised through invoking local planning regulations. Often, it is the cumulative effect of local pressure groups that produces a demand for changes in the law.

However successful voluntary campaigns turn out to be, there is always a residual problem arising from the people who will not accept the overall interest of the community (or a particular interpretation of it) and still attempt to 'get away with it'. It is this reaction which can lead on to a cry for enforceable legislation to which recourse can be made. Sometimes this can appear to be based on an 'equality of suffering' argument: if I am going to toe the line in a specific case, I have a vested interest in making sure you do too.

There ought to be a law

The most common way in which governments have attempted to control environmental matters has been through the introduction of laws which prevent certain actions taking place. We are all familiar with the regulations and restrictions laid down by various planning laws, irrespective of what country we are working in.[1] In some countries, the planning regulations bite more fiercely than in others, but the general intention is the same — to prevent industrial activity or development in certain areas.

Management has also been affected by restrictive regulations within the workplace. The various factories acts lay down minimum acceptable conditions for employment, but the protection of working conditions has gone far beyond the provision of guards for machinery. In the case of certain industries which are known to have health hazards, such as working with asbestos or working in high concentrations of dust as in mining, the governments have introduced stringent restrictions defining the conditions in which work is permitted to continue.

The importance of restrictive legislation is not merely in the restrictions that it imposes, but in the mechanism of enforcement. The existence of the necessary inspectorates inevitably introduces a degree of control over the operations of managers.

One of the perennial problems of restrictive legislation is the demand to make it encompass an ever widening number of processes or products. There tends to be continual agitation that the incidence of a particular disease in a particular industry, must be connected with the substances or the process used. As it inevitably takes a long period of time to establish whether there is a causal relationship, there can be long periods in which the argument continues as to

[1] In Britain the first Town and Country Planning Act was given Royal Assent in December, 1909. The purpose of the Act was to establish proper sanitary conditions and a sense of amenity in laying out land for development.

whether or not a particular process or product should be allowed. If we are going to cease every activity over which there is a trace of suspicion or concern then we have to be prepared to face up to the resultant cumulative loss of employment and general worsening of social conditions, which in many cases, will prove to be totally unnecessary.

You can't do that

There is a long tradition of legislation in the Western world, particularly in Great Britain. The first legislation which could be said to be connected with the environment was, in fact, apparently aimed at conservation. As far back as 1534, an Act was passed 'to avoid the destruction of wilde fowle'. It had no long-term conservation motive and its aim was far more practical and immediate, concerned with protecting the eggs of the birds which the gentlemen of England wished to pursue with either falcons or guns. The legislation was therefore concerned with conserving prey for the falcons, but not with conserving the prey themselves!

We have already considered how the working environment became one of the earlier subjects for protection in mid-nineteenth century legislation concerning working in urban areas. In Great Britain, the Board of Health was set up in 1848, with the aim of improving environmental conditions in towns, by providing a water supply, street scavenging and mains drainage. These aims would hardly seem to be over-ambitious, but they certainly brought about a revolution in the environments of the rapidly growing industrial towns.

The need for such efforts was by no means confined to Western Europe. The condition of towns in the United States was regarded as being a scandal in the first half of the nineteenth century. One foreign ambassador wrote back to his native country commenting that, in the capital of the United States, they relied on pigs in the streets to do their scavenging for them. The situation was little better in terms of sanitation. As late as 1900, in the town of Baltimore, it was estimated that no fewer than 90,000 dwellings had to make do with backyard privies and were devoid of mains drainage. Coming even nearer to our own day, Washington in the 1930s was still alleged to have 70,000 dwellings in the same category.[2]

Most of us are familiar with the story of the way in which food and drugs legislation had to be introduced to actually prevent people being poisoned by the adulteration of food by either unscrupulous or unthinking providers and purveyors of foodstuffs.

We may not realise the time and effort it has taken to reach our present standards. Two Acts in 1727 and 1730 introduced penalties for adulteration for that most British of institutions — the cup of tea. Apparently the eighteenth century Englishman was more concerned with his drink than his food,

---

[2] See Constance Green's *The Rise of Urban America.*

because Acts prohibiting the adulteration of coffee and cocoa followed. Somewhat surprisingly, it took until 1861 before a similar act was brought in to protect the working man's beer and port.

The second half of the nineteenth century brought forward a number of Bills to protect foodstuffs. The need for them perhaps was not surprising. The growth of towns, and the increasing demands for foodstuffs which had to travel a long way to the consumer, resulted in an increasing number of preservatives being added to food, some of which had very unpleasant consequences.

The concern over the adulteration of food and drink, which resulted in the Report of a Parliamentary Select Committee of Inquiry in 1856, finally resulted in the Act for Preventing the Adulteration of Articles of Food and Drink of 1866. This Act provided penalties for any person selling any article of food and drink which, to his knowledge, had been mixed with ingredients injurious to health. It became an offence to sell any articles as pure, if in fact they were not. In intention the Act was commendable, but as the penalties imposed were only £5 and costs, it proved to be largely ineffectual. Not until it was strengthened by the Sale of Food and Drugs Act of 1875, which provided for the appointment of inspectors and public analysts, was legal control over quality of foodstuffs exercised to any real effect.

In the United States, the first legislative control was through the Flour Inspection Act of 1824, which covered the County of Alexandria, in the District of Columbia. Between 1880 and 1906 more than one hundred bills were introduced into Congress to control various aspects of adulteration, but none of them passed through both Houses. The first major Act in the United States was the Food and Drugs Act of 1906, which gave a specific definition of adulteration, although it left loopholes on specification.

Attempts to obtain amendments and improvements in the law proved fruitless in the face of unrelenting opposition from various vested interests. As has all too frequently been the case, it needed the stimulation of a major disaster to win agreement that something needed to be done. In 1937, seventy-three people died in the United States after taking a substance known as 'Elixir Sulfamlamide'. This proved to contain diethylene glycol which can produce kidney and liver damage. In the aftermath of this tragedy, proponents of tighter control were able to secure the passage of the Federal Food, Drug and Cosmetic Act. This Act made no attempt at close definition, but prohibited the sale of any foods which were considered a danger to health.

Make it safe

The working environment was first tackled in terms of number of hours worked. Even then it was pictured as being the aim of protecting those who were too weak to protect themselves, primarily children. Inevitably, the

The industrial revolution: unplanned congestion with no thought for the environment. Top: factories in the centre of Birmingham (Architectural Press). Bottom: workers' back to back housing in Burnely, Lancashire (Aerofilms)

The use of landscaping to humanise or conceal. Top: a shelter belt of trees around an oil refinery (Clifford R V Tandy). Bottom: garden-like landscaping for a factory (ICI Fibres Ltd)

Opencast operations in progress and the same site restored to the environment
(National Coal Board)

Before and after: restoration carried out on sites by the sand and gravel industry, both for agricultural and recreational purposes (Tilling Construction Services Ltd)

Before and after: an improved landscape once the coal has been excavated
(National Coal Board)

The old and the new: the coal mine in the top picture started production before 1900; the new coal mine, opened in 1960, is planned to have a minimum effect on the environment (National Coal Board)

The Frankfurt-Nuremberg autobahn well sited into the landscape through existing woodlands, and with swinging horizontal curves which follow the rhythm of the undulating topography (Bayrischer Flugdienst, Munchen)

legislation that was passed to provide a measure of protection for children, women, and young adults, had side effects on the working conditions of all sections of the working population.

Legislation on hours of work was followed by restrictions on how the work should be organised and carried out. In other words — safety legislation.

The impetus for safety legislation came from the growing loss of life in the expanding coal mining industry. After a series of frightening colliery disasters in the late 1840s, Parliament passed a Coal Mines Inspection Act in 1850. This Act provided not only for the state inspection of mines, but laid down minimum requirements on light and ventilation. The provisions of this Act were soon amplified by further acts. In 1855 an Act was introduced which, for the first time, drew up a code of 'general rules' for collieries. This was followed in 1860 by the Coal Mines' Regulation Act, which laid down new general rules.

Throughout the 1860s, the miners agitated for better legal protection, resulting in the Coal Mines Act of 1872. At the same time, a companion Act was brought in, relating to metalliferous mining; significant, because it introduced a major restriction on the freedom of the colliery owners to carry out the work in any way they thought fit. For the first time, colliery managers were compelled to have some basic qualifications in their draft and had to obtain a State certificate indicating they were competent to carry out their duties.

The creation of a Health and Safety Authority in Britain in 1975 has given a new emphasis to safety regulations there. A series of mining disasters in the USA in the early 1970s heralded a more stringent attitude to safety in mines there also, with a much enlarged and more powerful inspectorate.

We don't want your rubbish

The increasing industrialisation brought with it major problems of pollution. The first of these to be tackled, however ineffectually, was the pollution of the water supply. In 1876 a major piece of legislation was passed in the United Kingdom to control pollution in rivers, caused by sewage and industrial waste. However, increasing technological 'progress' increased problems of water pollution and further Acts became necessary.

In 1951 an Act prohibited the discharge of poisonous, noxious or polluting matter into streams. It also prevented effluents from trade premises (including farms) or sewage effluents, being discharged into non-tidal rivers without the consent of the appropriate River Authority. These powers have since been extended and other countries have taken major steps in the same direction.

The need for pure water is widely recognised, yet it is often forgotten that water itself is never pure. Rainwater, which we tend to regard as being one of the purest sources, picks up such impurities as carbon dioxide, nitric acid, sulphur and ammonia from the atmosphere. In recent years, one increasing problem has been the enrichment of water by plant nutrients, often arising from the over-fertilisation of agricultural land in an attempt to maintain or improve crop yields. The over-enrichment of water in this way, known as eutrophication, leads to the development of algae and this, in turn, has major implications for rivers and lakes. The most striking example of this development is the Great Lakes Basin in North America, where the concentration of the outflows of municipal sewage and industrial effluents produced a frightening situation, which could have led to the 'death' of the Great Lakes as we know them. Now the problem is known, preventive steps can be taken.

Many of the problems deriving from industrial effluents arise from the amount of phosphorous in detergents. It has been estimated that in the United States some seven per cent of the phosphorous in municipal sewage arises from phosphorous-based detergents. Fortunately, there would appear to be a way out of this particular dilemma, as it has been found possible to obtain at least a partial replacement of phosphates in detergents without reducing their cleaning power. In the light of this development, the Canadian Government decided that detergent manufacturers must reduce the phosphate content of laundry detergents to a maximum of five per cent.

It is not only liquid effluents which can cause problems. The growing sophistication of our industrial processes has resulted in some alarming waste materials being left for disposal. Potentially the most frightening of them all is the radioactive waste which arises from the creation of nuclear power. Further down the scale there are many other poisonous products which need to be handled with great care and understanding, if they are to be disposed of in a way that will not cause potential danger to the community. There have been all too many instances where refuse tips have not been properly controlled and which subsequently have claimed the lives of people working on or near them.

Increasing concern with the pollution of the atmosphere has brought forth various clean air laws. Some are more advanced than others and, although in the United Kingdom we have tended to concentrate on visible air pollution, legislation in the United States, aimed at cutting down the emission of noxious gases from car exhausts, indicates the way the future lies. The demands for 'pure' air and water are unlikely to diminish. In the United Kingdom, the Clean Air Acts have been very effective in removing the visible signs of air pollution, but the air is not yet clean. In physical terms, it has been estimated that the emission of smoke has been reduced from an annual rate of 2.4 million tonnes to 0.4 million tonnes in the last 25 years but, in the same period, the emission of sulphur dioxide has risen from 4.7 to 5.1 million tonnes.

Legislation on the amount of noise that industry is allowed to create is a relatively new phenomenon but, given the mounting pressures to cut down on many activities, together with increasing knowledge and concern about the health hazards arising from excess noise, it would appear likely that we can expect more and tighter noise legislation.

There is also a need to protect purchasers of articles from dangers which are not already apparent and which were not anticipated by the manufacturers. We can all think of examples, the most obvious ones being lead in the paint used to decorate children's toys, and the noxious fumes which can be given off by certain plastics when burned. Unfortunately, manufacturers cannot assume that their products will be used safely for the purchase they were designed. Even if their products are only dangerous when they are misused, the manufacturer is still in trouble.

The other major area of restrictive legislation is in the control of all forms of industrial, or even residential, development. All countries now have some form of planning control which attempts to ensure that new activities involving the change of use of land must be supported by carefully argued submissions as to why such developments should take place, and provision for people to object to the proposed development.

In the United States, the move towards the introduction of compulsory environmental impact analysis is now well under way and this would seem to be a movement which will be repeated throughout the Western world. The aim of environmental impact analysis is to ensure that there is a formalised assessment of all the possible effects on the environment of a proposed development, before consideration of such a development takes place.

If governments decide that a certain type of activity does constitute a danger to the environment, then it is right that legislation should be introduced to control the activity and to make it conform to the required parameters.

For firms engaged in such activities, the danger is that governments may act out of ignorance or prejudice and may be making a purely political response to the growing influence of interested pressure groups. If they do this, governments may well create a legal framework which makes no sense in relation to the activity itself. Legislation introduced without full understanding of the effect on the activity concerned can be very dangerous indeed. Besides failing to achieve its direct objective, it can produce totally unexpected and unwanted results. Industries could be pushed from marginally questionable methods to much more potentially dangerous (but still legal) ones.

This is a good reason why, even though industries or firms may wish to resist restrictive environmental legislation with all the force at their command, they would be well advised to meet the arguments rationally and to develop counter-arguments. If they remain aloof and assert that no regulation or control is needed, because there is no problem, and do not attempt to see where there is need for improvement in their current practices, then these firms are likely to have standards imposed upon them which are either unworkable or are unnecessarily strict. The legislation will be based on the views and objectives of the conservationists or the environmentalists, and not the practising industrialists.

This situation has been very apparent in the United States in relation to the proposed legislation to control the operation of strip mining for coal. The coal operators alleged that the provisions brought forward in the Senate Bills were so restrictive that they would effectively prevent the realisation of the country's objective of reaching self-sufficiency in energy in the 1980s.

One of the reasons for paying close attention to the arguments of the pressure groups is to see whether they are concentrating on parts of the activity which are in fact hard to defend, or whether they are basing their allegations on misconceptions.

At times it is argued that even where there are weaknesses in certain environmental controls, an individual industrialist cannot afford to take steps to remedy them because it will put him at a commercial disadvantage in relation to his competitors. In itself this is an argument of somewhat doubtful validity. Although it might be true in the short-term, it is equally arguable that if you put your own house in order, fix your own standards (which by definition are attainable and reasonable), you are helping to establish an appropriate bench mark for any legislation which might be brought in and you will by then be ahead of the field.

If the government does not want to use the 'stick' approach, the possibility of a 'carrot' is still available. If it is policy to attract industry (or particular types of industry) into (or away from) particular areas, this can be implemented by means of tax concessions or financial grants, providing an economic inducement for the required result.

Pressure groups

Legislation is not a primary response to the impact of industry on the environment, but a secondary one. Before legislation is introduced, the desire or the demand for such legislation has to become manifest. The way in which this occurs is usually through the efforts of increasingly well-organised pressure groups. There is nothing new about this concept of pressure groups; all legislation starts out as the idea of a pressure group of some kind.

Although it is quite true that some pressure groups start out with a membership of one, unless they can build from this narrow base, then their hope of achieving success is somewhat limited!

Because pressure groups are effective in securing legislation, it is not surprising that counter-groups emerge aimed at either preventing or modifying the proposed legislation in such a way as will be more acceptable to the group concerned. We have to recognise the existence of such groups and not to work on the assumption that the existence of a pressure group indicates that the whole project is suspect. The debate must always be on the validity of the arguments of the pressure groups and not on the existence of a particular pressure group itself.

The biggest pressure groups of all are the organised political parties. The nation itself can be a pressure group, as can be seen very readily in the attitudes of different countries towards the definition of home coastal waters. But in the domestic context, the most important pressure group is the political party. If a political party, particularly one which has legitimate aspirations to becoming the government, adopts a particular idea or concept, then the likelihood of this becoming embodied in the law increases. Small pressure groups, therefore, generally try to work on political parties in order to gain support for their own ideas. This has a two way reaction, because the parties themselves hope that by adopting a particular pressure group's programme, it will secure the support of the members of that group.

In the environmental field a number of these pressure groups operate on an international, and not just on a national, basis. This has advantages for them, but it can also lead to disadvantages, the most obvious one being that it is tempting for the pressure group to translate the experience of one country into the ethos of another country, where it may not fit. As an example, the traditions, techniques, and practice of restoration of opencast mining in North America are not the same as those in Great Britain. Therefore it is totally misleading to translate the arguments for or against opencast mining in the United States, to proposals in Britain, or vice versa.

Most pressure groups, it should be accepted, are directed by dedicated people, with an intense conviction that the arguments they are putting forward are valid and should carry the day. Pressure groups should be recognised for what they are, a group of people with a committed view about a particular topic and, as such, their arguments should be listened to with respect and, where ill-founded, should be refuted, but only on the facts of the situation. The problem with pressure groups is that they tend to be totally unresponsive to counter-arguments, particularly if these in any way appear to undermine the basis of their own particular faith. In the same way that you would hardly hope to get the better of an argument concerning the validity of differing religious beliefs, you should not expect to convert the apostles of a particular environmental faith to your own. What you can hope to do is to convince the uncommitted.

Most pressure groups tend to promote counter-pressure groups for those who want to maintain the *status quo*, and vice versa. This has been much apparent in recent years, in groups such as the anti-abortionists and those who want wider availability of abortion for those who want it.

In the environmental field a pressure group as such, aimed at countering the more extreme arguments put forward by the environmentalists and the conservationists does not seem to have appeared. The impression has been that the reverse applies. Whenever industry or an activity comes under attack from pressure groups, there has been a tendency to attempt to avoid meeting the arguments and, in some instances, not to proceed with the activity. Even where battle has been joined, there has been a tendency to try to switch the basic grounds of the argument. Propositions based on the disturbance of the environment have been countered, not with the response that such effects are minimal or not of crucial impetus, but rather with attempts to justify the end result of the activity — not an approach calculated to win environmental friends or influence conservationist persons. More importantly, all too often this is unnecessary. Very often the environmentalists have either over-stated their case, or based their opposition on subjective grounds. In such cases it is far better for a counter-pressure group to be built up, making the facts clear and attacking the claims made by the protectors of the *status quo.*

He who pays the piper . . .

One of the ways in which governments are being pressed to exercise control over the 'despoilers of the environment' is through taxation. There have been many arguments put forward based broadly on the principle that 'polluters must pay' or that users of scarce raw materials should have to pay an additional tax for the privilege of doing so.

On the face of it, these arguments have much to commend them. Where an industrial activity does harm to the environment by pouring out noxious waste, polluting land or water, then it would be reasonable and common sense to charge that company with the full cost of the damage it is doing, so that the social costs of the operation are taken into the overall equation.

The 'polluter must pay' argument is unfortunately not quite as straight-forward as that. The advocates of putting a tax on this type of activity seem to have missed one fundamental point. The effect of such a tax could be to make the firm spend money to escape the taxation by ending its polluting. If that can be achieved, then it would be reasonable to argue that such a system of taxation was securing the right results. But supposing that the activity is producing something which is in strong demand, then the likelihood is that the industrialist will simply add the cost of the tax to his selling price to ensure that his return remains the same. If this is done, then the 'pollution tax' is not being 'paid' by the polluter, but by the consumer. The results being that not only the industrialist's financial return but the pollution will remain the same. It is a dubious moral principle to allow an offender to buy his way out of trouble just because he can afford to. This failure to appreciate the importance of what the economists would call the 'incidence of the tax', casts a doubt on the whole 'pollution must pay philosophy'. If the slogan was not 'the polluter pays', but 'the consumer pays', the emotional reaction to such a taxation policy might be very different.

Nevertheless, it might be argued that it is still a sensible policy because, if the consumer is to secure the benefit of the activity which has produced the pollution, then it is right that he should pay in the price of the product the cost of dealing with such pollution. Unfortunately, this again is not as simple as it appears because, by definition, the product or service is in very strong demand, otherwise the manufacturer, or producer, would not be able to pass on the pollution tax in the price. If it is in such high demand, then the implication is that the product is regarded by the consumer as some form of necessity. In such an event, all increase in price of such an end product is likely to cause a major diminution in the satisfaction of the purchaser and one which he may not be either willing or able to accept. He may therefore argue that any 'pollution' costs should be borne out of general taxation, rather than fall on the particular product.

Perhaps it will make the position clearer if we take a practical example. Unfortunately, the production of all the major types of energy — coal, oil and nuclear power — have some adverse effects on the environment. (The exception, natural gas, is now a rapidly depleting asset.) The effect of charging the industries concerned with the full cost would be to increase the fuel bills of the consumer. The consumer is therefore going to look for the cheapest source of energy to meet his needs. However, as the energy market is an international one, and as taxation is a local issue, it must follow that it is possible that the net effect of a 'pollution tax' would be to transfer the demand from the indigenous energy resources of the home to an overseas country. If the standards or pollution control in the overseas country were not as rigorous as in the home country, then the net effect of such a tax would merely be to export the pollution. However satisfactory this might be for the consumer, it is hardly a soundly based moral argument for the policy. Although it might have a short-term beneficial effect to the home country, the effect on the world's ecology must be just as bad wherever the pollution occurs. Making the polluters pay only makes sense where it can be assumed that this will drive people into alternatives which will cause less pollution in the world as a whole. This would be a very rash and optimistic generalisation. To achieve this objective requires detailed analysis rather than a blunt instrument approach.

The problems of attempting control of any activity by taxation derive from the fact that, as has been all too readily discovered in relation to income tax, it is almost impossible to formulate a water-tight law. Although it sounds simple to 'make the polluter pay', in practice, it could well be that the pollution tax could become as much a 'voluntary' tax as income tax. If the objectives are clear, then it is far better that these should be covered by direct legislation rather than by trying to adapt the price mechanism to make it do the work.

The same argument is not so applicable to the suggestion for a 'natural resources' tax on all people wishing to use a scarce natural resource, so as to minimise its use. In this case it would be possible to alter the rate of value added tax on the individual raw material components being utilised to manufacture a final product, to make it always relatively more attractive to use the resources in greatest supply.

Another way in which governments have attempted to do something about pollution is by intervention in a positive, rather than a negative fashion. This has been done by the creation of such bodies as the Tennessee Valley Authority in the United States, which was an attempt to overcome the environmental problems of lack of water and power by co-ordinating the management of the river basin, irrespective of state boundaries. This combination of power development, irrigation, drainage, purification and flood control, was a fundamental environmental issue. It has undoubtedly achieved many of its original objectives, but it is interesting to speculate what would have happened if the project had been put forward in today's environmental atmosphere. Undoubtedly, it would have been opposed on the grounds that it would be bound to have devastating effects on the ecology of the region and, as such, should not be allowed to proceed. If that had happened, would the quality of life of people in the area have been improved? I very much doubt it.

Governments often react positively in this way in response to pressure groups. The movement in Britain to clear up derelict land received great impetus from areas outside government, but resulted in government deciding to take direct steps to encourage the clearance of unsightly areas through campaigns and the provision of financial assistance to approved schemes. Sometimes the effect of government is on the level of exhortation, in an attempt to persuade people to protect the environment in which they live. Another area in which direct interference has had a tremendous effect, has been tree planting. The deliberate planting of trees to provide shelter has been a very long practice and was in fact decreed by the Parliament in Scotland as long ago as 1457. One of the earlier Russian Five Year Plans included the proposal to plant gigantic wind-breaks across the Steppes. In the United States, the Timber Culture Act of 1873 aimed to secure the planting of trees in the Great Plains and Prairie States, which it was hoped would foster rainfall and help to eliminate hazards to agriculture. As an indication as to how long it can take ideas to get firmly off the ground, there was an attempt as late as 1934 to resurrect the shelter belt project for tree planting on the Great Plains.

Governments, whether local or state, can have an effect on the local environment by either allowing or not allowing visitors to particular areas. Where the area is one of great natural beauty, then a fine balance has to be drawn letting people come to experience the peace and beauty of the place (which is one of the main intentions of having such a nominated area) and, on the other hand, the arrival of such an influx of visitors which could destroy the nature of the place. This is particularly true if uninterrupted access of cars, or even of walkers, is allowed.

The control of people in this way is becoming more and more necessary as populations grew and, in Western countries, the leisure time they have to spend increases also.

One of the main difficulties is getting international agreement on standards, whether voluntary or otherwise, because, as we have seen, individual countries could preserve their own environment by exporting their environmental problems. It is clear that, with the depth and complexity of the real environmental issues facing us (ignoring the false alarms which are so often made the forefront of environmental alarm), the call for government intervention — the policeman at the gate — will get louder and louder.

7   The silver lining

Can we afford it?

So far we have been concerned mainly with problems rather than solutions. We have looked at the ways in which mankind has abused the environment and not at examples where some consideration has been shown.

The future may well appear to be one of almost unrelieved gloom and at this point to hold out little hope of improving. But are we so ostrich-like, so blind to our own long-term interests, that we will not make some attempt to learn from our mistakes?

The task is to engender a greater concern with the reality of environmental issues and a greater awareness that — whatever our own preconceptions — we are in the world of necessary compromise or what the Americans call 'tradeoffs'. Unless compromise is possible, then we are embarked on a collision course. In this chapter, I want to examine some of the ways which, in recent years, societies have been able to show that they are capable of making moves towards limiting environmental impact in some very sensitive areas.

Even a cursory examination of differing attitudes towards the environment, whether over a period of time, or between different locations, will soon show that awareness of environmental issues and a determination to do something about them, are the result of increasing affluence. This seems a pretty paradox indeed. Increasing affluence and the desire for higher living standards, produce the very pressures on the environment that lead to unease, yet without the wealth thus created, there is little that can be done either to prevent or to curtail their worst excesses.

A little more thought tells us why this is not paradoxical but merely a matter of logistics. Improved living standards result from changes in industrial and agricultural techniques, changes in the types of activity we wish to undertake, and major new developments, such as the growth of motor and air travel. Such changes cannot be brought about without affecting the environment in some way. This applies whether one is talking about agricultural improvements, such as the Enclosure Movement in the Middle Ages, or the upheaval caused by the Industrial Revolution and the absorption of agricultural workers into the new factory system.

It is the changes themselves that ultimately produce a counter-reaction, complaints about environmental mutations which are in fact a direct consequence of technological developments in society. While man is searching for improvements in basic subsistence, such considerations tend to be ignored, being of secondary importance, but as living standards rise and immediate problems of survival retreat into the background, then people become more concerned with the environment in which they have to live[1].

Once primary objectives are taken for granted, secondary objectives more become important. The problem is, as we have already seen, that of a conflict between these demands for higher and higher living standards and the need to preserve the environment as we know it. Demands to clean up some of the mess and excess left from the earlier industrial revolution reduce the amount of resources available for improving, or even maintaining, current general living standards. This conflict between the environment and the maximum use of the resources that are available to mankind, is bound to grow and therefore it is of interest to examine ways in which these conflicts have been resolved so far. There is much in the present environment which is man-made of which we need not be ashamed.

A roof over your head

The most obvious way in which environmental standards have improved is in the general mass of housing in developed countries. We are all aware of the almost indescribable conditions which accompanied the Industrial Revolution in Western Europe and parts of the United States. The overcrowding of towns, which burst at the seams in their attempt to hold the influx of workers required by the new industrial processes, is only too familiar.[2] The overcrowding, the festering side alleys and the dingy, despicable courtyards; the complete absence of sanitary facilities, and the meagre attempt to provide even such elementary amenities as a pure water supply, all combined to condemn much of the working population of Western Europe to lives which Thomas Hobbes would certainly have seen as typifying his view of human existence in a primitive society, as 'nasty, brutish and short'.[3]

---

[1] This attitude can be reversed just as speedily. If, after a succession of mild winters, you have one that causes fuel shortages and people find that their factories go on short time because they lack supplies, and that they cannot heat their houses, then there will be cries for urgent action to meet the crisis. Environmental considerations will then drop down the scale of priorities.

[2] See Engels *Condition of the Working Classes in England*; William Booth *In Darkest England*; Charles Booth *Life and Labour of the People of London*.

[3] We must not conclude that no one cared about the appalling housing conditions that the masses of the population had to endure. The Society for Improving the Dwellings of the Labouring Classes had set out a programme of better housing and improved lodging houses for the homeless poor as early as 1847. The great philanthropist Lord Shaftesbury introduced Housing Bills in 1851 which made the licensing and inspection of all common lodging houses compulsory. There were further Acts in the 1860s and 1870s. The degree of public concern was reflected in the membership of the Royal

The whole atmosphere of the towns themselves was one which should have been a source of shame to any civilised country. Although there are many hair raising contemporary descriptions, perhaps the feel is most graphically caught in Dickens' description of his fictional Coke Town, in *Hard Times*.

'It was a town of red brick, or of brick that would have been red if the smoke and ashes had allowed it; but as matters stood it was a town of unnatural red and black, like the painted face of a savage. It was a town of machinery and tall chimneys, out of which interminable serpents of smoke trailed themselves forever and ever, and never got uncoiled. It had a black canal in it, and a river that ran purple with ill-smelling dye, and vast piles of buildings full of windows where there was a rattling and trembling all day long and where the piston and steam engine worked monotonously up and down like the head of an elephant in a state of melancholy madness. It contained several large streets all very like one another, and many small streets all very like one another, inhabited by people equally like one another, who all went in and out of the same houses, to the same sound upon the same pavements, to do the same work, and to whom every day was the same as yesterday, and tomorrow and every year the counterpart of the last and the next.'

There has been much criticism of the new town developments in the United Kingdom since the war.[4] They have been described as soulless and antiseptic and the general impression has been created that they are not very desirable places in which to live. However, one has only to read Dickens' description to see how far we have progressed and the enormous improvements that have been made in providing reasonable environments for people. One does not, however, have to look only at the new towns. Throughout Western Europe the average quality of housing has improved enormously over the last half century and this type of planning, with care taken to ensure that the urban environment gives people a chance to live a decent life, is now taken for granted. This is one area where management has taken into account the

---

[4] The development of Garden Cities (the idea was suggested by Sir Ebenezer Howard in 1878) and subsequently 'New Towns', is a fascinating chapter of social history and a case study of how we have learned to compromise with our environment. The proposal to build 'satellite towns' as the 'New Towns' were originally called was violently opposed by the then local agricultural and other vested interests. It is interesting to contemplate what would have happened if the environmental movement had reached its present strength. The New Towns would not have been created and the housing problem would have remained that much worse.

Commission on the Housing of the Working Classes which was set up in 1884 under the chairmanship of Sir Charles Dilke. It was 'Royal' indeed having the Prince of Wales as co-chairman. Other members included Cardinal Manning and the Marquis of Salisbury. In the event, its membership was more distinguished than its impact on the problem. Things might have been different if another pioneer of better housing — Mrs Octavia Hill — had been allowed to be a member, but her nomination was overruled by Mr Gladstone.

problems of the environment and has tackled them in a reasonable way. There are many signs of the inevitable compromises that have had to be made, and there are some disasters, such as the passion for tearing down structurally good property instead of refurbishing it, but the general result is an improvement and not a deterioration.[5]

The industrial environment has also seen much needed change. While it is true that there are still far too many industrial premises whose conditions bear all too clearly the stamp of their nineteenth century parentage, new types of industrial development bear no relationship to the same family. Modern factory buildings are often almost indistinguishable from office blocks or hospitals. Not only that, but the evolution of the concept of industrial parks where factories are brought together in properly landscaped settings with a judicious grouping of associated industries, has transformed our ideas on what constitutes a good working environment.[6]

The idea of grouping industrial activities together, away from the areas where the employees live, removes the problems associated with living cheek by jowl with industry. (It does, however, accentuate the problems of transport, and these may well have a severe effect on people who live on the access routes to the factory estate.) It would be hard to deny on any criterion that present day industrial buildings are an immeasurable improvement for employees on the industrial workhouses which we inherited.[7]

Not only the buildings have improved: inside them, far more attention is given to safety, heating, lighting and hygiene. Proper attention is paid to all those aspects which could be collectively described as the workers' environment. In many cases this increased concern for the wellbeing of the worker has borne fruit in increased productivity and better industrial relations.[8]

A start has been made on clearing up our inheritance of industrial wastelands and we have learned how to exercise control over those activities which are, or could cause, major health hazards. There remains a lot to be done but it would be foolish to decry the progress that has been already made.

---

[5] The changing approach to housing is one of the best examples of the way in which conditions have been improved out of all recognition, but we must realise that there is still far to go. The numbers still without adequate housing in so called developed societies are a disgrace. My argument is not that all is well, merely that the relative improvement for most people is marked indeed.

[6] The working environment has been much influenced by the growing strength of factory legislation which first concentrated on working hours but later increasingly on health and safety.

[7] Perhaps the industrial archaeologist would argue that the new buildings no longer have the magnificence of the old castle-like mills and factories, but perhaps our illusions of grandeur have finally disappeared for ever.

[8] In recent years, with the growth of flextime in some fields of activity, the employee has even been able to shake himself free of the tyranny of the clock and has begun to enjoy some control over the actual hours he wishes to work — a facility which many a senior manager must envy!

Isn't there a better way to get there?

The development of roads and motorways throughout the world, over the last quarter of a century, illustrates aspects of the argument over environmental concern.

A great deal of time, effort and ingenuity has been put into the careful design of the road system. Attention has been paid to the future projection of traffic flows and the needs of the community in assessing just where the road system needs improvement. Care has been given to the engineering design of roads in an attempt to cut down the appalling carnage caused by road accidents. Indeed, one of the main arguments in favour of introducing motorway systems has been that, as well as reducing journey time, (thus, in commercial terms, the cost of transportation) they would be much safer and reduce the accident rate. The elimination of crossings, traffic lights, roundabouts, numerous feeder roads, etc., has produced an inherently safer road. Unfortunately, it is true that care in safety design can be offset by poor driving standards. This is particularly true if people believe that because the road is safer, they can drive at much higher speeds. However, most figures indicate that the net result of the introduction of motorways is to reduce the accident rate in terms of miles travelled and that obviously represents a major improvement in our environment.[9]

Safety standards have been further improved by the attention given to the lighting of roads. Decisions taken to put permanent lighting on long stretches of the motorway have also had an appreciable effect on accident reduction. The significance of lighting in improving safety standards can easily be appreciated by anybody who is driving on a motorway at night and moves out of a lighted stretch.

It is now hard to believe that motorways were originally built without central reservations or crash barriers; their introduction has done much to minimise the seriousness of motorway accidents by eliminating the cause of the most terrifying of all accidents, traffic crossing from an up to a down stream.

Ever since the invention of the motorcar, progress has been made on improving traffic flows, traffic and road systems. We forget how much work has been done, because the improvements have been swamped by the fantastic rise in the number of vehicles using the road system. This growth in traffic has apparently obliterated the hoped for effects of the improvements that have been carried out.

It is not only in the area of safety that the design of the road system has taken major steps forward. We have learned to look at the motorway in terms of how it fits into the landscape. One has only got to travel on a protracted journey, over motorways constructed at various periods over the last fifteen years, to see the lessons that have been learned and the ways in which major

---

[9] See the various Reports of the United Kingdom Road Safety Research Laboratory.

attempts have been made to ensure that the new motorways fit more harmoniously into the countryside and the local environment.

It can be argued that this improvement is visual proof of the effectiveness of pressure put on the motorway engineers by environmentalists and conservationists, and that it would not have come about otherwise. Be that as it may, the net result is undeniably better. Looking at the motorway carefully it will be seen that now the aim is to blend into the countryside rather than to cut starkly across it. Contours are followed rather than bisected. The monotony of the same standardised bridges across the roads has been avoided. It seems that motorways are now being accepted as an integral part of the landscape, in the same way that we accept railways and canals; those major intrusions of earlier times.

It is now hard to believe the furore that greeted the introduction of railways into the landscape in the nineteenth century. The outcry even reached into the realm of English literature. Wordsworth commented on the Kendal and Windermere Railway:

'Is there no nook of English ground secure from rash assault?'

John Ruskin was equally outraged. Not only did he hate the visual effect of railways, he also detested their fundamental purpose:

'Now every fool in Buxton can be in Bakewell in half an hour and every fool in Bakewell in Buxton; which do you think a lucrative process of exchange — you fools everywhere.[10]

Despite these outbursts the remarkable thing in retrospect about the impact of the railways on the landscape was that they became an accepted part of the scenery. In fact, so much an accepted part of the scenery in the current century, that the closure of railways has raised the shouts and protests of the very types of environmentalist who would certainly have opposed their introduction in the first place. This success story of the introduction of a major technological innovation into a total landscape, is particularly important because it was carried out in Britain at a time when we had a highly developed environment and landscape, one which had been adjusted and made by mankind for over two thousand years.

In retrospect, railways are a success story in environmental terms, but that they had a major impact on the environment cannot be doubted. In many ways their impact was precisely the same as that of the introduction of a road system. They required access to the centre of large towns, and they needed to be able to move in relatively straight lines avoiding severe gradients.

Railway companies in running into the hearts of cities (in particular into London), bought up property on the proposed routes. Although most of this was slum property, it nevertheless housed thousands of people and in destroying it to lay their lines and build their stations, the railways caused

---

[10]Both quoted in Michael Robbins *The Railway Age*.

major environmental distress. The poor, as always, had a less powerful voice than their more affluent neighbours, and therefore their personal upheavals caused less concern in government and policy making circles.

From the design aspect, motorways, like railways probably can be regarded as a modified success story. Successful in that it seems highly likely that, in a few years' time, they will be regarded as a natural part of the landscape rather than an intrusion in to it. A modified success, because inevitably, landscapes have been affected and towns and villages will have been radically changed.

It is often forgotten that these changes can be for the better: motorways and by-passes have been the saving of many villages and market towns. Some have taken on a new lease of life because the new road system has reduced damage to old buildings from traffic vibration.

Roads and railways crystallise the two opposing forces in the environmental approach to change. Although it can be demonstrated that environmental aspects are being given the fullest possible consideration in introducing new roads into the landscape, the fact remains that inevitably they must have some major effect on the environment as it exists. This effect is a mixture of good and bad. It is always possible to say that the introduction of a road had affected the view, the ecology, and the general pace of life in a particular area. Such proposals must imply some sacrifice for somebody. The questions that arise are whether the balance of sacrifice has been assessed correctly and whether the net effect is to the overall advantage of the community.

Insofar as the 'quality of life' is a purely subjective concept, then Ruskin's comment about enabling the fools in Bakewell to be in Buxton in half an hour is not valid. So long as the 'fools' believe that their lives are improved by this facility for rapid movement, then it is arguable that it must represent a genuine increase in the quality of people's lives. We are back to the impossible problem of comparing one person's notion of 'quality of life' with another's. This is not an argument to be pursued at this point, but it does show the weakness of adopting any set of arguments in isolation from those of your opponents.

Motorway madness

The conflict between various environmental issues is well illustrated by the road building programme in recent years. The general wish of communities has been to improve their road facilities, to avoid the frustrations, the delays, the economic costs and the pollution, arising from over-crowded roads and city centres. It is not surprising, therefore, that the 1960s were a period of major road building. Attempts were made to improve traffic flows with by-passes, major motorways and the re-designing of traffic systems. Although this raised problems in the countryside it also raised more fundamental conflicts in some towns.[1] In Britain far too many impressive Victorian and Georgian buildings have been destroyed in order to facilitate the passage of the car. Whether these conflicts were inevitable, and whether some of them could have been solved by more intelligent forethought and planning, is a matter of some conjecture but, in the context of this argument, the point is that there was a very real conflict between the environmental objectives pursued. An attempt to improve the environment in certain ways seemed likely to produce a worsening of the environment in others. As the protection of the glories of previous ages is usually a minority interest, we are faced again with the question as to how far the minority should be able to impose their will on the majority and vice versa.[11]

Motorways, therefore, illustrate the fundamental problem of conflict between different environmental priorities. It is important to realise that there are such conflicts, otherwise it is easy for one side to become so absorbed in its own case, whether for or against a proposal, that it fails to appreciate the strength as well as the weaknesses of the opponent's point of view.

Transport has been in the forefront of environmental news for reasons other than motorways. The increasing use of bigger trucks — the so called juggernauts — has raised many environmental issues. The pounding of the ancient village high streets has caused every conceivable form of environmental protest. As the competitive margin of road against rail has increased the commercial advantage of using ever larger vehicles, this particular issue has been put into the forefront of the debate. Apart from the damage that such vehicles may do to the ancient fabric of our buildings, they also raise the problem of safety. A tired driver of such a vehicle is a major hazard. It is of the utmost importance that everything be done to reduce the chances of accidents. We go to great lengths to ensure that airline pilots have sufficient rest and relaxation so that they are always alert when working, and we are going to have to do something similar for truck drivers who are responsible for potentially dangerous loads.[12]

It will be readily appreciated that there is a conflict between differing environmental aims in trying to limit the impact of the juggernauts on our countryside. One solution is to build more roads to by-pass village and town centres and to build more motorways to enable faster journeys and turnrounds. But these very solutions raise further environmental objections. The building of a new stretch of motorway, while helping the villagers and the users of the present roads, is hardly likely to be acceptable to the indefatigable zealots who oppose on principle the building of any further motorways. Looking at the problem from the opposite point of view, it would be legitimate to argue that the building of the motorway solved more environmental problems than it created.

---

[11] See Professor Buchanan's famous Report — Traffic in Towns: — A Study of Long Term Problems of Traffic in Urban Areas.

[12] One of the problems here is the conflict between safety and the driver's earning power and perquisites. The argument about the introduction of the tachometer, the so called 'spy in the cab', illustrates this point. But we must not allow these difficulties to blind us to the fact that there is a solution to this safety aspect. We have to find acceptable ways of getting it implemented.

Modern road systems are a contribution to the solution of many problems. We must not be misled by propaganda into believing they only create problems. Whether the particular disadvantages of a specific proposal outweigh the advantages is a question that society has to find an acceptable answer to. It is often forgotten that the rejection of the motorway solution may effectively sign the death warrant for some of our older towns and villages by robbing them of the only feasible and acceptable solution to their own environmental problems.

'All at sea'

Apart from the roads, we are now faced with new problems at sea. At one time it would have been difficult to envisage that events out at sea could cause any environmental problems. However, with the coming of the super tanker, the situation has changed. Collisions at sea, with the spillage of huge amounts of crude oil which inevitably end up on neighbouring beaches, has become a matter of major concern, particularly in those areas which rely heavily on the holiday trade for their economic wellbeing. The effects of the wreck of the Torrey Canyon, off the south-west coast of Britain, was an example of what can happen.[13]

The oil companies realised that they would have to take steps to allay the very real apprehension this incident created. It was, however, something more tangible than mere apprehension. There was the question of financial compensation to those who had been, or would in the future, be affected by such incidents. One of the difficulties is the international implications of any such incident. While discussions were going on between governments, through the Inter-Governmental Maritime Consultative Organisation (IMCO) — a specialised agency of the United Nations — the major tanker and oil interests decided to take action on their own. They set themselves the task of ensuring that governments and persons who suffered damage from oil pollution caused by tankers anywhere in the world were compensated fairly and quickly. To prevent such mishaps, tanker owners were to be given encouragement to take prompt measures to prevent, or mitigate, pollution damage.

The main need was seen as being some means to reimburse governments which had spent large sums on cleaning up the oil pollution. To bring this about, companies entered into a voluntary agreement, The Tanker Owners' Voluntary Agreement concerning Liability for Oil Pollution known as TOVALOP. Before this was established, any government wishing to recover costs incurred in cleaning up oil pollution on its coastline, faced major legal problems. It had first to establish which court of law had any jurisdiction over

---

[13] See *The Wreck of the Torrey Canyon* by Gill, Crispin and others. (David & Charles, 1967).

the owners of the tanker concerned and was also necessary to establish the fault and liability of the crew or captain of the vessel concerned.

TOVALOP dealt with the question in the following way:

1. It resolved the question of jurisdiction by an undertaking that, where a TOVALOP tanker spilled oil the owner would either remove the oil himself or would make reimbursement for reasonable clean up costs without waiting to be sued. In the event of dispute the owner agreed to go to arbitration.
2. The question of negligence was dealt with by giving assurances that the owner would assume responsibility for clean up costs unless he could show that he had not been at fault.
3. A maximum liability was stipulated for any one incident of ten million dollars. More that ninety nine per cent of the worlds tanker tonnage is now covered by TOVALOP.

There are two other agreements of relevance in this field. Firstly a Contract Regarding an Interim Supplement to Tanker liability for Oil Pollution — CRISTAL. This is a scheme of the oil owners, as distinct from the tanker owners, which enables individuals, as well as governments to obtain compensation for pollution damage. It also increased the amount payable for any one incident to thirty million dollars.

The increase in the amount of offshore work being done by oil companies, and the increasing spillage of oil offshore, resulted in the Offshore Pollution Liability Agreement — OPOL. Initially this applied to United Kingdom and North Sea waters and it is intended to provide for speedy settlement of claims and responsibility.

These agreements show how the question of compensation has been tackled. Once financial liability has been acknowledged then there can be little doubt that the usual incentives to minimise liabilities by preventing the occurrences will come into full play. With the increasing size of tankers, and the possibility of spillage increasing, it is important that every effort should be made towards preventing such happenings. The voluntary agreements outlined above represent a step in the right direction.

A further type of transport which has been in the forefront of environmental attention is air travel.

Up in the air

We are all only too familiar with the arguments about aircraft and the difficulties of living in the vicinity of airport flight paths. The problem here seems to be one where the increase in volume of activity has transformed the issue from a quantitative to a qualitative one.

Those of us who do not live within the immediate vicinity of an airport tend to have a vested interest in being able to secure a flight as and when we want it and as cheaply as possible. We therefore tend to support the technological arguments in favour of bigger and more economic aircraft and flights all round the clock. However, those people living in the vicinity of airports are concerned in entirely different ways. Their lifestyle is affected totally by the impact of their airport neighbours. They want to see the amount of traffic reduced and if this means smaller planes, no night flights and higher prices for airline tickets, then so be it.

This is not the place for an argument on the merits or demerits of the respective cases because, again, this clearly depends on whose 'quality of life' we are talking about and on the need to define the general interest of the community in acceptable terms. However, there are certain managerial points which are well worth making as until recently the aircraft industry had tended to grow like wildfire.

Many cities are served by airports that were first established in the days before we had any real conception of the volume of traffic that might be generated. Few of the early airports were sited with any regard to the wider issues of accessibility, capacity for growth and minimum impact on the local environment. What has happened is that once they were established, there became an inbuilt tendency, sometimes a vested interest, to see that growth of traffic was either entirely or mainly contained at the original airport site. This meant the extension of runways, and the eating up of more of the undeveloped land around the airports, not only for the runways and passenger facilities themselves, but for the ancillary services such as catering, baggage handling, etc., which are essential requirements for a modern international airport.

Airports are now trying to handle levels of activity which were never anticipated when they were originally sited. This has resulted in the ravaging of the local environment in ways never anticipated. The answer in many cases is to start again in a more suitable locality. The economics usually seem to be against such a move but, these will worsen rather than improve, and the environmental problems will remain. But when proposals are put forward to create alternative new airports, then the residents in those new areas who might be affected, and who fully appreciate the disturbance to the environment caused by airports mount the strongest possible opposition — after all they have heard the protests of local airport residents for years. This can result in Governments finding that the least politically expensive way out is to carry on developing existing airports, and so worsening the environmental impact on such areas. It is ironic that the newest form of transport would appear to have received the least attention from environmental planners.

The silver lining here is that the solution of building brand new airports has proved possible where there has been a determination to face up to the problems involved, and to tackle them as a way of avoiding tomorrow's intractible difficulties — the Charles de Gaulle airport outside Paris, is a prime example of this approach.

The fundamental objection to airports is the noise they create. As aircraft became larger, to improve the economics of flying, they went through a period when the noise of the engines appeared to be ever increasing. This argument, which has now been extended to the problems of supersonic noise from aircraft such as Concorde, is by no means over. But it has established that the noise generated by an aircraft could well be a major factor in its commercial potential. Most other remedies are attempts to mitigate the existing problems — double-glazing, restrictions on the number of night flights, restrictions on flying speeds in the vicinity of residential areas. Here again, we are in the realm of competing objectives in society.

Energy

In the fuel industries, which traditionally seemed to have little concept of care for the environment, there have been substantial changes in Britain. The development of the pipeline network for transmitting natural gas throughout the length and breadth of the land, has been carried out with efficiency and imagination. The pipelines have been buried and the land restored with the minimum of disturbance. The national electricity grid often causes adverse comment, but this is a clear case in which society was not prepared to pay the enormous additional costs which would have been involved in any viable alternative. A great deal of attention has been paid to the design construction of power stations and many would regard them as creations of some industrial magnificence. The new generation of coal mines bear no resemblance to their Victorian forebears, and I have already commented on the success of the restoration work which is carried out after the extraction of opencast coal.

Progress can be made. The examples I have quoted show that. But they also indicate how much there is still to be done, and the time and resources that have to be devoted to the problems to get acceptable and workable solutions.

8 Energy — a case study

The first of the many

The problem of the conflict between demands for the maintenance or improvement of living standards and the needs of the environment, which is the underlying theme of this book, has already come to a spectacular head in the world's demands for energy. Insofar as the developing 'environmental problem' is on the one hand the product of inevitably increasing calls on natural resources, and on the other a growing awareness of the importance of the environment, the aftermath of the artificially induced energy crises which followed the Yom Kippur War of October 1974 has highlighted the kinds of choices we are going to have to make in the future in respect of all kinds of natural resources. It exhibits many of the strands of the argument we have been discussing so far. Perhaps because it was unanticipated it encapsulated the running tide of events and compressed an emerging series of difficulties into a relatively brief span of time. How these questions are being handled demonstrates in a graphic way the reality of all resource conflicts.

When the petrol pump runs dry

While this is certainly not the place to become involved in a discussion of the rights and wrongs of the Yom Kippur War, we need to remind ourselves of one or two facts to put the oil crises in perspective.

As most people will remember, the Arab nations decided to intervene by attempting to bring pressure on Israel through third parties. They thought that this would be helped by cutting off supplies of oil, especially to those nations which were thought to be sympathetic to or actively supporting Israel.

The Arab nations were convinced that such actions were necessary to bring about what they would regard as a satisfactory outcome of the war. They had appreciated the crucial nature of oil supplies to developed nations. In the event, their actions can be seen as having a profound effect on the attitudes of these countries to the problem of energy supplies. It was, as the Arabs had foreseen, a direct attack on the jugular vein of developed nations, who had lulled themselves into the belief that supplies of cheap oil would continue for ever and ever and when any attempt was made to cast doubt on this belief, the argument was dismissed as being the biased product of special interests. For example, although the National Coal Board had been pointing out throughout the 1960s that Britain was becoming increasingly vulnerable to any curtailment of its oil supplies, no serious consideration was given by governments to this viewpoint and the proportion of the country's energy needs met by oil continued to increase. Only the fortuitous finding of oil in the North Sea has saved this country from irretrievable disaster.

To get some flavour of the official thinking of the time in Britain, it is worth looking at the White Paper on fuel policy, Cmnd 3438 published in 1967 which assumed the continuance of cheap oil supplies into the foreseeable future. It concluded, 'On the evidence available, it seems likely that oil will remain competitive with coal, and that pressure to force up crude oil prices will be held in check by the danger of loss of markets.' (paragraph No. 53).

Table 4   *World energy consumption, 1950–1970*
(million tonnes coal equivalent)

	1951–1955 Average		1966–1969 Average	
	Amount	Percentage	Amount	Percentage
Coal, peat, etc.	1,669.4	56.3	2,276.3	38.6
Oil	802.0	27.0	2,327.7	39.5
Natural gas	359.6	12.1	1,149.3	19.5
Other*	135.4	4.6	139.4	2.4
Total	2,966.4	100.0	5,892.7	100.0

*Hydroelectric and nuclear.
Source: The Wharton School, University of Pennsylvania, *Materials Requirements in the United States and Abroad in the Year 2000*, Washington, DC, 1973.

Table 5   *World proven solid fuel reserves, 1968*
(million tonnes oil equivalent)

Country	Proven*	Inferred*	Total	Percentage share
Western Europe	32,350	44.350	76,700	1.3
Poland	26,000	14,800	40,800	0.7
U.S.S.R. (including Asian U.S.S.R.)	166,000	3,575,000	3,741,000	63.6
South Africa	24,500	24,500	49,000	0.8
Other Africa	4,000	5,570	9,750	0.2
China	—	680,000	680,000	11.6
India	8,500	64,750	73,250	1.2
Other Asia	6,500	15,750	22,250	0.4
South America	95,000	990,000	1,085,000	18.5
Central and S. America	2,500	21,950	24,450	0.4
Australasia	35,500	40,500	76,000	1.3
World Total	400,850	5,477,350	5,878,200	100.0

Sources: Commodities Research Unit and National Coal Board estimates.

Table 6 *World's 'proved' oil and natural gas reserves, 1973*

| | Oil Reserves | | Gas Reserves millions of | |
	millions of tonnes	percentage share	tonnes oil equivalent	percentage share
Western Europe	2,115.0	2.5	4,735.0	9.4
Caribbean, South America	4,303.0	5.0	2,252.0	4.5
Middle East	47,622.0	55.8	10,193.0	20.4
Africa	9,153.0	10.7	4,629.0	9.2
Indonesia	1,428.0	1.7	370.4	0.7
Other Asia	355.0	0.4	1,147.0	2.3
Australia, New Zealand	343.0	0.4	1,300.0	2.6
North America	6,001.0	7.0	7,339.0	14.6
U.S.S.R.	10,880.0	12.8	17,410.0	34.8
China	2,720.0	3.2	493.0	1.0
Other Communist	408.0	0.5	232.0	0.5
World	85,388.0	100.0	50,144.0	100.0

Source: *Oil and Gas Journal*, 31st December, 1973.

The Arab oil embargo caused many rapid and agonising reappraisals, not only at government level, but down to the policies of individual companies. In practice, policy proved difficult to implement, because it is hard to keep a tight control over the ultimate destination of oil once aboard the tanker and off into the wide blue yonder. But it was effective enough to show the power of the weapon which the oil-producing nations had forged. Inevitably, once the immediate crisis was over, the oil producers decided that they should seek to take greater advantage of their new strength, in order to build up their economies to face the day when their own particular supplies dried up. In a very short space of time, therefore, the consuming countries found themselves presented with a fivefold increase in oil prices.

Should we buy bicycles?

Overnight, countries had to wake up to the fact that what had been 'cheap energy' the lifeblood of their economies, had vanished from the scene and that they had to face a world in which energy costs would be a heavy and rising part of the cost of living. Anyone who installed oil-fired central heating prior to October 1974, should not need convincing of the truth of this statement!

For a while, many commentators argued that this 'unnatural' increase in the price of oil was merely a direct product of the Arab-Israel conflict and that, before long, it would fall back to a more realistic level.[1] The argument was that

---

[1] See the editorials in the *Economist* of the time. The *Economist* must be one of the best written periodicals on business and public affairs in the world today, but it seems at times to have a touchingly naive faith in the ability of a supply and demand curve to solve the most profound of humanity's problems.

the consuming nations would reduce their demand for oil and the producers would be left with a surplus. This would weaken their general resolve to maintain the higher price, the unity of OPEC would be broken and prices would fall to a 'normal level'. In practice it looks as though the best we can hope for is a mitigation of future price increases.

This approach that there would be an inevitable reduction in price ignored the fact that the pressure for substantial increases in oil prices did not come exclusively from the Arab nations. Leaders among the pressure groups for increased prices were Venezuela and Canada. There is now little doubt that, had Britain's North Sea oil reserves been a little nearer commercial exploitation, Britain itself would have been a fervent advocate of a major price increase to cover the costs of this development. As the energy crisis increases, Great Britain, with its massive reserves of coal and enormous finds of oil in the North Sea, has come to have a vested interest in a high oil price. The reason for this is simple. Where you find you have substantial physical reserves of natural resources vital to your economy, but where your own production costs are relatively high, then you have a strong incentive to do everything possible to raise the price to a level that will enable you to absorb your higher costs and make the overall operation profitable. A similar argument applied to Canada and to Venezuela. The net effect of the quintupling of oil prices almost overnight, has been to make more reserves of oil available to the world, by making it increasingly economic to work them. Similarly the world's more economic coal reserves have greatly increased. In the case of Great Britain, it is now sensible to embark on the 'Plan for Coal'[2] with its major investment in new and reconstructed mines to maintain, and eventually increase, capacity. In the United States attention is now focused on the 'new' coal fields of the West. In Canada, the price increases have resulted in the exploitation of the almost mythical reserves of the tar sands.

Things will never be the same again

These events will, in their turn, have a profound effect on local environments in all these countries. Areas which were previously undisturbed by industry, such as the north-east Coast of Scotland, and the mid north-western states of the United States, have now become boom areas and their way of life has been transformed. Whether for better or for worse is, of course, the nub of the argument.

Because of this activity, and the fact that, until mid 1970s the talk had been of oil surpluses, many assumed that the 'energy crisis' was a politician's crisis,

---

[2] The policy for coal in Britain was considered by a tripartate body representing the National Coal Board, the Government and the mining unions. The findings of this group were set out in the *Interim and Final Reports of the Coal Industry Examination* published by the Department of Energy in 1974. These Reports set out the guide lines for the industry to follow in the next decade.

rather than a 'real' one. There is a widespread belief that the crisis was always artificial. Some people have gone as far as to argue that it was partly manipulated by interested parties in order to boost the price of their products. This feeling was not helped when the major oil companies announced record profits in the years immediately following the major price increases.

This superficial analysis hardly bears examination. Whatever may be the truth or otherwise of the short term motivation behind the actions of energy producers or suppliers, the fact remains that, even at these higher prices, we are consuming our resources at a frighteningly fast rate. Total reserves of oil represent far fewer years of anticipated consumption than any other major energy resource. Although new reserves will be found, it is probable that a major proportion of these will be found in the Middle East, or in other

Figure 1.   1973 Crude petroleum production and petroleum product consumption for major producing and consuming areas (MB/D)

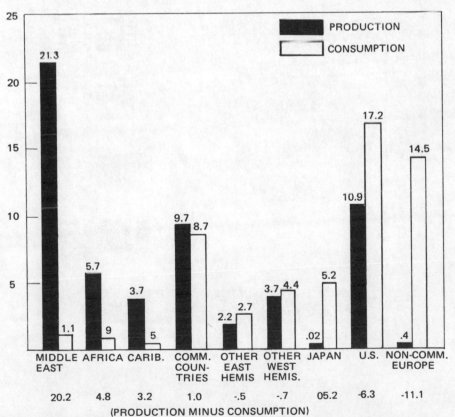

Source: Project Independence Report, November 1974, Federal Energy Administration

Figure 2. 1973 Crude petroleum reserves for major producing areas

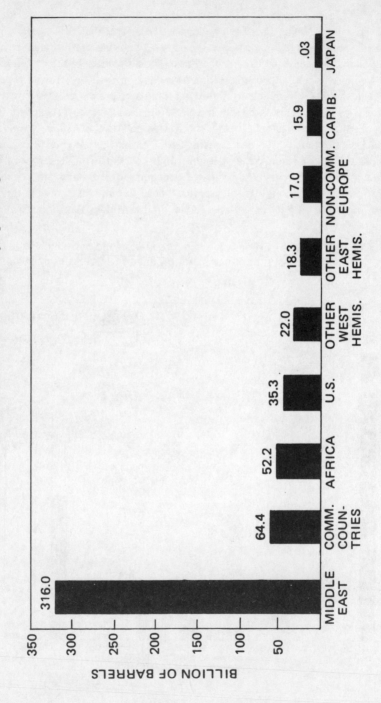

Source: Project Independence Report, November 1974, Federal Energy Administration

countries which, for one reason or another, might be regarded as unreliable sources of supply. It must be faced that the world will have to adjust from an era of a cheap and plentiful energy supply, to one of scarce, dear, energy. The result will be a consequential need to avoid unnecessary additions to production costs and to find acceptable ways of maximising supplies.

To each his own

It is not surprising that faced with this situation, countries have embarked on a scramble for energy self-sufficiency. This is likely in many areas of activity to lead to a confrontation with environmental interests. In this context, the problems that arise are exemplified by those in the United States.

Until November 1973, the level of imports in the United States from Arab sources alone, was some three million barrels per day or seventy per cent of total demand. The effect of the short embargo was marked. Apart from the inconvenience caused by petrol shortages, during the period, the gross national product of the United States dropped by some ten thousand million dollars, and unemployment rose by some half million workers.

Worried by these considerations, the United States Government has embarked on the so-called 'Project Independence'. The professed aim of this programme is to achieve self sufficiency in energy within a period of ten years.[3] This target seems far too ambitious. It has aroused expectations which probably were never likely to be fulfilled and, as it was adopted at a time when Federal and state governments were in the process of tightening the environmental standards for air, water, nuclear generation and strip mining, any hope of making the target a reality has been effectively killed.

The Project Independence Report considered three broad strategic options:

1. An increase in domestic supplies of energy;
2. Conserving and managing energy demand;
3. Establishing standby emergency programmes.

What is significant is the speed at which the change came over the American energy scene. Until 1950, the United States was self-sufficient in energy. The situation deteriorated rapidly in the following twenty-five years for three main reasons. Firstly, coal production remained static. Secondly, crude oil production has been in decline since 1970 and, lastly, natural gas consumption has been exceeding annual new sources since 1968. Thus, by 1973 the dependence of the United States on foreign oil had grown to thirty-five per cent of domestic petroleum consumption. (It is interesting to note that the Report comments that the strategic implications of oil imports were highlighted by the Arab-Israeli conflict, rather than created by them.)

[3] This theme has been taken up by President Carter in his attempts to encourage energy conservation and to secure replacement prices for all types of consumption.

Do you want to see the strip show?

The Report sets out a strategy for increasing energy supply within the United States, as a first and fundamental aim, although it also acknowledged that this raised major environmental problems, the main reason being that one of the quickest ways of increasing energy supply was to go for a major expansion in coal production. In terms of reserves, there was no problem: in 1974 coal production was running at some 600 000 000 tons, whereas reserves were estimated as being more than 400 000 000 000 tons. Project Independence calls for a doubling of coal production by 1985 but the immediate problem is that, given this period of time, most of this increase would have to come from surface or strip mining production. Strip mining of coal in the United States has built up over the years a bad reputation for its environmental record, derived from the method of work, and the relatively scant attention that has been paid to the environmental problems it created.

In its simplest terms, strip mining consists of nothing more than removing the top soil, rock and other strata in order to recover the mineral or fuel deposits, below them. The problems arise in relation to what you do with the overburden (i.e., the material that you have to remove to get the mineral you want, both during and after working). There are many ways in which this simple-sounding process can be carried out, some of which have far more profound effects on the environment than others.

In the United States, a particular method of surface mining, known as contour mining, has caused considerable environmental damage. Contour mining consists of removing the overburden above the coal by starting where the coal outcrops and proceeding along the hillside. Frequently the overburden is just cast down the hillside. The result is that a shelf, or bench, is formed on the hillside while, unless controlled or stabilised, the overburden cast down the hillside can cause severe erosion and landslides. The most notorious areas of this activity are in Appalachia where some 20 000 miles of benches were created and, in some cases, completely isolated entire mountain tops. In Pennsylvania, large areas of woodlands, that had helped to retard run-off, have been destroyed. Material washed from the overburden banks has seeped over adjoining downhill areas and choked streams. Effluent from the mine has formed in pools and become acid. Many areas spoilt by mining operations were abandoned, without any attempt at restoration. There is no doubt that environmental degradation, caused by surface mining, has become widespread and serious in some parts of the United States.

But, this is not the whole story. The problem has been appreciated for some time. In fact, the Indiana Coal Producers' Association was founded in 1919 to re-vegetate part of the banks spoilt by coal operations. The first strict mine legislation was introduced in West Virginia in 1939 and other states have subsequently passed their own regulations. These are of differing quality but in recent years the number and severity of them has increased. At the time of writing, some thirty-three states have surface mining and mined land reclamation laws, and new regulations have been proposed by the Department of the Interior.

Do we want a cover up?

For a variety of reasons much of the strip mining in the United States in the past, was done without any thought being given to an end use for the land or the possibility, or practicability, of restoration. There are considerable areas of previously strip mined land in the United States which have not been in any way restored. It has often been argued that the cost of restoration would far exceed the worth of the land 'created'. This is to miss the point entirely. Landscape in this sense has no economic price and the cost of restoration should be seen as the cost of working the area in the first place. This action on the part of some operators naturally caused considerable resentment, both in the community where they had operated, and amongst environmental protection bodies and conservation societies.

When it was understood that, in order to double coal production in the United States in the ten year period, it would be necessary to more than double the area of land to be strip mined, then it will be appreciated that considerable concern and opposition was aroused. Congressmen were under severe pressure to prevent what the opponents of the extension of strip mining saw as despoilation of the country. The result was that much lobbying took place and a great deal of effort was put into a bill aimed at controlling surface mining. This bill, a very comprehensive piece of legislation, provided for the following:

1. Environmental production standards,
2. Regulatory procedures;
3. Provision for states to introduce control over surface coal mining operations;
4. Federal programmes of control where states failed to come forward with the appropriate programmes;
5. Procedures for applying for permission to work strip mining;
6. Provision for public notice and public hearings;
7. Methods of control.

The purposes of the bill were said to be:

1. To establish a nation-wide programme to protect society and the environment from the adverse effects of surface coal mining operations and surface impacts of underground coal mining operations;
2. To ensure the surface mining operations are not conducted where reclamation as requested by the Act is not feasible;
3. To assure that surface coal mining operations are so conducted as to protect the environment;

4.   To assure that adequate procedures are taken to reclaim surface areas as contemporaneously as possible with certain surface mining operations;
5.   To assure that the coal supplies essential to the nation's energy requirements and to its economic and social well being are provided and strike a balance between the protection of the environment and agricultural productivity, and the nation's need for coal as an essential source of energy.

The bill was in fact vetoed by President Ford, on the following grounds:

1.   It would result in 36 000 jobs being lost;
2.   Fuel bills would rise;
3.   The nation would become more dependent upon foreign oil;
4.   Coal production would be unnecessarily reduced at a time when the country needed increased production.

It was argued that the introduction of the bill would reduce the amount of coal production by somewhere between 40 and 160 million tons a year.

This seems to be a classic case of conflict between the apparently incompatible aims of having the economy working at its maximum efficiency and preserving the environment, but it would be a false conclusion. In the hearings on the present veto, the aim was succinctly stated by Mr Zarb, then Administrator of the Federal Energy Administration: 'We want to work out a Surface Mining Act that would achieve reclamation and will get our energy produced and, at the same time, stop any erosion of our environment, not only with respect to this area, but clean air and clean water.'[4]

Here is a clear example of 'managers' in their day-to-day activities having created a situation in which rules are being invoked, to prevent desirable industrial action being taken, even at a time when the nation has an obvious and desperate need to maximise its production of coal. It demonstrates the weakness of relying on economic arguments alone for your product to carry the day. If the general reputation of some of the operators in working and restoration had not been so abysmally low, then it is most unlikely that they would have had to face up to the demands for such stringent legislation. Is there an answer or is this now an inevitable conflict?

Have we any choice?

In its environmental assessment of the possible options open in the United States, the report on 'Project Independence' stated that: 'The United States does not have to make an absolute choice between energy development and a clean environment. These goals are not mutually exclusive, or their actions

---

[4] See first session of the Committee on Interior and Insular Affairs (Ninety-fourth Congress) on The President's Veto of H.R. 25, June 3, 1975.

taken to develop energy would inevitably have environmental implications, and certain environmental standards would strongly affect energy growth. Environmental protection must be placed in perspective with other national goals, such as, economic development, social welfare and energy security. To a large extent the energy and environmental decisions, made in the near future, will determine our future lifestyles.'

To see how things might be done better, the Americans have looked in the direction of Europe and, in particular, at Germany and Great Britain. The experiences here have been different and the head-on conflict facing the United States, so far has been avoided.

Opencast mining in Britain and Germany: a practical example

Of all the industrial activities that arouse the wrath of the environmentalists and conservationists, it is hard to think of one that causes as much of an outcry as that of strip mining. Strip mining, in many people's minds, has become synonymous with attack on civilised living standards, the epitome of all that is wrong in the attitude of industry to the environment in which it lives.

That this attitude exists is hardly surprising. Strip mining, by definition, involves the removal of the immediate land overlying the mineral and it is hard to think of anything more potentially destructive. The whole operation is seen in highly emotive terms as the rape of the countryside, the tearing apart of the natural landscape. These are all phrases that spring to the mind of even moderately well-informed conservationists or environmentalists.

The question is, therefore, why do people try to persist with opencast mining and is it really ever defensible? In the terms that I have been describing, is it possible to imagine a compromise between the needs of the environment and the industrial operation itself?

In raising these questions, whether or not strip mining should be 'banned', either in part or whole, the various issues that I have been discussing so far are brought into focus and, for this reason, I think the example of the way a compromise on opencast coal mining in Great Britain has been sought is worthy of detailed study. The lessons, both good and bad, have, I think, much to offer industry in general.

Opencast coal mining in Great Britain began in 1942. The date is significant, because it was in the middle of the Second World War, at a time when the German Atlantic blockade was proving very effective and the nation's attempts to built up its armaments and fighting power were being gravely handicapped by lack of fuel. In those days, the only way in which additional volumes of fuel could be made available was from the coal mining industry. The deep mined industry was already producing as much as it could, and the situation was so desperate that manpower was being put into the pits by the simple expediency of making work in the pits the equivalent of serving in the armed forces. A scheme was adopted whereby, under a process of ballot, men who were being enrolled for the armed services found themselves instead being drafted to a colliery to work underground.

Against this backcloth of national emergency a number of civil engineers in Great Britain suggested that there might be pockets of coal that could be produced by adopting the American method of stripping off the covering of the coal and simply digging it out. It was agreed that this should be done, American expertise and some machinery were imported and the whole operation got under way. It will be appreciated that the unity of purpose inspired by the war effort was such that arguments against producing the coal in this way because of the effects on the landscape, were hardly likely to be given great weight. But it is significant that from the very beginning, the British Government provided that all areas which were being opencasted should be restored to their previous use. This turned out to be a fundamental and well thought out decision. It meant that from the beginning the industry had to become accustomed to handling the restoration problems as well as those of production.

After the war ended the need for coal continued at a high level, but the immediate pressure of the 'enemy at the gates' had receded and, not surprisingly, pressure to improve restoration techniques began to grow.

Although restoration had to be carried out during war-time, there was little insistence on getting the best possible standards. The immediate problem was to keep the coal production flowing and there was a strong tendency to have plant and men transferred from restoration to further production sites as rapidly as possible. This was not an argument that could be used once the pressures for supplies lessened.

This did not happen in the immediate post war period. Shortages of energy, in those days almost entirely coal, were seen as the fundamental problem holding back economic development. The then British Foreign Secretary Ernest Bevin said that the greatest help he could have for his foreign policy was a surplus of coal to export. Then, about 1957, the situation changed.

Helped by a well-mounted and conceived selling campaign. and backed by heavy rebating, the oil companies made major inroads into the market, which had traditionally been supplied by the coal industry. The demand for coal dropped very sharply and the long-term investments which had been made in the coal industry in the 1950s, with the object of increasing annual coal production in Great Britain by up to 240 million tons a year, began to appear ill-conceived. As demand dropped, pressure was brought on the coal industry to reduce, if not eliminate, the production of opencast coal. By this time a major commercial problem was that the opencast coal production was far more economic and, as such, made a major contribution to the coal industry's efforts to fight oil competition. In those circumstances, the industry was having to deprive itself of its most economic source of production, at a time when it needed the maximum production in order to keep its average prices down and so compete with its rivals.

A further difficulty was that opencast production happened to produce some very high quality coals which were not readily available in deep mines and it was essential that production of these coals should be maintained.

In 1957 the government decided that the whole issue of opencast mining should be dealt with under a special planning law. They therefore introduced the Opencast Coal Act which laid down in detail the ways in which the Coal Board could attempt to get approval for the working of opencast coal sites. Specific provision was made to enable any local objectors, who had a direct interest in the operation, to make their views known to the authorities and if they maintained their objections to proposals for working any particular site, then the Minister in charge of the coal industry had to call a public inquiry under an independent inspector to assess the merits of the Coal Board's case for working the site, together with the arguments against such working put forward by the objectors. Following the inquiry, the Inspector would then submit his report and recommendations to the Minister.

In such a situation it was essential (in fact it was provided for in the Act) that a detailed description of the proposed restoration should be provided

Over the years, detailed practices have been built up in applying for sites, and it is worth while considering them in detail.

When the National Coal Board wish to work a coal deposit by opencast methods, they first of all drill the proposed area to see whether they have an economic and workable site. If this is the case, they then call a site meeting with all the interested parties: the land-owners, the tenants, their agents, the Ministry of Agriculture and local authorities. This meeting is held on the site and its purpose is two-fold. Firstly, it enables the National Coal Board to explain to the people most directly concerned what would be the effect of the proposals if adopted. Secondly, it enables the people on the receiving end to make their comments and to point out difficulties or objections that would arise if work proceeds.

If the National Coal Board wish to go ahead, they have to make formal application to the Secretary of State for Energy under the terms of the Opencast Coal Act of 1957.

Britain is one of the most densely populated countries in the world. The task of trying to work surface mining, with due regard to the environment, is made doubly difficult because it inevitably affects far more people, both directly and indirectly, than would be the case in a more sparsely populated country. In Britain the technique used is most probably area strip mining, in which a series of parallel cuts are made with the overburn from each cut being deposited in the void created by the previous cut. In some countries, the final cuts are left open, in Britain they are always filled with the overburden from the first cut.

Objections to opencast coalmining in Britain have always been made on environmental grounds. They cover two important, but distinct, aspects:

1. The disturbance to the environment and to the people living in the area, which takes place during the working of the site;
2. The danger of permanent changes in the landscape and damage to the land itself.

It is interesting to note how the weight of objections has moved from the second category to the first. This is basically because, in Britain, opencast mining has always been under centralised control. Originally under the control of the Ministry of Works, later the Ministry of Fuel and Power, until in 1952, final responsibility was given to one central body, the National Coal Board. But from the very beginning complete restoration of a site has always been mandatory. The fact that all major opencast work in Britain is under the control of a central body is a great advantage in terms of restoration. It means that the National Coal Board does its utmost to ensure that standards of restoration are high throughout its activity. Any signs of omission or commission on a site in one part of the country, are quite likely to be quoted against the National Coal Board by organisations or industries trying to prevent it being allowed to operate in another part of the country. The Opencast Executive have built up a world-wide reputation for the quality of the restoration carried out on opencast sites. The way in which this has been done, has been the subject of much study from abroad, particularly the United States, faced as it is with the current concern to protect the environment while getting the additional coal needed from surface mining.

Because in Britain, opencast mining has been under unified control, it has been possible to incorporate the cost of restoration as a 'prime cost' in planning the feasibility of any particular operation, thus reducing the need to cut corners or to make economies in cost at the expense of the restoration. This is of the utmost importance. As it is the aim of the Opencast Executive to build up production on a long-term basis, it is clearly essential that they do nothing which could tarnish their reputation or make further applications to the sites more difficult to obtain. This, in itself, provides a strong degree of self-policing and control.

As in Germany, restoration is planned when the site is conceived and, frequently, it is found possible to provide something new in the restored land area which meets a social or economic need. For example, it is quite possible to create a country park, a recreational area or a golf course, as part of the restoration, if this is what the local community and the landowners want. There is therefore no reason why the landscape should be affected in the long term although it is true that the landscape will be changed, it not being possible to replace a wood or a hedge overnight. The crucial point here is to make sure they are replaced in the long term, if this is what people desire. People may be making some sacrifices in relation to the landscape as they have always known it, but these changes need not necessarily affect the succeeding generations, who will be faced with a different but, nevertheless, totally acceptable landscape.

An increasing amount of opposition to opencast sites is based on the disturbance that is caused during the working of the area. This is a very difficult problem. Working sites by opencast methods near urban areas does result in a number of disturbances — albeit mainly of a temporary nature — to the local inhabitants. The point here is that the effects can be mitigated, if not eliminated and an increasing amount of work is being done to tighten up on the protection of amenities during site working, while the costs of this must be seen as an essential part of the operation. New ways to control operations, so as to minimise disturbance, are thus constantly being investigated and brought into operation.

As many of these problems as possible are discussed and thrashed out, both within the Executive and with the Planning Authorities concerned, before the application on site takes place. Following authorisation on the site, the Coal Board offer to set up a liaison committee with the local residents and their representatives, to keep a careful watch on the progress of the site and to discuss any worries or concerns that local residents may have. It is obviously of the utmost importance to do everything possible to remove the reasons for such complaints as may arise.

The opencast operation in Britain has worked and restored well over 100 000 acres of land, the vast majority of which is back in full-scale agricultural production. The operation has produced much needed coal (a high proportion of the coal produced from opencast methods in Britain is of a high quality, and in short supply from the deep mines). It has thus made a major contribution to the economy of the country whilst, at the same time, through intelligent land use and not leaving behind the moonscapes seen in parts of the United States, has restored Britain's rolling countryside. The operation is still far from perfect, but it does represent a major step forward in reconciling the twin objectives of economic prosperity and concern for the environment.

The German experience

West Germany has massive reserves of brown coal (lignite), amounting to some estimated sixty thousand million tons; providing as it does a third of all power generated in German thermal electric power stations, this resource is of crucial importance to the economy of the country. This vital role has been recognised by the West German Government, and a tremendous modernisation programme has been undertaken. Since the end of the Second World War, more than a thousand million dollars have been invested in the industry, which has been fully consolidated. Many shallow surface mines, formerly common in the Rhineland, have been replaced by larger and more efficient open pit operations. This is demonstrated by the fact that, whereas the number of active mines in the Rhineland has decreased over the last twenty-five years from twenty-three to six, the annual production of brown coal has increased from 64 million to 100 million tons.

The main companies have merged to form the present day Rheinische Braunkohlen Werke AG. The size of the operation and its unity have been important factors in allowing it to institute enlightened land reclamation practices. The discarded spoil material is filled back into the mined-out pits and then levelled off. The land is returned to agriculture, forests are planted and new lakes created. It has become customary to follow the coal, even to the extent of moving villages that lie in the way, and new towns have been designed and built for displaced people. The basic resettlement costs are borne by the mining company, with local and state governments providing supplementary funds to pay for the incremental costs of better schools and other community services.

This comprehensive approach has shown how integrated the solution to the problem needs to be. By accepting the need for the end result, in this case brown coal, and meticulously planning for it in advance, it has been possible to minimise the environmental effects and, in many cases, create something better than that which existed before. This tremendous achievement shows what can be done if intelligence is applied to solving the problems.

Lessons to be learnt

The above examples show how it is possible to answer apparently irreconcilable differences between the needs of the economy and the interests of the environment. I am not suggesting that the environmentalists have been totally satisfied with the solutions. Neither, for that matter, have the people involved in the exploitation of the mineral. In Britain, in reaching agreement on those areas which can be worked, a number of areas of coal have been excluded, at high cost, for environmental reasons. (Where these decisions have been made as the result of the recommendations of an inspector at a public enquiry, the cost of the environmental protection may not be known, because inspectors' recommendations to pull back a boundary for a few hundred feet, may remove the most economical part of the coal area and result in an economic nonsense.) Nevertheless, compromises have proved to be possible.

The German experience is perhaps the best example, in that it shows what can be achieved if, at the beginning, the overall long-term objectives are accepted and the concentration from then on is aimed at meeting the very proper environmental concerns.

It will be seen that in these examples a tremendous amount of work and effort has to be made in planning the site from scratch, to minimise the environmental impact during the period of working and maximise the quality of the restoration once the mineral has been extracted. To get this right does involve a major application of money and resources. Experience has shown that an attempt to take cheap short cuts is always the most expensive in the long run.

It should also be noted that in the planning and during the period of operation, it has been found essential, as well as worthwhile, to involve the local inhabitants and planning authorities to the maximum possible degree. Problems are not necessarily solved through such means, and it would be foolish to believe that this might be the case, but we must try to reach a real appreciation of each other's aims and objectives, and see what might be done to make them coincide a little more closely.

Use something else

One argument often put forward in relation to the strip mining of coal, is that alternative fuels should be used instead, the assumption being that these must be somehow less inherently destructive of the environment. The U.S. Federal Energy Administrations Report did not take such a simple way out. It suggested that, whatever happened, there would have to be what it called, 'major environmental tradeoffs'. In terms of the United States, it defined these as:

1. New versus existing areas of production

This is because most of the major coal reserves are in areas where coal production has not expanded on any considerable scale. There is therefore the problem of accustoming new areas to the environmental impact of coal.

2. Nuclear power versus fossil fuels

Whereas nuclear power is undoubtedly a clean operation and, on the face of it, has major environmental advantages, its potential, even if not probable, environmental drawbacks are severe indeed. There are major problems of waste disposal: it is becoming increasingly unacceptable to think of dumping waste in 'concrete overcoats' to the depths of the sea, because no one dare envisage the effect of such waste eventually seeping into the sea and subsequently, into the human habitat. The potential seriousness of any accident hardly needs elaborating and there is a further critical complication in that it now seems clear that countries can easily develop nuclear energy into atomic weaponry. This poses a major threat to the stability of the world and, as such, is a fundamental environmental objection to further massive nuclear expansion.

3. Location of facilities

The difficulty is in deciding whether to site the production capacity near the source of supply or near the source of demand. If near the source of demand, the environmental disadvantages associated with the form of energy being used, will be existing cheek by jowl with large centres of population. If, on the other hand, they are sited near to the source of production, then there is the problem of transporting such energy to the centres of demand. This can lead to requirements for major electricity grids or pipelines, with all that this means in terms of environmental disturbance.

4. Renewable versus non-renewable resources

How far should we concentrate on the rapid use of non-renewable resources, particularly oil, at the expense of more renewable ones, such as wind and water?

5. Degrees of environmental damage

Some pollution can be rectified and we have discussed already the rectification of major environmental upheavals caused by strip mining. Other types of pollution are irreversible — particularly nuclear.

All these tradeoffs have to be taken into consideration when deciding what is in the overall interest of a community, in terms of energy policy. In practice, the arguments tend to be conducted at a very localised level indeed, i.e., it is the individual who is effected directly who will raise the strongest objection. It is right that this personal aspect should be given sympathetic attention and, where appropriate, provision be made to alleviate the disturbance. The people who have to accept a worsening of their own environment should be compensated. It is not right, however, that such considerations should necessarily always be the deciding factor in how the policy is decided. It is all too easy to wish the problem from your own doorstep on to somebody else's.

We must, in the example of energy, as with all scarce natural resources, maximise the use of those categories which have the least effect on the environment. But we have to remember that all of them, to some extent, have some effect — we cannot eliminate, we can only minimise the problem. Even hydro-electric plants affect land use and river ecology, although these would normally be regarded as minor disturbances. The issue we have to face is not whether the environment will be disturbed, but in what way will it be the least disturbed, and what can be done to alleviate the difficulties caused to individuals by the disturbance. We cannot live without energy; every effort must be made to maximise our production of energy. The world economy depends upon having sufficient energy to keep it moving. In such an area of primary concern it is of vital importance that all concerned do everything possible to fulfil the essential needs of the community with the minimum impact on the environment.

1 : Summary of the provisions of the United Kingdom Opencast Coal Act of 1957

Prospecting

Prospecting is carried out under the terms of the Opencast Coal Act and of the General Development Order. The National Coal Board may carry out prospecting after the service of forty-two days' notice on local authorities and after having obtained the consent of landowners and occupiers. If consent is not obtainable, the Board may compulsorily enter land after obtaining a direction from the responsible Minister (at present, the Secretary of State for Trade and Industry). Compensation is payable for any damage or disturbance caused during prospecting.

Site working

No site may be worked by the National Coal Board without the grant of an authorisation by the Secretary of State for Trade and Industry.

When preparing working proposals, the National Coal Board are required by the Act to take into account any effects their proposals may have on the natural beauty of the countryside; flora, fauna, buildings of historical or architectural interest and any other relevant features must be given due consideration.

Before application for authorisation to work a site is made, the National Coal Board must advertise its intention in the press, and it must serve notice on all local authorities and statutory undertakers concerned; and on all individuals with an interest in the land. A period of twenty-eight days is allowed for objections to be made. If objections are raised by bodies or individuals who have an interest in the land cannot be resolved, the Secretary of State for Trade and Industry must order a public inquiry to be held. He may also order a public inquiry at his own discretion even if no objections are made by the above parties.

The application submitted by the Board must consist of:

1. Map showing the land which it will require to occupy, and the parts of that land on which coal will be worked by opencast operations.
2. Description of the operations to be carried out on the land.
3. Description of the restoration operations.
4. Statement of the Board's case for working the site.
5. The application must be made available for public inspection.

If authorisation is granted, the Board must advertise the fact in the press and it must serve notice to this effect on each of the interested parties. The authorisation must be made available for public inspection.

Environmental aspects of opencast coal working in the United Kingdom

1. Restoration code of practice

(i)   Before working commences, topsoil (to a depth of twelve inches if available) and subsoil (to a depth of twenty-four inches if available) must be separately stripped from the site and stored in separate mounds. After working, the soils must be replaced on a graded overburden which is free of rocks, shale and blue clay (which might impede a plough) to a depth of three feet.

(ii) After working and the grading of the site and replacement of subsoil and topsoil, the land is managed for five years on the Board's behalf by the Ministry of Agriculture. During this time, fences, hedges, ditches, farm roads and other farm fixtures are re-established and permanent under-drainage installed. Trees are planted in hedgerows, shelterbelts and woodlands, and the land undergoes intensive agricultural management and treatment.

(iii) Provision is also made for the land to be restored to forestry. In this case, the land is managed for five years by the Forestry Commission, after being regraded to the contours required for planting.

2. Environment protection during site working

Measures taken vary according to individual site conditions, but generally include the following:

(i)   Mounds of subsoil, topsoil and overburden are sited so as to screen the site from the surrounding neighbourhood and to act as baffles against noise and dust. They are grassed to improve their appearance.

(ii) Blasting is limited to specific hours of the day.

(iii) Wheel-washing bays are provided to prevent lorries depositing mud on public roads.

(iv) Site roads are watered in dry weather to reduce the incidence of dust.

(v) The use of electrical machinery is specified wherever possible to reduce noise.

(vi) The diversion of streams and watercourses crossing the site, and the construction of settlement lagoons to reduce the possibility of sediments leaving the site.

The Board will detail proposed environmental protection measures in the application for authorisation, and the authorisation will contain conditions enforcing these measures and any others which the Secretary of State for Trade and Industry deems desirable.

2: United States Federal Energy Administration 'Project Independence'

The preceding chapter has made some references to this Report. It is a most comprehensive document and is essential reading for anyone who wishes to get an understanding of the complexity of the choices facing society. The details will be different for each country but the principles and lessons of the analysis will remain equally valid. The following brief *précis* gives a little more background than could be contained in the chapter.

Alternative energy strategies

1. Accelerating domestic supply

The report concludes that this action could be inhibited by key constraints:

(i)   Shortages of materials, equipment and labour.
(ii) Availability of drilling rigs.
(iii) Financial and environmental control problems in the utility and railroad industries could hamper their ability to purchase convenient facilities and equipment.
(iv) Water availability will be a problem in certain regions by 1985.
(v)   Accelerating nuclear power plant construction does not have much effect on the reduction of imports in general. It replaces new coal-fired power plants.
(vi) Accelerating synthetic fuel production would require by-passing key research steps and may not be cost effective or practical by 1985.

2. Energy conservation and demand management

Energy conservation actions can reduce demand growth to about two per cent per year.

Actions can be taken which result in switching from petroleum and natural gas consumption to coal or coal-fired electric power. However, increased coal use in the pre-1985 period, by conventional building of coal-fired power stations, must be weighed against the possibility of increasing coal use by liquefaction and gasification in the post 1985 period.

The potential for coal development is virtually unlimited under accelerated conditions if no equipment, manpower or demand constraints are assumed. Coal production could be over 2000m tons per year in 1985 under these assumptions. Although demand limitations are likely to keep production to about 1000m tons in 1985.

Crude oil

The first fears of 'running out of oil' were expressed in the early 1920s and American companies were urged by the government to develop oil production abroad to augment domestic supplies. In the 1930s the depression caused a break in demand and, with the subsequent development of the East Texas Field, the problem became one of containing the surplus oil production. As a result of these circumstances, oil production was concentrated in large vertically integrated companies, and state bodies became the regulators and conservers of crude oil production. State agencies began to control well spacing, restricting production to maximum efficient rates to prevent reservoir damage, and rating well production on the basis of market demand.

At the close of World War II, capacity was barely sufficient to meet market demand. By the mid 1950s, spurred by strong demand and rising prices, these lags were overcome. But oil reserves and the capacity to produce the required surplus stocks, began to decline.

Production peaked in 1970, reserves having fallen each year since 1966, and drilling effort has only recently reversed its long-term downward trend.

Foreign oil became available at costs far below those of the United States' domestic production. Therefore major international oil companies expanded production in foreign areas. Federal government, concerned over the national security aspects, encouraged voluntary import restrictions in 1955 and 1957. In 1959, President Eisenhower invoked the national security provision of the Trade Agreement Extension Act to establish mandatory oil import quotas. Nevertheless, by 1970, the dependence of the United States on foreign oil sources had grown to twenty-six per cent.

On 18 April 1973, the President suspended the Mandatory Oil Import Control Programme, replacing it with a system of licence fees that escalate with time. The Licence Fee Programme is designed to support the long-term restoration and domestic capacity, while providing for the short-term need for imports.

In 1969 a major oil spill in the Santa Barbara Channel, and another on the Gulf Coast, directed attention to the environmental risks of off-shore production. As a result, the Department of the Interior suspended the leasing of Pacific Continental Shelf acreage, pending the development of operating procedure and regulations to minimise the potential for future significant environmental damage.

Future supplies of oil will be determined by four fundamental factors:

1. The amount of oil resources remaining to be found.
2. Success in finding the remaining supply.
3. Ability to recover what is found.
4. The costs of the necessary exploration and production efforts.

The Federal Agency found that:

> 'The cost of the long lean times required to bring new petroleum fields into production is an important factor. Domestic production of crude and natural gas liquids will continue to decline for a few years regardless of higher prices or policies designed to encourage exploration. The major new source of oil production is Alaska. It is expected to provide between 3 and 5 million barrels per day. By 1985 Alaska could produce up to a quarter of United States oil, although, at present, it accounts for less than two per cent.'

The Federal Government controls about forty per cent of the remaining producible oil. How much of it will remain available for exploration and development depends upon consideration of environmental and ownership questions. The terms under which the government lands are made available affect the availability of capital, the rate at which these areas are explored and produced, and the proportion of oil in the place ultimately recovered.

Oil extraction, manufacturing and distribution processes affect the quality of the environment. Oil spills can affect the marine environment, as well as creating aesthetic problems. Development of petroleum production has social and economic implications, especially in frontier areas. The Alaskan North Slope, with its fragile ecology and unpopulated areas, presents a particular series of problems. Its abundance of resources suggests that an extraordinary effort is needed to minimise environmental impact.

Natural gas

The first natural gas well was put into production in 1821. Large discoveries took place in association with the development of the oil industry. The first large scale use of natural gas was in the manufacture of steel and glass, in plants located in Pittsburgh. Initially, its use was confined to areas near gas or oil fields, but the development of long distance gas transmission systems in the 1930s, broadened its market. Immediately post war, the availability of abundant supplies and improved quality enabled the gas utility industry to expand rapidly and widely. Marketing gas production increased from 4 trillion cubic feet in 1946 to 8 t.c.f. by 1952 and continued to grow at 6.5 per cent in the 1950s and 1960s. It now represents about a third of the total energy consumed by the nation; including almost half of the non transportation uses — and about twice that supplied by either oil or coal. One half of the gas used is for residential and commercial purposes, one sixth for the generation of electricity and one third for industrial uses.

In the 1970s the demand for gas has exceeded its supply. The Federal Power Commission has set priorities on gas use.

The Natural Gas Act of 1938, gave the Federal Power Commission authority to regulate inter-state pipelines and natural gas imports and exports. In the Phillips Petroleum case in 1974 the United States Supreme Court held that a firm which produces and compresses gas and sells it to a pipeline company, is a Natural Gas Company. As a result, the Federal Power Commission began regulating the well head prices at which gas is sold in inter-state commerce.

The Federation found that natural gas will continue to decline in production at regulated price, until the 1980s. A sharp real increase in price could improve supply, but this will be dependent upon oil prices. In the meantime consumption of natural gas is running at two or three time the rate of proving new resources.

Coal

Since 1950 the declining use of coal in American energy structure has been accelerated by government actions. The development of nuclear electric power reduced the need for coal in generating electricity. The elimination in 1966 of world import quotas for residual oil on the East Coast resulted in many large coal users converting to cheaper and more convenient foreign oil. The implementation of the Clean Air Act during the 1970s has created significant uncertainties as to how much coal will be permitted to be burnt.

Coal reserves are estimated as being more than four hundred thousand million tons, and more than half of them are located east of the Mississippi. Whereas nearly all of the coal reserves in the East are privately owned, most of the Western coal reserves are owned by the Federal Government. Although sixty per cent of the nation's coal reserves contain not more than one per cent of sulphur, and most of this is in the West, a far smaller proportion of reserves can meet the sulphur dioxide performance standard for large boilers (i.e., 1.2 lb of SO_2 per million btu's) established by the U.S. Environmental Protection Agency.

Coal production has not increased as fast as it could have because of the reluctance of owners to invest the major capital necessary to open up new mines. The capital has to be recovered over twenty to twenty-five years and this level of markets had not been foreseen in the recent past. The future of coal

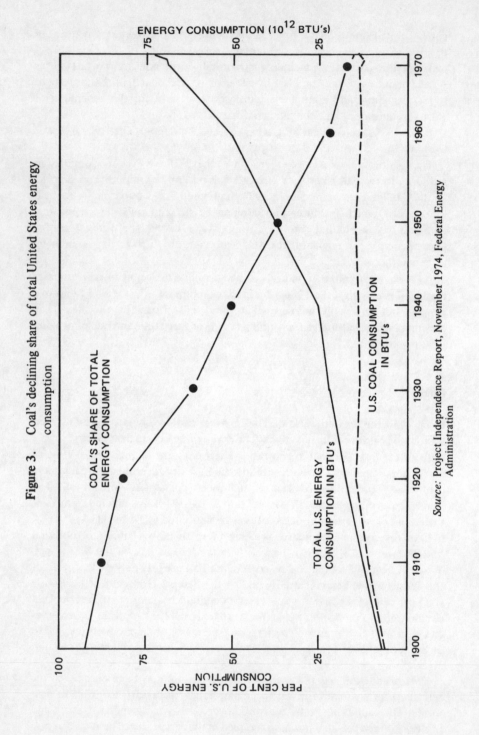

Figure 3. Coal's declining share of total United States energy consumption

Source: Project Independence Report, November 1974, Federal Energy Administration

has been clouded by uncertainties over strip mining legislation, Western Coal Lands Leasing Policy, Clean Air implementation, oil import policy, natural gas pricing policy and electricity demand forecast and nuclear capacity forecast.

The crucial factor here is whether the current emission regulations of power stations are enforced.

Nuclear fuels

Early nuclear fuel production operations were sponsored by the United States government, with some private involvement. However, after the enactment of the Atomic Energy Act in 1954, private initiatives occurred in all phases of fuel production, with the exception of enrichment and permanent disposal of high level radioactive waste. The government continues to be responsible for the regulation of nuclear operations storage and permanent disposal of high level radioactive waste, and has a major role in the development of most nuclear fuels. It remains the sole supplier of enrichment services. In order to meet the projected accelerating nuclear generating plant schedule, nuclear fuel production and uranium enrichment would have to more than double between 1980 and 1985. Constraints are:

1. Limited amount of uranium resources.
2. The mining and milling capacity for uranium.
3. The capacity for enriching uranium.
4. The re-processing capacity for spent fuel.
5. Uncertainties about the schedule for nuclear generating capacity coming on stream.

The relatively low price of uranium has limited the exploration efforts and the uncertain role of nuclear power in electric power generation has had a major limiting effect on development. (More recently, environmental concerns have come to the fore.)

Recovering usable uranium by reprocessing 'spent' nuclear fuel could reduce new uranium requirements by about fifteen per cent and enrichment requirements by about twenty per cent.

Public acceptance of nuclear power is an important factor in overcoming the current problems constraining the use of nuclear power and the exploration and mining of uranium.

Shale oil

Commercial production of liquid fuels from oil shale began in France in 1838. The Scottish oil shale industry started in 1850 and lasted until the 1950s when production ceased due to the availability of lower cost substitute fuels.

The Federal Government owns seventy-two per cent of oil shale lands, and although there is a potential for major development of up to 200 000–300 000 barrels per day, the development would affect the environment. It is possible for levels to be expanded to over a million barrels per day by 1985, but this will only be considered if the price of oil remains high.

Synthetic fuels

The economic production of low btu fuel gas is dependent upon the development of new technology processes. Commercial production is expected to commence in the 1980s. At costs of $2 or more per million btu's in 1974 it was regarded as uncompetitive with natural gas. The decision is whether the existing technologies is whether rapidly to deploy the existing technologies or wait for more efficient technologies.

Reliance on imports has generally positive domestic environmental effects, since many of the environmental impacts occur outside the consuming country.

However, adverse environmental effects from conventional energy development can be considerably mitigated through abatement measures such as surface mine reclamation, oil spill prevention technology, and emergency reactor core cooling systems.

9   What can management do?

Up to this point, we have been more concerned with analysing the true nature of the problem facing management than with considering possible remedies. I have tried to establish and clarify certain basic issues, namely:

a)   Why there has been a growing interest in the environment and the reasons why this interest will become increasingly important;

b)   The areas which give cause for genuine environmental concern;

c)   The importance of distinguishing between environmental issues of intrinsic significance and those which are fundamentally subjective judgements;

d)   The imperative need to find ways of reconciling the environmental needs of society with its other objectives;

e)   That tomorrow's environment will be shaped by countless managerial decisions;

Whilst we must consider the wider implications of the effects of our industrial and commercial activity and the possibility of environmental 'doomsdays' which we may be approaching with unexpected speed, it is hard for us to relate our day-to-day actions to these consequences. It is difficult, but important, to appreciate that the cumulative effect of thousands of relatively innocuous managerial decisions can be environmentally disastrous.

It is all too easy to regard our own contribution, whether for good or for evil, as being insignificant. However, I hope that I have said enough to indicate that I think this would be a calamitous state of affairs, inevitably leading to increasing conflict between the environmentalist and the industrialist. Such a conflict cannot be in the interests of society as a whole, and we must therefore take whatever steps we can to avoid it.

Practical managers are involved continually in making decisions which inevitably affect the environment for better or for worse. It follows that such decisions need more careful thought, analysis and monitoring, than they have previously been given, if we are to achieve the necessary improvement. This chapter attempts to provide some assistance to practising managers in tackling these day-to-day problems and to suggest an approach to integrating consideration of environmental consequences into the company's decision-taking processes.

Much of what follows may appear to be self-evident, but the crucial test is whether you can honestly claim that your own particular approach to managerial problems stands up to close scrutiny.

Put yourself in your opponent's shoes

The fundamental requirement is to bring yourself to accept that there may be a problem to be tackled. We can all accept that our competitors have a problem. We can also accept that firms in other types of activity may well have problems that they haven't handled in a very sensible manner. It is hard, however, to apply such criticisms objectively to one's own organisation. We are all victims, knowingly or unknowingly, of custom and practice. If, something has been done in the same way for many years, and in terms of the results of the company apparently successfully, then it is not surprising if it seldom comes up for analysis and reappraisal. However long your company or organisation has been in existence, you should beware of the argument that suggests that you have no environmental problems simply because you have not encountered any. It could be a costly complacency to assume that you will continue to remain in this happy position.

The first step is to try to put yourself in your opponent's shoes. Suppose that you had been given a brief to attack your company's environmental record. Forget for a moment how fair or unfair such an attack would be, but just assume that you have a barrister's brief, i.e., you must do your utmost to prove that the record of the company was reprehensible in the extreme. Remember, the barrister is not paid to present an objective picture but to convince the judge and jury. He will therefore try to ignore any favourable aspects or mitigating circumstances (these are matters for the defence counsel to bring out) of which you are aware, and will concentrate on those points at which the company is most vulnerable. The preparation of such a brief by yourself can be an eye opener and it is the first essential in understanding the strengths and weaknesses of your company's position.

It is important that this analysis should be done in detail and not on the proverbial back of an envelope. A great help in preparing such a review, is to enlist the aid of someone who is knowledgeable about your activities, but not necessarily committed to them, for help in formulating criticisms. It is surprising what a candid view you can get from members of the family, (particularly one's marriage partner) who very often see aspects of your operations in a very different way to yourself!

You should jot down all the possible criticisms of your past and present activities that you believe might be made (however unjustly). Then, in relation to each point, ask yourself whether there is any action, which is conceivably within the power of the company, which would contribute to removing or reducing the cause for criticism. At this point, do not consider the practicality or advisability of such actions, merely whether they could reduce the objections. If there is anything at all that would help, then outline the reasons why it has not been done already. The answer may be simply that nobody had thought it necessary to do anything.

Having established why remedial actions have not been taken already, the next step is to decide whether they should be introduced now and if not, why not. Such objections as there are may be on the grounds of practicality but, most often they tend to reduce themselves to purely financial considerations. Once you move out of the area of technical possibilities, you tend to find yourself arguing that the money needed to reduce the environmental effect is more urgently needed for different purposes or objectives. Perhaps it is a question of financing expansion, or modernising certain other aspects of the company's activity. If this is the case, then you should be clear in your own mind why you are not carrying out remedial work, because the accusation could be thrown at you that you are carelessly damaging the environment simply to enhance your own profitability! You should not expect criticisms of your conduct either to be fair or just, but you should try to arm yourself so that you can give a satisfactory and truthful reply. The basic reasons for not carrying out work that would reduce the environmental impact are:

1. Technical inability.
2. Lack of worthwhile return on the money invested.
3. Money needed for different purposes or objectives.
4. The adverse reactions of more senior management, right up to, and including, the board and the shareholders.

How far the last three of these objections should carry weight, is a matter of managerial judgement. A view has to be taken on the validity and seriousness of potential environmental opposition, and how necessary it is to try to meet it.

In trying to reach such managerial decisions, a very important factor is that failure to take action may inhibit future proposals and plans of the company. Take a simple example. If you are operating a process which is causing some avoidable environmental damage, which you decide to ignore, then you are severely weakening your case for any planning permission which may be required for extensions or even the continuation of the process. In considering this last point, you should not think of it purely in relation to the site of the present operation. Your company's reputation is indivisible and it is more than likely that any proposal to establish a similar process or operation, even hundreds of miles away from the original plant, may be opposed on the grounds of the damage you have caused at your original site. Unless you can be seen to be aware of the problems and are taking all reasonable action to see that they are overcome, you may become an unacceptable neighbour.

The day after tomorrow

Most sizeable concerns these days attempt to carry out some form of long-term planning. This is usually in terms of a five year rolling programme. But, it is becoming increasingly common to look beyond this period. It follows from what I have said above, that any long-term development programme that ignores the environmental aspects of the proposals put forward is asking for trouble. Whether or not inevitable trouble, depends upon the nature of the proposals in the programme!

The incorporation of environmental considerations in long-term planning is really a part of the wider issue of including social objectives in the aims of the company.

It is becoming more generally argued (and in many cases accepted) that no company, public or private, can simply pursue the criterion of profit as a sole measurement of its contribution to human affairs. Peoples and governments are increasingly expecting industrial and commercial concerns to include the wider needs of society in the formulation of their objectives. In some instances, this responsibility is imposed on the company by law. I have in mind statutes which in some countries impose an obligation on employers above a certain size to employ a given percentage of registered disabled people, or which provide by statute for the removal of discrimination between potential employees, on the grounds of sex, race, creed or religion. This is an example of society accepting that it has a duty to protect the interests of those of its members who want to make a contribution, but who need help in finding the opportunity to do so.

Many companies have not needed the spur of the law to make them move in this direction. They have assumed wider responsibilities and have taken social acceptability as being an objective of company policy. Some of these companies have been accused of being too paternalistic in their approach. It has been argued that they put the worker into a state of complete dependence on the firm, almost from cradle to grave. This is regarded as bad in some quarters because it inhibits individual development and detracts from personal responsibility. It is a difficult dividing line to draw. Perhaps the best test is the aim of the firm. If the intention is to help meet the needs of the local community, then this would seem to display a praiseworthy acceptance of social responsibility. On the other hand, if the driving force is to get a tighter control over the workers and weaken their allegiance to outside bodies, then this might well be seen as undesirable paternalism.

To most companies this argument would seem academic, as they would not accept any obligation to pursue social objectives that were not imposed on them from outside. In many cases, they would not accept it because it would be anathema to their shareholders. There can be no doubt, however, that the movement toward companies accepting social responsibilities is rapidly gaining pace. In some instances, it represents a defensive reaction on the part of large companies who fear that they have a poor public image. With the arrival of the concept of 'small is beautiful', so cogently argued in Dr Schumacher's book, the large monolithic corporation has lost its mystique of being the all-wise and all-powerful provider of goods, services, and employment and is now under increasing pressure to justify its existence, or has to face growing demands for its dismemberment or takeover by the state.

This growing awareness of the necessity to adapt to changes in the character of business and social organisation is well documented in Hargreaves and Dauman's book *Business Survival and Social Change.* They outline the development of the relationship between business and community in Britain in the nineteenth century, and attempt a definition and classification of social responsibility:

1. *Basic Responsibilities* which they define as being the continuation of the bedrock prerequisites of the company's activities i.e., it must obey the law, pay its taxes and have honest dealing with suppliers, customers and workforce.
2. *Organisational Responsibilities*, the need to obey the spirit as well as the letter of the law.
3. *Societal Responsibilities*, contributions to the wider community.

Hargreaves and Dauman conclude that social responsibility objectives are not just a question of social duty, moral obligation, or corporate conscience. They represent the need to promote a healthy external environment, in order to survive. That is the hard business justification for including them in the company's overall objectives.

This is particularly true in relation to environmental matters. An analysis of how reaction to these may move during the next decade, is a matter of crucial concern in formulating a company's long-term plans. A clear example of this in relation to investment can be seen in those areas of the world which are likely to undergo traumatic changes of one kind or another over the next ten years. How can you make a rational decision on investment in Africa, particularly Rhodesia or South Africa — or in Latin America — without trying to form a view as to which way these societies are going. It is even more relevant to consider how the policies or approach of your company could influence these developments. These are not areas which are amenable to the disciplines of cash flow or any kind of quantitative analysis. They call for a judgement to be made on the quality of society that we are trying to create. We have to remember that we are making tomorrow's environment, not just today's money and that we shall be judged on that basis.

If environmental considerations are taken into account in formulating the long-term development programme for the company or organisation, then it will follow that some items may be discarded from the company's long-term proposals on the grounds that they would raise too many environmental objections. It is at this point that considerations must be given to ways of overcoming any potentially damning objections. Undoubtedly, this would increase costs and it is very often on grounds of increased cost that such projects would be dropped.

There is another side to this particular coin. If the proposed development has strong environmental objections, then these are most likely to apply where the product or the service is produced or provided. This being the case, the company first in the field with a way of meeting the demand whilst preserving the environment in an acceptable manner, will be in a very strong competitive position, because it will be able to expand its production where others will not. In such a situation, the full costs of providing the necessary environmental protection might be recouped through an increase in price. Very careful consideration should be given to environmental aspects before it is decided either to include, or exclude, a new project or development from the long-term programme.

One of the major difficulties in trying to foresee environmental reactions is that you can never be sure what impact almost unrelated activities can have on your own. For example, if there is an escape of poisonous fumes from any form of chemical plant, then all chemical plants tend to come under local suspicion, even though they may be producing totally unrelated products. Even when a similar product is being produced, there may be no comparison between the safety precautions taken by one firm and those taken by another.

An added complication is that of working overseas. In some cases, firms have established plants overseas to carry out activities which have a higher than average environmental hazard. This is sometimes because the restrictions in the home country have become unnecessarily severe. The receiving country is often in such need of foreign investment that it is prepared to accept a level of risk higher than in the home country. How long this latter state can continue is debatable. It will not always be possible, let alone desirable, to continue to 'export' pollution in this manner. It is also arguable that it is sensible to 'export' pollution to countries that have the ability and processes to deal with it that the 'exporting' country has not. The only exceptions I can see are those where it is accepted that activity, up to a certain level, can take place without undue risk, in a given area, but that expansion beyond that level, will bring risk with it. In such circumstances, it might not be unreasonable for a country to allow expansion of such activity, up to this level, by overseas companies who have already reached the permitted maximum in their home territories.

There are, of course, political implications in trying to establish in a foreign country an activity which is no longer permitted in one's own. These are areas in which emotion often ignores the effects of the situation. In Great Britain, there was considerable concern and opposition to the Atomic Energy Authority's proposal to import from Japan nuclear waste material for re-processing. We have to work towards the ideal of having environmentally hazardous activities carried out in the safest and most suitable locations, irrespective of country.

You want to change the rules?

In trying to assess what might be the reaction to our long-term plans regarding the environment, the first requirement, and in any ways the most difficult, is that we have to face up to the fact that our objectives as managers differ from the objectives of other people. There is nothing revolutionary, new, or indeed wrong, in this concept. We have only to consider our day-to-day relationships with trade unions or employees and the government, both local and national, to realise that those objectives that we regard as being of primary importance are not necessarily held in the same high esteem by the people sitting on the other side of the table. We have already established that people concerned with environmental matters do not see, and will not see, things in the same way as management. Objectives are therefore going to be different. What we have to do, is to try to strip the argument of its emotionalism and false premises and to accept that we will, most of the time, be working towards some form of compromise. Often the best we can hope for is some form of acceptance on both sides that ideal objectives are unrealistic and never totally attainable. Unfortunately, being human, we always want to assume that it is the other side that has to make the compromise and that our own position is unassailable. If we continue to work from that premise, then we are likely to end in deadlock, which can lead to tremendous difficulties and the complete frustration of each party's aims.

The first step should be to establish the respective objectives as honestly as possible and not to fool ourselves and become victims of our own propaganda. If we are proposing a development in a certain area, because that is the cheapest place in which to operate and maximise our profitability, then we should be prepared to say so. We should not be ashamed of trying to produce the maximum economic benefit to the community by working to optimum efficiency and providing local employment. If that is the strength of the case for a particular proposal, we should say so. It is then up to our opponents to demonstrate why it should not be accepted. If, however, it is the sole reason for the development being in that area rather than in another, it does not help to try to argue that, without it, we may have to consider the relocation of existing operations. If this argument is used as an idle threat then, in the event of the development being rejected, we have our bluff called. The credibility of future statements will be nil. This leads to a fundamental proposition: in stating the case, never use false or unsustainable arguments; always state the facts correctly and, where you are expressing an opinion, make it clear that you are doing so and give your reasons.

Similarly, we should not make the mistake of assuming that our opponents are whiter than white and nor should we always assume that their arguments can be taken at face value. They are likely to start from what they regard as a morally superior position of wanting to prevent what they term 'a desecration of the environment', or 'the destruction of a rare ecological pattern', etc., etc.

These will undoubtedly be some of the reasons inspiring a few of the more ardent crusaders. But, equally, much of the opposition could come from people who have little concern with these wider philosophical niceties.

Do not attack your opponents for what you may think are stupid or shortsighted opinions — they may be sincerely held. What you must do is establish the facts and make your opponents distinguish between facts and opinions in their arguments. If they have genuinely, but wrongly, formed the view that your activities would cause a health hazard, then you must demonstrate the lack of foundation for this view, rather than just dismiss the argument.

Much of the opposition will come from people who simply do not want to see any change in their particular locality. We must accept that this is not necessarily a bad motive. Consider your own reaction if somebody wished to build a motorway, a factory, an opencast site, a housing estate, or a chemical plant outside your own front windows. In logic we might be prepared to admit that, when we bought the house, we did not buy the rights to an uninterrupted view. Yet having got it, we do not propose giving it up without a fight. In fact, we should probably fight most strenuously and, if we can find reasons other than our own particularly rather selfish ones, then we are going to use them. It is sensible to examine your opponent's views carefully and not to accept them necessarily for what they purport to be. There will be genuine objectors on realistic ecological and environmental grounds, but there will also be plenty of people who want to jump on to the bandwagon for their own particular reasons. It is up to you to try and separate out these two categories and to argue with each of them on their own chosen ground. Of course, it is not beyond the bounds of possibility that objections might be encouraged on the grounds of environmental disturbance when in fact, the prevention of such a development could coincidentally have commercial advantages for someone or other.

Only through analysing the aims of both yourself and the potential objectors, is it possible to assess the impact of your proposals and to gauge the reaction to them. This also provides you with the opportunity of determining which are the strongest areas of objection and whether anything can be done to meet them.

To get a clear picture, it is necessary to analyse in detail just how the proposals could affect, or could be seen to affect, the local environment in all its aspects. This analysis should be carried out under the following headings which cover the basic ways in which the environment can be affected: Sight; Sound; Smell; Dirt; Danger.

Let us consider each of these in more detail.

What will it look like?

The immediate impact on the environment of any new development is its appearance. This causes direct concern to the people living in sight of the proposed development. Sometimes it can be argued that the visual amenity will be improved because perhaps land will be reclaimed or derelict structures will be replaced with new ones. This is not, however, the most likely situation in which you will find yourself faced with strong objections. If there is any form of view whatsoever, then you can expect that somebody is going to be upset by having this taken away. In this context, the people who object may not even live in the area — they may be people who like to stroll through it, or to visit it from time to time. Yet they will have strong opinions about what should and should not be there.

Whatever the proposal, the first questions are therefore:

1. Will it require structures of any sort?
2. Will it affect the present visual scene in any way whatsoever?
3. Whose sight lines will be affected?
4. If a new structure is required, what height will it have to be?
5. How large?
6. Of what material will it be built?
7. Will it blend into the area?
8. Will it be temporary?
9. Will it require additional car parking facilities and amenity blocks?
10. Will it be self contained?
11. Can this visual impact be lessened or improved by the planting of trees or by landscaping, by fences or walls?

If you are proposing a new process, then although you may not want an immediate extension to your works, is it possible that you will want an extension should the process prove successful? If this is the case, then you will have to face up to overcoming this type of visual objection.

You do not have to build structures to have an impact on the visual environment. Car parks, stock yards and, of course, surface mining activities, can have a very substantial effect on visual amenity.

In a mining operation, the landscape itself will be completely changed, certainly for a number of years and, in the case of quarrying, it could be for ever. Even in these circumstances, there are occasions where it is possible to provide for restoration of the land so that, in the long term, the visual impact is minimal and, in some cases, beneficial.

If the proposal is to build new roads, then that will alter the visual amenity because, instead of seeing a panorama of fields with cattle grazing, the local inhabitants will have to get used to speeding traffic and exhaust fumes, juggernauts and traffic jams. (Relatively minor new access roads to a motorway can cause considerable upset by increased traffic on local roads.) Even if the land is to continue in a use which does not alter the existing visual amenity, access to it may be altered by closing existing footpaths or rights of way. In time, this will alter the character of the locality.

Sound and fury

In recent years, noise levels, in our society, whether from industry or pop music, seem to have gone ever upwards. The result is a cacophony of sound which people are all too anxious to get away from. When they have been successful in finding a relatively peaceful spot, they thus tend to oppose strongly anything that would bring additional noise.

In the past, people have accepted levels of noise in certain activities which are becoming less tolerable in modern day society. The type of noise levels acceptable in, say, weaving sheds, which were so great as to require operatives to be able to lip-read, is not the type of industrial environment that we now regard as being satisfactory. The feeling has grown that it is not the absolute level of noise that is so important, but the difference in noise levels. This is why, when assessing the impact of a new activity on the noise levels in an area, you start with the general level of noise as it exists in that area. Known as the ambient noise level, it is regarded as the bench mark against which all noise intrusions should be measured. One has to be very careful in dealing with noise levels because, although no measurements can be made with a good degree of accuracy, there are so many other changing factors that it is easy to think that you are making a scientific comparison when, in fact, many of the basic elements differ on each side of the equation.

Noise is a difficult area. Rupert Taylor in his book on the subject has called acoustics 'the unknown science' and we would do well to remember that we are travelling in unexplored country.

All developments in technology have produced increases in noise levels. Although we know how 'noise' is produced, we do not know how to define it with universally acceptable standards, partly because 'one man's noise is another man's music'! 'Loudness', 'intensity', 'duration' and 'character' of sound act together to make some 'noises' acceptable and others not.

To get out of one's mind the fact that loud noises are not necessarily unpleasant is difficult. In many areas, the sound of the dawn chorus gives a far higher reading than much of the industrial activity in the area and yet it is the industrial activity that undoubtedly will be criticised.

Although much fundamental work still needs to be done on noise, we have to learn to design quiet machines. In the meantime, we must protect those who have to work with noisy machinery. The usual response of providing ear muffs of varying effectiveness is not always satisfactory. They give protection not only from unwanted noise but also from wanted noise, such as speech. The isolation that this causes can be dangerous to the individual — the noise of the engine is blotted out but so is the warning shout of 'look out'!

Noise has to be looked at in relation to the working environment and to nearby residents. The latter can be affected by the strength of, and changes in, the prevailing winds, and whether it is winter or summer (are windows open or shut?). In terms of residents, it has to be remembered that there are many noisy domestic appliances at work in every home. Try listening to a dishwasher or waste disposal unit, or even to the common vacuum cleaner.

In Britain, an experiment is taking place to see whether noise levels can be appreciably reduced in a town. A campaign has been instigated to reduce all noise levels, including those emanating from domestic appliances. This should demonstrate how far noise has become an accepted part of our way of life.

Can you breathe easily?

Naturally people object most strongly to industrial processes which result in an all pervading smell permeating the locality. No one wants to live near the sewage works, the glue factory, the fish processing plant or the gas works, if they feel they will never be able to get its presence out of their nostrils! But, far more insidious and dangerous than these obvious pollutants of the atmosphere, are those which may not affect the sense of smell, but may cause permanent damage to health. The possibility of lead poisoning, arising from too great a concentration of lead being allowed to escape into the atmosphere from a processing works, is a matter of considerable concern. Of course the Alkali Inspectorate will be keeping a close eye on this aspect, but it is no consolation to have to close your factory to ensure you are not causing any permanent harm. This type of problem can sometimes be tackled by extraction in the process of potentially harmful emissions. Electrostatic precipitators are used, for example, to remove sulphur from the chimney stacks of power generating stations.

The crucial point is to consider what *might* happen in terms of emission of gas, as well as what should happen. The tragedies that can occur were exemplified at the Icmesa Plant at Seveso, near Milan, in July 1976, by the accidental production and venting into the atmosphere of the poisonous contaminant TCDD (tetrochlorodibenzo-para-dioxim). In the immediate after-math, more than a hundred people were treated for ailments, ranging from skin irritation, to nausea and diarrhoea. Cats, dogs, chickens, mice and birds died, and much of the foliage in the area was killed. The long-term effects cannot yet be assessed. This disaster has caused a number of firms to abandon the production of 2,4,5 trichlorophenol until they are satisfied that their processes will not lead to accidental production of TCDD. Chemical firms have had to take a closer look at all their potentially dangerous processes to see whether risks have been minimised, and it has become evident that not all instances of potentially dangerous occurrences or outbreaks have received the attention they require. It is therefore important to ensure that you are fully informed about any process you propose introducing, as you must assume that your opponents will have done their homework, but may have an interpretation of the facts far different from yours.

Where is all the dirt coming from?

Many industrial operations are inherently dirty. They produce dirt and dust which in the first instance affects the workers but, all too often, can affect people living around the operation. Much of this can be prevented. Roads can be kept clean so that each vehicle passing does not produce a swirl of dust that settles on the fabric and furnishings of nearby houses. Industrial good housekeeping, with the right kind of equipment, can make a major contribution to good neighbourliness.

Is it a danger to life and limb?

One of the most effective ways of preventing any form of development is to stir up the feeling that it might cause some type of danger. This danger might be to the general environment, in forms as radioactivity, lead poisoning, or merely worsening the atmosphere and therefore increasing the risk of bronchitis. (The latter was in fact one of the main reasons for the introduction of the Clean Air Act in the United Kingdom in 1957.) On the other hand, the danger might be more specific. It might relate to the people working on the new process, people living in the neighbourhood, or the consumer of the product. Recent history is full of examples of occupations turning out to involve a hazard to people exposed to particular working conditions over a period of time.

Perhaps the best known example was in the coal mining industry, where exposure to high levels of coal dust over a period of time resulted in men contracting pneumoconiosis. This tragic illness, known in many parts of the coal mining industry as simply 'the dust', focused attention on the need to maintain good environmental standards in the working place, in order to minimise the chance of contracting such diseases. In the coal mining industry in the United Kingdom, the strictest controls are now exercised on the levels of dust in which men are allowed to work and the coal faces are subject to examination to see whether or not they can be 'approved' as being fit for men to work in. Protection is also ensured by regular examination of the men who work in such conditions to ensure that a tendency to the disease is spotted at the earliest possible moment. Such men are then put to work in conditions which are environmentally more suited to them. This continual effort has brought about the desired reduction in the numbers of men affected. The battle continues to identify those men who have the greatest susceptibility to the disease so that they are not exposed to any risk, but the progress made so far in reducing the incidence of the disease has been marked.[1] Before these controls

---

[1] Regular surveys of over a hundred collieries between 1960 and 1975 showed a drop in all categories of the disease from 14 per cent to 8.5 per cent and in its more marked form from 6.1 per cent to 2.6 per cent. See the Annual Reports of the National Coal Board Medical Services for more detailed information.

were introduced pneumoconiosis represented the type of condition that could cause illness and sometimes death to work people without management being aware that they were exposing men to such a risk.

It is not only in the mining industry that occupational health hazards have arisen, and not only to men. In the late nineteenth century there was a major outcry because of the onset of 'phossy jaw' among women and girls manufacturing matches. This disease, which resulted from exposure to the phosphorous then used in the manufacture of the matches, was brought to public attention during the 'match girls' strike in the 1880s. The strike would probably have gone the same way as so many others of the time had it not been that the plight of the girls aroused the interest of some middle class radicals — including Annie Besant[2] — who were able to drum up sufficient public indignation to see that, not only were the wages of the girls restored, but action was taken to control the health hazard.

Recently the full impact of asbestosis has come to be realised. This disease, which results from working among the fine grains of asbestos, is a major industrial scourge and one which was certainly not fully appreciated for many, many years. The allegations and counter allegations of failure to enact or enforce strict regulations are currently continuing.

We are aware of the potentially fatal effects of exposure to radiation and the greatest care is taken to protect operators. This has not always been the case and it is a well-known story how one of the inventors of the X-Ray — Madame Curie — had her life shortened as a result of being exposed to the rays that even she did not fully understand. Whenever anything new is introduced, we must assume that there may be side-effects which may not come to light for many years but which will then be traced back to the particular process.

The effect of the hormones used for the rapid fattening of poultry and cattle, on the people who have been working with them over a period of time is another example. The alien hormones enter into the human system and disrupt the natural hormone balance.

All these examples are sufficient to remind us that, if what we propose involves a new or substantially modified process, then somebody ought to have the task of examining the operation to assess whether or not there is a possibility of affecting those people who are employed in the process, if not immediately, then over a period of time.

Trade unions have become well aware of this type of problem and, whereas at one time irresponsible management and union representatives tended to buy their way out of trouble with 'danger' or 'condition' money, a more socially responsible attitude is emerging. Even if some managers are not influenced by

---

[2] Annie Besant, a very active socialist in the last quarter of the nineteenth century. She was first notorious for her atheism (especially as she had married a Church of England clergyman). She was an early member of the Fabian Society and later became an ardent Theosophist.

the humanitarian arguments, the possibility of claims in common law, not to mention the damaging effect that such occurrences have on the company's image, should be sufficient to bring home the need to keep the tightest control over working conditions, particularly where new products are involved.

All manufactured products must be safe in respect of their final user. In normal circumstances, this would appear to be a straightforward operation. If you are manufacturing a patent medicine, or a food, you will certainly ensure that it is non-toxic and will have no harmful effect on people taking it. However, this is not necessarily such a simple operation. There are many things which, taken by themselves, are relatively harmless but, when mixed with something else, can prove lethal. Therefore it is crucial that the manufacturer tests his product, not only in isolation, but also in relation to other substances which might be taken in conjunction with it. For example, there are certain chemicals which should not be taken at the same time as cheese, because the mixture of the two may produce most unfortunate results. We are brought up with the idea that it is not very sensible to mix our drinks and we now have to learn that it is even more unwise to mix our chemicals without knowing what we are doing. It is not now just a question of checking what is inherently dangerous, but what is potentially dangerous. The manufacturer has to think his way through all these permutations and combinations, to provide adequate instructions for the circumstances in which his product can or cannot be used.

Apart from danger to the employee and to the customer, there is a possibility of danger to people living close to the factory. This can arise in a number of ways, but chiefly through either the risk of explosion or of the escape of poisonous gases. The experience at Seveso has already been described. The danger of explosion was all too tragically demonstrated in the explosion at the Nypro plant at Flixborough in the United Kingdom, which caused the deaths of twenty-eight people working at the plant and damaged property over a wide area.

It has been established on a number of occasions in recent years that the emission of lead fumes into the atmosphere, as a result of the manufacturing process, has resulted in a concentration of lead in the atmosphere exceeding safe levels and producing abnormally high lead concentrations in the blood of children and adults living within the vicinity of the factory. In such cases, the Public Health Inspector can close down the factory until the dangerous emissions have ceased, and this can have a catastrophic effect on the future of the firm concerned.

Therefore it is of the utmost importance that in any new product or process the likely effect of emissions of either liquids or gases into nearby water, or into the atmosphere, will not constitute a danger to the local inhabitants.

Even if the pollution is not sufficient to affect the human species, it may still have a fatal effect on animals or insects and, this again, could have unacceptable environmental consequences.

The release of effluents and sewage into waterways has resulted in the destruction of a tremendous proportion of the fish population and, in recent years, strong attempts have been made to try and reverse this process.[3] The powers given to the various river and water authorities are now extensive and will be brought to bear against any malpractice in this field.

It follows that in any new process which has unwanted by-products, the greatest care has to be taken in the disposal of these by-products and waste. Recent legislation in Great Britain has tightened up considerably on the disposal of poisonous waste. The disposing of noxious or poisonous waste is now very difficult and adds greatly to the costs of any firm faced with the problem. However it is good commercial, as well as good environmental, sense to determine whether the process can be adapted to avoid, or minimise, the manufacture of such noxious products, and to treat the products within the confines of the plant, rendering them harmless before they leave the control of the firm. There are sometimes opportunities for recycling wastes, and these are to be encouraged. In this way, to some extent, both the environmental and the economic problems can be met. But if the costs of treatment render the process uneconomical, then it is sensible to be aware of this before embarking on the project, rather than having to face up to such costs as the result of an enforcement order laid on you by the local authority or the river or water authority.

Will you be long?

In considering the environmental effects on a community, one point which must be taken into consideration is the length of time the operation will continue. Something which might be endured for a short period of time may be intolerable as a permanent institution; we might be prepared to accept noise, dirt and inconvenience for a short period, but would not tolerate similar intrusions into our amenities for very long. Examples of this might be a circus, a motor rally or a pop festival, the improvement of a road, the building of a housing estate or additional air flights at public holidays. Therefore it is essential to make clear whether you are proposing something which would be there for the foreseeable future or whether you could make do with it for a more limited period. If the latter is the case, this may become your fall back position for getting the planning permission for your operation.

The objectors

Having identified the people who might be affected by the proposed development, we must then carefully look at the possible objectors, because

---

[3] The best known effects have been on the Thames, where fish are now being caught further downstream than has been recorded for over fifty years.

these are by no means always the same people. It is not at all uncommon for objectors to come from well outside the affected area to defend their own specialised interests. This type of objector normally represents a national pressure group which automatically comes into action when it feels that any of its concerns are threatened. Examples of the type of organisation I have in mind are the Conservation Society, the Friends of the Earth, the Society for the Protection of Rural England, the Society for the Protection of Rural Wales, the Royal Society for the Protection of Birds, the England Waterways Association and the Footpaths Preservation Society.

There is also the possibility that the local authorities may object to the proposals and it may be necessary to fight them through the process of a public inquiry.

Apart from the obvious effects on the environment in terms of the visual, noise, or effluent, there are other changes which produce strong reactions. A great deal of concern is shown these days for any proposals which generate more traffic on the roads, particularly if this involves juggernaut lorries. This is seen not only in terms of creating more traffic jams or worsening lines of communication for local residents, but also in terms of increasing the danger to pedestrians and cyclists, particularly children and old people. In examining the proposals, it is therefore necessary to analyse any trouble spots, such as blind corners (particularly narrow roads or narrow bridges, level crossings or poor road surfaces).

This last point can be used against the proposal in a more direct form, in arguing that the additional traffic will require repairs to the roads to be made more frequently and thus put an imposition on the rates which would not be offset by any apparent benefit. To establish the facts it is advisable to carry out a traffic survey to establish existing usage and to relate this to the estimated additional traffic. It is, therefore, necessary to be quite sure how much traffic *could* physically go by more acceptable routes (as opposed to more economical ones) and to analyse what would be the additional cost of using such alternatives. The disadvantages of the alternative transport should be well known to you, as they should have been taken into account in making the original decision to put the traffic on the road and on those particular routes.

Apart from traffic, other questions will be:
a)   Will the proposals lead to more jobs in the area?
b)   Will any additional work force come from the area itself?   ˙
c)   Can it be claimed that it will lessen the unemployment problem?
d)   Will it merely generate more pressure for existing skilled workers?

If it will generate greater pressure for existing skilled workers; then you can expect opposition from local employers, not wishing to see their skilled labour attracted away and their costs forced up.

If the proposals will require people to be brought in from outside the area, then this could create problems for the local authority in housing. Therefore you must ask yourself:

a) Will the influx cause pressure on the public housing stock?
b) Will most of the people coming in be prepared to buy their own accommodation?
c) Will there be sufficient housing available?
d) Will the local authority have to expect requests for planning permission for house building in areas which have so far been kept as green belt?

If the influx of new people is great, then this may create problems for recreation and it will certainly be argued that the whole character of the area may be changed.

All the problems discussed so far are, to some extent, affected by the length of time that the operation takes place in each working day. Are we talking about a single shift operation where, outside these periods, life will be relatively normal? Or will the noise, the effluent, the dust, the traffic on the road, etc., be continuous round the clock? This can have a marked effect on attitudes to the proposals: these may be acceptable in terms of single shift working, but not for multiple shift working. People are less tolerant of noise at night than during the day.[4] It is essential to be clear in your mind as to whether or not the proposal can be a viable proposition, if it has to go ahead on the basis of single shift working.

The other side of the coin

So far the discussion has focused on reasons for objecting to the proposal but, here and there, the attentive reader will have noticed one or two facets of the defence which can be argued in support of development proposals. If additional work is being brought into an area of unemployment, then this is a very distinct advantage and is a very strong argument in favour of the operation. Similarly, if the development is providing new openings for training for young people leaving school, this again can be a major factor in the locality.

Even on the question of roads, it could be that the additional traffic generated will be such as to make more immediately relevant the long postponed proposals for a new by-pass, or for widening the road, or a scheme for a new bridge. The pressure may be turned away from objections to the proposal in favour of getting on with the favoured road improvement scheme. Similarly, it could be that the additional work which might be generated for the railways is sufficient to make them think twice about closing the local railway line, or even to persuade British Rail to invest money in improving local railway facilities.

It is important not to overestimate the advantages of your proposals. If the advantages which you are claiming can be brought about without having the

---

[4] This is partly because the ambient noise level always tends to be lower at night and, as most of us are trying to sleep, we react very strongly to anything that makes it otherwise.

inconvenience of the new development, then the opponents of your project will assume that they can have their cake and eat it. They will argue for improvements without accepting that their price is the alleged inconvenience of your proposals.

What shall we do about it?

Compromise is a word which arouses vastly differing emotions. Some people are proud of the fact that they 'never compromise'. They see the very suggestion of compromise as an indication that people either do not know their own minds in the first place, or that they are weak or vacillating when faced with any opposition. On the other hand, compromise can be regarded as being one of the cardinal virtues.[5] It can be seen as an attempt to show sweet reasonableness, by endeavouring to find a way out of a situation without either imposing one's will or having another's will imposed upon one. Whatever the moral merits, or otherwise, of the concept of compromise, there is little doubt that, in practice, there is frequently no alternative if a stalemate is to be avoided.

Given that you have to compromise, it is sensible to analyse all the various objections which you conceive could be thrown at you and evaluate whether there is room for concession on any of them. At this point, the argument should be seen in terms of whether there is any possibility of concession, i.e., whether is it physically possible, and not whether it is desirable. At this stage, the aim is to analyse the cost of trying to meet any of the objections, taking the broad types of objection in turn:

Visual

There may be little that you can do to avoid affecting the visual amenity of the area, but there may be a lot you can do to make sure that the visual impact is not as unpleasant as it might be. If you are involved in a mining, or quarrying operation, it is sometimes possible to screen the actual work by mounding and shaping the overburden and, if it is to stay there for some time, putting it down to grass. Similarly, if structures are to be erected, it often costs more to have a structure which is made of attractive materials, or designed to be relatively pleasing to the eye, but it can be done. In our own domestic lives, we prefer to see our neighbours build the additional garage out of brick, and not out of corrugated iron. The same applies to our industrial structures. Of course the aim is to build them economically but, in the situation of compromise, it is necessary to know just what the additional

---

[5] We might do well to heed the words of Edmund Burke 'Every human benefit and enjoyment, every virtue and every prudent act is founded on compromise and barter.' Or, perhaps more down to earth, George Herbert's comment 'A lean compromise is better than a fat lawsuit.'

costs will be in providing a suitable facing or altering a building in such a way as to make it more acceptable.

Noise

This may be capable of being tackled at the source, by equipping the machines with suitable silencers and ensuring that these are kept in good condition, and are always in use. This again, would be an additional cost and, in some cases, could result in lowering efficiency. It is also possible to consider sound insulation in one form or another to protect the worst affected areas. Where a lowering of the noise level does not prove to be possible, compromise can be sought in reducing the period of time in which the noise is made: it might be agreed that the noise activity should not be carried out on the night shift or at weekends.

Effluent

This can normally be tackled by installing treatment plant within the operation, which can, however, be an expensive and limiting factor on the operation. But, if some treatment can be introduced, and the appropriate authority can be shown that you are making a genuine effort within reasonable economic constraints to provide relatively pure effluent, then this is perhaps all that can be reasonably expected.

Traffic

The issue of additional traffic on the roads can be one of the most intractable problems to tackle. Compromises here can normally be in the form of agreeing a route for your traffic, which may not be the most direct or economical route, but which minimises the environmental and danger hazards to the local population. If the traffic which you are putting out is very heavy indeed, then it might be regarded as being reasonable to make some contribution to the improvement of the particular bottlenecks, such as the blind bends or narrow passing spaces.

Also of the greatest importance is to ensure that the positive side of the proposals receives full publicity. If the proposals are beneficial in providing additional work, then it should be possible to win the support of the trade unions and to present a united front in presenting them. The importance of the support of your employees and their union cannot be overestimated. They can be your best ready made public relations team; but you must ensure they are fully informed and that they accept your arguments. It is doubly difficult to face objectors if you have, at the same time, to face objections from your own workforce while, conversely, there are no better ambassadors for your case than your own workforce, if they are persuaded of the proposal's importance to them. It is therefore essential that they be kept fully informed of potential

environmental problems that might cause a reaction from local residents or the
local authority.

Whom should we tell?

It follows from the various difficulties already discussed that any form of
proposed action which can effect the environment in any one of the ways
described, should be the subject of the most careful thought and consultation,
with both the workforce and those bodies and people likely to be affected by
the proposal.

Timing can be a problem here if ideas are leaked and become public before
you are ready for general discussion. The difficulty is that it is extremely easy
for the media to describe the proposals in a sinister way, and to give the
impression that you have been quietly concocting proposals which you knew
would be hazardous to the public at large. Thus, implying that had it not been
for the enterprise and initiative of the reporter working on the story, the
general public would have been kept in the dark until it was too late!

It can be equally awkward to start discussions with the people concerned
before you have been able to think out the various consequences of the
proposals, the likely sources of objection and possible ways in which you
might be able to meet these objections. In such a case you may be criticised for
not appreciating the problems you might create and of having no acceptable
way of meeting them. It may then be said that your scheme is hasty, ill
prepared and not to be trusted.

Either approach could therefore lead to trouble but, as there is a great deal to
be said for being open and candid in discussions with local authorities, the
sooner you can give a broad indication that you have an interest, the better.
Again this is not always easy, because there may be commercial deals that you
need to finalise before the proposal becomes generally known. For example,
you may require an additional piece of land to make the proposal practical and
yet, if the seller of the land became aware of your particular interest and your
overriding need for his piece of land, then the price may rocket astronomically.

Despite the difficulties, the broad rule of thumb should be to consult as soon
as it is practical, to be honest about difficulties that you have not yet been able
to face up to, and to arrange to have further consultation when you are in a
position to give more positive replies to the questions and objections being put
forward. It may be advisable to hold open public meetings to which objectors
can come along and hear the proposals outlined in detail so that, at least, there
can be no less room for disagreement as to what the proposals actually consist
of. By no means is it uncommon for a great weight of objections to be based on
a fundamental misunderstanding of what the proposals involve, and who will
be affected and for how long. An alternative to this would be to circulate every
local resident with an outline of the proposed development in order that they
can see for themselves what you intend doing.

The disadvantages of an open meeting are self-evident. It may well be taken over by an organised group of specialised protestors whose objections may be altruistic, but may equally fall into the category of vested interest.

People who perhaps were willing to listen to both points of view can get swept away in the tide of objections once the snowball of objection gets rolling, and the open meeting can fulfil the purpose of creating a forum for organising the objectors, rather than the reverse. This is always a tricky matter to decide but, if the principle adopted is that the local citizens have a right to know what the proposed changes on their locality and their lives would be, then some way of giving them the detailed information has to be devised and implemented. It has been said that, in the long run, people get the kind of government they deserve. It certainly seems likely that the amount and depth of consultation they receive, will depend on the way in which they use it.

If it is agreed that consultation is a desirable activity in itself, it should follow that the consultation should carry on beyond the stage of reaching an agreement on the planned development. In the course of the necessary compromises arrived at to reach agreement, many undertakings and promises will be made on behalf of the company, and objectors like to claim that the promises are not worth anything. This is often an admission that, if the policies could be kept, then some of the weight in the objections would fall by the wayside. It is therefore necessary, from the objectors' point of view, to try and weaken the effectiveness of such undertakings. In order to counteract such objections it is highly advisable to create a mechanism through which your promises can be monitored.

In recent years, in opencast coalmining in Great Britain, it has become increasingly the practice to offer to local residents the creation of a liaison committee to be operated should the site be approved. This liaison committee consists of local residents, the contractors working the site and the National Coal Board's Opencast Executive as the initiators of the project, and, sometimes, although not always, local authorities. The committee itself decides on the frequency of meetings and it considers issues raised by anyone who is affected in any way by the site. It therefore forms a focal point for objections to the way in which the site is being worked. Should there be any suggestion that the conditions originally included in the authorisation are not being adhered to, then this would be raised in the first instance at the liaison committee. This committee has a far more widespread use than simply a complaints forum. It ensures that the promises made in good faith by the National Coal Board are being implemented by the contractors operating on their behalf. The existence of such a committee makes it more difficult for people to argue that the promises and undertakings, made in seeking approval for working the site, will not be kept. It also ensures that work is carried out in ways which have been agreed and, therefore, helps to preserve good relationships. Such a liaison committee is far more than a public relations exercise.

The manager and the democratic process

So far we have been concerned mainly with the outside world but the company's own labour force is also directly concerned. The great changes that have taken place in attitudes towards participation in all types of social and political activity over the last ten years, can only be ignored by the manager of today at his peril. This is not to make a moral judgement on the desirability of such developments, but merely to note the fact that participation is becoming an essential ingredient in any managerial process, whatever happens to the 'Bullock' proposals.[6] All managers should therefore achieve a clear understanding of the political and democratic processes involved in planning and control, if they want to enjoy a good grasp of the potential difficulties.

The movement towards participation has been a by-product of wider educational opportunities. The concept of fixed social stations in society — 'The rich man in his castle, the poor man at his gate, God made them high or lowly and ordered their estate' — as Mrs Frances Alexander, the Victorian hymn writer, put so positively, has completely collapsed. The idea of equal votes and an equal say in government was bound to lead to a similar view in industry. The improvement in living standards has meant that individuals could look to something other than the battle for personal survival in their day-to-day activities. People have begun, in varying degrees, to seek job satisfaction. It is easy to argue that there are many people who do not wish to participate in any way and it is beyond dispute that there are many who are more than happy to let other people take decisions for them. Some actually resent any attempt to bring them into the decision-making process.

Despite all this, it is becoming more and more evident that increasing numbers do wish to be involved. This is true even where they do not have any self appreciation of the fact. The classic example of the latter condition is where a firm decides to shut down the business and the workers refuse to accept the managerial decision and press for direct action, whether by a 'sit-in' or a workers' co-operative. Determined to have a say in their own future, they do not accept that their interests can be served by decisions taken by what might be a remote board of directors, or by management who may be simply trying to withdraw its investment in that particular activity so as to put it elsewhere. Such views may be ill-founded. The co-operative set up, with its high hopes, may prove to be as unequal to the economics of the situation, under the banner of workers' participation, as under the flag of management. The difference is that the workers will *know* from first hand experience and not from an edict from on high.

On the industrial front, the pressure for participation on the Continent has been very firm and the legislation now provides formalised mechanisms whereby all firms over a certain size must provide for worker participation in

[6] Report of the Committee of Inquiry on Industrial Democracy, Chairman, Lord Bullock, Cmd. 6706.

the decision-making process, in certain clearly defined areas of activity. The two tier board, with mandatory rights for workers' representatives on the supervisory board, is now the accepted pattern in most of Western Europe, but not in Britain. While it is true that there are as yet few signs of pressure for participation in the United States, it should not be assumed that they have some form of immunity.

It is sometimes said that these mechanisms are mere window dressing and that the companies act in the same way as they did before the mechanisms were created. If one examines the situation in detail however, it does not seem quite so clear cut. Traditionally boards of management have taken the decisions as to where their capital will be invested. They would decide, for example, whether or not the new factory should be near the existing one, or perhaps overseas in the country where it is planned that sales would take place. This has long been the natural behaviour of management and only recently has been challenged.

One of the first major challenges was to the decision by Volkswagen to start assembling their cars in the United States, where they had developed a major market. The workforce, and their representatives on the supervisory board, did not regard this as being in the interest of the work people in Germany. Their argument was that if Volkswagens were to be assembled in the United States, then this would take away work which had previously been done in Germany and, in the face of the then likely recession in the car industry and a drop in the level of activity, this was, in effect, a decision to export jobs from Germany to the United States. This was seen, not unnaturally, as being undesirable, and certainly not in the interests of the German labour force. The supervisory board (which in the case of Volkswagen was in a 50:50 relationship) was able to prevent this action on the part of Volkswagen, and precipitated a change in senior management.

Similarly, attempts by the British Steel Corporation to introduce what were interpreted as arbitrary cutbacks in levels of manning, or changes in conditions of service, met with strong opposition from the workforce.

Since the war, there has been much pressure for the creation of works' councils, consultative committees and the like, where the people employed are able to express their views on policies proposed by management and, in fact, to impose some policies of their own. The first act of Nationalisation by the post-war Labour Government — the Coal Industry Nationalisation Act of 1946 — provided for mandatory consultation at all levels in the industry. Consultative committees were established at every pit and at area divisional and national levels. There has now developed a Joint Policy Advisory Committee through which all the problems and future plans and programmes for the industry are considered. The Labour Government of 1974 introduced the concept of Planning Agreements, which call for industry to prepare, discuss and give detailed plans for the future with the unions concerned — potentially a change of profound importance.

There has grown up a parallel desire for increased information and consultation in the community in general. We all now expect to be fully informed about changes which may take place in our own locality and, where appropriate, to be consulted on such changes. Governments have introduced elaborate mechanisms to see that we are properly consulted, culminating in Great Britain with the national referendum on whether or not the country should remain in the Common Market.

Narrowing it down to the field of the environment it is now expected that, if any proposals are put forward, all amenity societies will be given a chance to state their views and to bring forward arguments as to why they do not agree with them.

The planning procedures which have evolved in this century have increasingly concentrated on the need to see that all points of view are considered and are seen to be considered. This is true even where it is overriding government policy that some particular action should take place. The recent major example of the latter is perhaps in the United States, in respect of the Environmental Protection Bill which Congress attempted to introduce to control the acticities of American strip mine operations. This interesting case is dealt with in some detail in Chapter 8.

The important point of this example is that it demonstrates that, even where there was a clear-cut government decision in favour of increased indigenous coal production, the processes had to be gone through to establish the desirability of such production in the face of the potential damage which its opponents felt it could do to the environment. The likely damage to the environment was probably exaggerated, because it was based on an examination of what had already occurred in the country, rather than what the best practices could achieve. Battle lines were drawn between the producers — many of whom seemed to be solely concerned with minimising the restoration costs — and the environmentalists and conservationists. In some instances the latter seemed to be more concerned with maintaining the *status quo* in respect of the environment than with analysing out the overall needs of the country — or trying to establish ways in which restoration could take place which would make the development of new strip mines acceptable.

It is, therefore, unwise to assume that the strength of your own particular case in economic terms will necessarily be sufficient to win the day. Unless you are prepared to back up your proposals with strong arguments in relation to environmental considerations, you may be in for a nasty and expensive shock.

The businessman is often fully aware of the consequences of actions that might be taken by planning authorities, but he doesn't always make an attempt to involve himself in entering into the public debate with the intention of influencing the final decision. This is regrettable. At this stage in the development of our democracy, it is becoming more important that people 'stand up and be counted' in relation to every aspect of activity. If you fail to make the economic argument in favour of your particular development, do not be surprised if it goes by default; you be left vainly expostulating that decisions are taken on the basis of inadequate or emotionally biased information. With the increasing inter-reaction between the environment and industry, it becomes more and more important that the manager or businessman has a clear understanding of the role of democratic planning.

He must understand how the game is played, and intervene at the appropriate points, to ensure that his case is heard. In doing this, in relation to a proposal affecting the company, it is a cardinal error to enter the battle in a political way. The aim should be to inform politicians of all shades and opinions of what you are trying to do and to convince them that it is right. You must avoid the temptation of only talking to those politicians who happen to share your own prejudices. It is involvement in the political process, and not in the political battle, that is required.

10 Crossroads

Is it straight on?

I have called this chapter 'Crossroads' because I believe that as a society we are at a point where we need to stop and think before deciding which direction to go in. To continue blundering straight ahead is not good enough. We are at one of those infuriating crossroads without a signpost that are so often found in a strange country. We have certainly equipped ourselves with inadequate (not to say positively misleading) maps, and consequently it is not surprising that there is real confusion as to precisely where we are. In such a situation, it always pays to stop for a while and consider all the alternatives with great care. This becomes very necessary if one has reason to doubt whether the petrol in the tank will be sufficient to take you down more than one wrong turning.

We are in a similar situation in our attitude to the environmental problems facing us. Whatever our differing views, we ought to be able to agree that, in our present dilemma, we no longer have sufficient resources to permit us the luxury of making many further fundamental errors of judgement.

The analogy is worth pursuing a little further — let us consider the alternatives facing us at these particular crossroads. The first and most obvious option is to keep going straight ahead; to carry on as we are doing. I hope that the preceding chapters have shown that such a course should hold few attractions for us. It may be that we can carry on going through relatively pleasant countryside on roads which are not too bumpy for a mile or two yet, but it would seem highly probable that the going will become increasingly unpleasant and we shall run out of road before we reach our destination. If we agree then that to carry on as we are is not an acceptable solution, what other choices have we got?

You're the navigator

The first thing to do at our crossroads is decide precisely where we want to go. What is our destination? It is bad enough if we have doubts as to where each road leads; the task of deciding becomes almost impossible if each passenger has a difficult opinion as to where we ought to go. Unfortunately this seems to be the situation we find ourselves in. Some may opt for the tranquility of the country, some the bustle and bright lights of a busy town, while others the remoteness of a desolate moor or lonely marshlands. No matter where we want to be, with us all in the same vehicle, we stand little chance of making progress until we have a consensus of agreement. In such a situation, we are likely to try and reach either a majority verdict or some type of compromise. Similarly, this is what we need to be doing in the environmental field. We are all passengers on 'spaceship earth' and must agree an order of priorities for our objectives. We cannot consume the cakes we like if an increasing proportion of the ingredients available are needed to make bread.

This is an easy proposition to make, but a very difficult one to put into operation. It brings us back to the root problem of all societies: how to establish the 'will' of the community so that its aims and goals can be defined. This is not just a problem affecting environmental issues, but it does have special relevance to them because it is an area in which the 'will' of the people is so confused and crosses normal political allegiances.

At certain points in history, the objectives of a society can be relatively easily defined in terms of priorities. If we take the Western world in the twentieth century, then it is not too gross an over simplification to say that most of its first decade was concerned with trying to eliminate grinding poverty and lay the foundation for some form of social 'security net' which would conquer the starvation and degradation which so disfigured the apparent prosperity of the nineteenth century. The next two decades were dominated by preparations for fighting, and recovering from, the First World War. In the 1930s the first overriding issue was that of the Great Depression and how to remove the scourge of mass unemployment. The second was the growing conflict over democratic values. The 1940s was another decade of war, but the next quarter century seemed to usher in the millenium. We had a run of rising material living standards and the apparent elimination of the economic 'boom/bust' cycle. This tended to make us think that our fundamental economic problems were behind us and we could concentrate more on the division of the cake than its baking. The consequences of the Yom Kippur War have given us a sharp reminder that this was a false dawn, night has closed in again, and our current economic astronomers (or should it be astrologers!) do not seem to be in agreement where to look for the silver lining.

Many people are now questioning the fundamental aims of our society. The idea that, in terms of the economy, we should be constantly aiming at increasing growth, has come under much criticism (informed and otherwise) in recent years.[1] It has been argued that we have sought the economic

---

[1] See in particular E.J. Mischon's perceptive analysis *The Costs of Economic Growth* for a critique of the economic case for growth. This needs to be read in conjunction with the counter arguments in F.J. Blackaby's *In Defence of Economic Growth*. Of perhaps more fundamental importance is E.F. Schumacher's philosophical questioning of the whole foundation of our economic approach in *Small is Beautiful*.

objectives of our Victorian forefathers without the benefit of the social cement that was provided by the moral and religious climate of those times. These are deep waters indeed and ones which, while deserving the most detailed examination, we have no need to swim far in for our present purposes. But we do need to note that the water is there and its depths have not yet been plumbed.

All environmental conflicts have to be seen against the background of different attitudes towards economic growth. This is a difficult area. There seem to be an equal number of advocates for the view that most of our global crises can be attributed to continuous and rapid growth, as there are for the contrary view, that the solutions to the world crises can be found only through even greater growth. For our purposes it helps to realise that, once again, we are involved in problems of definition. What do we mean by 'growth'? And is it the same in all parts of the world? Some types of growth may be undesirable but this does not mean that all types of growth should be avoided. If we call for a 'no growth' policy, does that mean that we accept that everyone's standards in the economic hierarchy will remain frozen? This seems very unrealistic; therefore, advocates of 'no growth' must face up to the consequential problems of the re-allocation of existing wealth (and entitlements to future wealth) between people with our society. This is something which many would argue has already reached practicable limits. Growth is a process, not an object. It should be used as a description of something that is humanly initiated, and not as an aim. In the *Second Report to the Club of Rome* the point is well made that to grow or not to grow, is neither well defined nor a relevant question until the location, sense and subject of growing and the growth process, are defined.

If we think about the level of material consumption, it is a fact that in the world's developed industrial countries, materialistic consumption has reached proportions of preposterous waste. In these regions we must take action to bring about a reduction in the waste of materials. On the other hand, there must be a continued growth in the use of some essential resources either for food or industrial production, to meet legitimate needs. There are far too many mouths that still need feeding, bodies that need clothing and homes that need building.

It is therefore no solution to the environmental problem[2] to argue that we should go for 'no growth' policies. That is a neat but meaningless slogan even for so called affluent societies. If taken at its face value, it assumes that we do not want any further growth in health or social care, or provision for the aged. It pre-supposes that leisure and cultural needs are fully met. As this is not the case, the most this particular injunction can mean is that we should not require growth for growth's sake.

On the other hand, it would be equally wrong to assume that the solution of

---

[2] Note that this does not mean there might be very valid arguments for pursuing such policies to meet *other* objectives. My concern here is that it should not be regarded as a short cut to environmental salvation.

all mankind's ills rests in finding a magic formula for improving growth rates. Dr Schumacher has argued that this could in fact make matters worse. He has suggested that the threefold crises of mankind — the crisis of resources, the ecological crisis and the social crisis — will still be with us, but in an accentuated form. He argues persuasively that more growth will result in everything becoming increasingly brittle and vulnerable. Whatever the underlying validity of this thesis, the answer is not an unmitigated policy of conservation. As the journal the *Economist* pointed out in September 1975:

'A major weakness of conservation has been a failure to relate programmes and projects to prevailing social conditions. Accordingly, there have been occasions when scarce money, expertise and effort have gone into projects with little chance of success. For example, an attempt to safeguard a substantial area of tropical rain forest in a small densely populated country, whose numbers are still growing rapidly, which can be expected to eventually cultivate every available bit of land to prevent starvation, is unlikely to succeed and probably should not be made at all. A similar project elsewhere might have every chance of success *provided* it includes the means whereby the local people can continue to grow food, obtain firewood and so on, as (or more) easily than before.'

The old adage of 'horses for courses' is a suitable one for environmental and conservation problems. We have been faced with far too many sweeping generalisations as to what we should or should not do in environmental matters. This book has been written in the belief that we are headed on a collision course between so-called environmentalists and so-called realists, and unless somebody starts changing direction very quickly indeed we shall precipitate the potential disasters already balanced above our heads. The parties involved are too concerned with their own narrow interests and seem to work from the assumption that if allowed to get their own way, then all danger will be averted and all will be well. The 'professional' environmentalist, with an increasing number of environmental disasters to which he can point, believes that he will be able to rouse sufficient public opinion to prevent the extension of almost any activity that changes the environment in one way or another.[3] The industrialist hopes that the sheer economic necessity for his products will, in the long run, overcome any 'misguided' opposition to the extension or continuance of his inactivities. Both parties therefore go flat out to eliminate their opponents rather than genuinely try to reach accommodation with them.

---

[3] This aspect is especially worrying when arguments are reduced to the skills of the respective sides' lawyers. Law is an essential framework, but the lawyers should not be left to design the building. There are areas of society's activities which are too crucial to leave to the dictates of the personal interests of any profession, and that includes the legal profession.

Meanwhile, most governments frantically seek the best of both worlds. The environmental lobby has grown in strength to such a degree that many governments feel it carries the full weight of public opinion and must be given a major say in influencing policies. Yet, at the same time, governments are desperately in need of an extension of industrial activity to provide the necessary ingredient of 'growth' and are seeking all means for promoting industrial expansion. That the laudable objectives of seeking to provide more employment, better material standards and an unaffected totally secure environment may be contradictory, is something that governments and electorates prefer to ignore. It is a case of the rule of the ostrich once again. There remains, nevertheless, a genuine dilemma which will not be solved by ignoring the issue and hoping it will go away.

The problem is made more difficult than it need be because of our reluctance to try and define it. We tend to want to see each issue in isolation and treat it separately, usually exclusively from the point of view of its possible environmental effects, rather than see the issues for what they are: different facets of the overall problem of how to reconcile the conflicting human desires of obtaining improved material well-being while not losing anything we value in the process.

No one should doubt the sincerity of those who campaign genuinely for a better environment. Organisations such as the Friends of the Earth have done a great service in highlighting areas of current or potential concern. They have offered their own solutions for policies which would meet the crises they envisage. Inevitably, however, their order of priority for tackling the complexity of problems facing humanity differs from those of other pressure groups.

Most people, if asked, would claim truthfully that they wanted to live in a better and safer environment. Unfortunately, very often they see this solely in terms of removing some existing undesirable features of their own neighbourhood (or preventing the incursion of a new development) while expecting all the desirable apsects of their living standards to remain unchanged. They see it in terms of a genuine improvement rather than a process of 'trading off' benefits against costs. This approach is not surprising, particularly as individuals in such circumstances expect, with justification, that the benefits will accrue to them while hopefully the costs will fall on somebody else. In fact this is the reverse of the situation that has appertained for so long, in which companies have accumulated the benefits while allowing the social costs to fall on individuals, without making them any recompense. People have yet to be faced with the reality of having to choose to make personal sacrifices in their own standards of living in order to achieve the environmental improvements they want. Faced with such a choice, it is doubtful whether as many would act so positively in support of environmental proposals.

It could be argued that one of the many reasons for the economic decline of Great Britain (and of other countries) in recent years, has been the growth of the 'do nothing, change nothing' school. The difficulty is that usually it is hard to show precisely where such losses have occurred and impossible to trace them back to individual standards of living.

One small example might illustrate the point I have in mind. As the result of pressure from local inhabitants and conservationists, the Inspector of a public enquiry decided to draw back the proposed line of working for an opencast coal site by a matter of some 200 yards. This had the effect of protecting a group of trees which was certainly beneficial to the area, but the price of this arbitrary withdrawal was some £7 000 000 increase in cost (because the most abundant coal seams happened to lie beneath the trees). The Inspector was not aware of this when he made his decision; he was doing it in order to meet the legitimate interests of people living locally. It did, however, add its morsel to the country's economic problems by depriving the nation of much needed coal and, at the same time, add substantially to the costs of this particular site.

While we cannot estimate the costs that have been incurred over recent years as a result of decisions made on environmental grounds, there can be little doubt that the amount is significant. While many of these costs were no doubt proper charges to protect the environment in most cases, the real costs are not known to the public and the judgement cannot be made! It is not appreciated that however desirable the interventions may be the general economic standards of living are that much lower than would otherwise be the case. This is not an argument that the costs should not be incurred and the consequences accepted, but that they should be known and appreciated when the decisions are taken.

Many good environmentalists argue that we should be prepared to accept such sacrifices as the cost of preserving our environment. In particular cases, they can undoubtedly command popular support, but not every time. The point I am trying to make is that the population at large is not being faced with the choice. We are not being asked to judge in specific terms, as opposed to generalities, whether we are prepared to accept the price of an improvment or the maintenance of current environmental standards. One fact that is often overlooked is that for a large part of our standard of living over the last hundred years we have depended on the exploitation of resources overseas, the workings of which have had major detrimental environmental effects. We have to beware of the self-righteous approach, which prevents possible damage to the environment in one country at the expense of 'exporting' it to another, where the local inhabitants may be too poor or unorganised to have the matter properly debated. Although, for example, the leaders of the campaign, to prevent the exploitation of copper by RTZ in North Wales, might be prepared to concede that logically they ought equally to resist the exploitation of copper in any part of the world where similar environmental problems will arise, it is more doubtful whether their supporters would follow such an approach, particularly if the consequential shortages of copper resulted in substantial price rises. This is the real choice that is facing people. Of course we would all like to preserve everything that is best in our environment and we would all like to carry out improvements to make the country a better place to live in. The question is, how much can we afford and how much should we afford?

In Chapter 2, I argued that we need to distinguish carefully what we mean when we use the word 'environment'. In terms of the natural landscape, we are in danger of making costly sacrifices at the altar of conservation for conservation's sake. We would do well to remember the wise words of Max Nicholson, in his classic *The Environmental Revolution*, when he writes:

> 'Each generation, therefore, mistakes for a natural permanent environment what is actually the outcome of a peculiar blend of natural and human forces, and mistakes a temporary transition stage as a settled end-product of evolution. Such false assumptions discourage thought and investigation concerning the natural and human forces responsible for the current situation, the means by which they operate, and the extent and rate to which they themselves are undergoing change and thus exerting changing types of influence upon a natural environment itself in the midst of change, already dictated by previous impacts or interventions. The process is highly complex and dynamic and is unlikely to be handled with skill or success by people who do not realise that it exists, or who brashly suppose that the particular views and attitudes which they themselves hold are the only ones possible for their community.'

We all accept the need for certain types of development (even those of us who believe in 'no growth' economics). We acknowledge the need for more and better schools, hospitals, old peoples' homes, etc. Most of us would accept the need for roads, to cut down delays and traffic frustration, power stations to provide light, better schools, abolition of slums, adequate prison facilities and humane psychiatric institutions to provide help for those who cannot help themselves.

Most people would support the need for industrial development to provide employment, particularly at times and in places of high unemployment. All these types of development, we might support to some degree or another, depending upon our own particular interests or concerns. But, despite our rational approach in relation to individual projects, we are still very much inclined to oppose any such development in our own neck of the woods. We do not want our own environment disturbed in such ways. We, of course, oppose it for the most rational of reasons — the danger to children, the additional traffic it would create, the change in the character of the area — but our objections normally focus on the argument that the development would be far better located in some other place! We always forget that we all live in 'some other place' to some other people!

The environmentalists should therefore accept that some types of development in some places will continue to be necessary, whatever the policies of economic growth that are pursued, and concentrate on getting the type of development which is most compatible with their objections.

I have argued that, irrespective of reductions in demands for improvements in individual living standards in the Western world, the total demand for resources is bound to increase rapidly because of the population explosion. It is hard to appreciate the rate at which our consumption of metals and minerals has been increasing in recent decades.[4] The total volume of workable mineral deposits is only one per cent of the earth's crust and each deposit represents some geological accident in the remote past. Deposits must be mined where they occur and this is often far from the areas of consumption. (Although, unfortunately, from an environmental point of view, not always far from centres of population.) Each deposit has its physical limits and, if worked long enough, must sooner or later be exhausted. The simple but crucial point here is that, unlike agricultural production, no second crop will materialise. Rich mineral deposits are a nation's most valuable but ephemeral material possession and we must learn to treat them as such. We cannot afford to squander these reserves and sacrifice the benefits they could bring later. Fortunately, there is no reason why we should make such a drastic decision.

In their stimulating study of resource conflicts in international relations *The Politics of Scarcity*, Connelly and Perlman, the authors, offer a note of optimism. They conclude that:

> 'The resource challenge confronting the international community is not the problem of halting consumption in the face of a fixed and diminished resource inventory. We have argued instead that natural resources have a fluid and ever changing nature and that grounds exist for optimism — albeit qualified — that technology will solve problems of exploration, extraction, substitution, and environmental impact.'

One thing is certain, however; that the problems cannot be solved without changing or altering the environment in some respect. It is a matter of whether it can be done in a way which is acceptable. In deciding acceptability, we must learn to assess the alternatives in order to decide whether these would be found tolerable. On the environment issue, Connelly and Perlman conclude that:

> 'Acceptable environmental standards can no doubt be achieved over time and at a cost by the application of a degree of technical effort and ingenuity commensurate with that devoted to the extraction

---

[4] These points are made graphically in the publication *Resources and Man* published by the American National Academy of Sciences, which points out that, in the thirty years following the Second World War, we managed to consume more metal than we had in the previous entire course of human history.

process itself. It is less certain that the "technocratic" solution will
mollify all the environmentalist groups whose aesthetic principles
have recently commended political support.'

It is unreasonable to expect the technologist and the industrialist to tackle the
very real problems of making sufficient resources available in the world with
one hand tied behind their backs. It is not sufficiently appreciated that this is
what society is asking them to do. This is an approach that is potentially
disastrous if it is done for non-essential environmental reasons. It is important
to note the qualification 'non-essential'.

In discussing the importance of precise definitions of the words we were
using, in order to understand the true nature of the problems we were faced
with, I stressed the need to avoid over-concern with *relatively* minor issues.
One of the themes I touched on was the difficulty in defining what is meant by
environmental protection or conservation. There is no doubt that in respect of
matters which could affect the survival of the human race, i.e. such matters as
the possible irreversible nuclear contamination that we could unleash on
ourselves, it is impossible to over-estimate the importance of such
considerations. But an argument that would be relevant to such fundamentally
crucial matters should not be conceded on those more mundane aspects which,
in the last analysis, are matters of subjective judgement. It may well be, for
example, that I prefer a particular type of landscape, architecture, or way of
living, but that is no reason why you should have to share my tastes, or vice
versa. I want to be clear on this point. I am not suggesting that it is in some
way morally wrong that people should concern themselves with what I term
'non crucial' environmental issues. Apart from the difficulties in reaching
agreement on what is crucial and what is not, it is highly desirable that people
should seek to protect those aspects of their lives and their environment that
they believe to be important. This is an essential virtue of a free society. But, in
forcibly expressing our views, we should not be so intellectually arrogant as to
assume that, because we believe them to be of overriding importance this
judgement must necessarily be accepted by everyone else. For example, while
some of us may be prepared to accept a lower economic standard of life in
order to protect what we believe to be of supreme importance, by what right
should we be allowed to impose such opinions on other people? We certainly
have no moral authority to follow such policies without the explicit acceptance
of those affected by both the proposed actions and the likely implications for
their living standards. It is dishonest to ignore the fact that some measures
proposed to protect the environment could have adverse consequences in
reducing available employment and the national wealth.

It is sometimes argued that the very work of enforcing environmental
protection standards has a positive effect on employment because of the jobs
which are created. This proposition, however, misses the point that, even in
such cases, most of the jobs created are 'service' jobs which have to be

financed out of existing resources and so, in fact, reduce even further the size of the economic cake available for other purposes.

When I was describing ways in which industries might consider how they could overcome potential environmental opposition, I suggested that one of the first questions to ask was whether there was anything that could be done which was not already being done. The problem here is that, all too often, no real attempt is made on the part of the industrialist to meet the specific problems which lead to general environmental opposition. If people feel that they will not get a satisfactory solution to aircraft noise, then they are going to object to extensions to airports or development of new ones. On the other hand, as more and more effort is put into eliminating the specific causes for objection, it is possible that the blanket objections may be overcome. The 'vested interest' objections will remain but there will be a better chance of identifying them for what they are. Industry must get out of the attitude of doing only the minimum necessary to 'get away with it' and do that which would be environmentally and economically sensible.

But let me return to those basic areas of environmental concern the importance over which there can be little disagreement — those areas where the whole future of the human race could be affected. In this context, overriding importance must be attached to the potential both for good and evil of nuclear energy.

Whereas it is impossible to set limits on the future universal demand for energy, the conventional means of supplying it, i.e., through fossil fuels, are very finite. Whatever view one takes of the attitude of the 'Club of Rome' about the imminence of running into catastrophic world shortages of metals and minerals, there can be no questioning their basic thesis that, sooner or later, the non-replaceable natural resources available to mankind will reach either economic or physical exhaustion. The argument is on the timing and not on the reality. In the context of energy, therefore, we must welcome the prospect of an infinitely renewable source of energy. It is therefore foolish to dismiss the essential nature of the contribution nuclear power may have to make to the world at some time or other. A more germane question is whether we need to go down such a dangerous road just yet? It is always possible that, given time and resources, we could find an alternative route or destination which may not involve the same type of hazards.

I would however accept the proposition put forward by some of the opponents of the 'Club of Rome' thesis that the classic pressures of supply and demand will reduce the present growth rates in the demand for certain resources and, therefore, their physical exhaustion could theoretically never be reached. But this is cold comfort for those who are priced out of the market and can no longer afford the resources they need even though in physical terms they are still available in the world. A 'let them eat cake' philosophy is no more acceptable because it comes carefully packaged in the sterile wrappings of basic economic doctrine.

While this is not the place for a dissertation on the merits or otherwise of nuclear power, certain facets of the arguments which are being deployed cast some light on the problems we have been considering.

In Great Britain, concern about these types of developments has been growing and the public debate has become more intense.[5] The most authoritative contribution to it in recent times has been *Nuclear Power and the Environment*, the Sixth Report of the Royal Commission on Environmental Pollution, under the Chairmanship of Sir Brian Flowers, which was published in the autumn of 1976. The Report brings out the overwhelming complexity of the issues. The question is not merely a matter of deciding whether electricity generating stations using nuclear fuel should be brought into operation as quickly as possible, because they are a cheaper substitute for boilers using coal, oil, or gas. The question of nuclear power transcends economics. The terrifying reality is that an inevitable by-product of all atomic power stations is the production of a wide range of dangerous reactive waste substances. Some of these substances are so dangerous and so toxic that a very few grains inhaled into the lungs can cause death. Although precautions can be taken in the handling of the materials, there is the further problem that the waste materials have to be safeguarded for unimaginable lengths of time. The most hazardous of them remain dangerous for so long, that safe disposal means creating storage methods that will ensure their isolation for more than a hundred thousand years.

On the other hand, it must be said that the safety record of the nuclear power industry in Great Britain is second to none. The likelihood that Britain and the world will want atomic power is almost beyond dispute. The main problem comes from the apparent need to develop fast breeder reactors which use plutonium as their fuel, probably the most dreaded of all poisonous radio-active elements, because of its toxicity and its life-span which runs into tens of thousands of years. One of the conclusions of the Flowers Report is:

> 'There should be no commitment to a large programme of nuclear fission power until it has been demonstrated beyond reasonable doubt that a method exists to ensure the safe containment of a long-lived, highly radio-active waste, for the indefinite future. We are clear that such a demonstration will require a substantial programme of research.'

---

[5] This is true of many Western nations. Legal action has been taken on an increasing scale in the United States to try to present specific nuclear development. In Sweden the development of nuclear power stations is of major importance in the country's present plans for meeting their energy requirements. However, calls for a phased withdrawal of even existing capacity have reached such sizeable dimensions that the Swedish Central or Agricultural Party campaigned in support of such a policy in the elections of 1976. Presumably, this had some appeal as the elections resulted in the leader of that party, Torbjorn Fallion, becoming Prime Minister of a three party coalition. How the conflicting objectives will be reconciled remains to be seen.

This illustrates one of the frightening voids that we constantly meet when considering the alternatives open to our society — the lack of basic knowledge. So far, much of the argument in the environmental field, whether relating to something as basic as the development of nuclear power, or as relatively unimportant as protecting a particular view or landscape, has been conducted in terms of protecting the *status quo*, because we fear the unknown. Very little fundamental research work has been done on the part of either side to demonstrate ways in which there could be some meeting of the other's point of view. The amount of money invested in trying to develop alternative technologies which would meet our needs in different ways, or enable the environment to receive a greater degree of protection while developing the needed resources, has been pitifully small. The critical importance in the medium and long term of measures to conserve energy is far from being recognised and accepted. This is partially the responsibility of accounting systems which inevitably conclude that there is no financial advantage in undertaking many such schemes because on current prices the rate of return is insufficient, coupled with an understandable reluctance to use pricing mechanisms to promote conservation of resources.

To revert to the Flowers Report, it is significant that they comment on the potential dangers of breeder reactors and the importance of looking at alternative courses of energy supply. But, whereas research into peaceful fission power is running at something like £80 million a year, the amount of money being devoted to developing alternative energy technologies (other than fossil fuels) is not much more than £500 000 a year. In the longer term, the possibility of harnessing tidal power and wave power must be of the utmost importance yet the amount of money being spent on it is pitifully small. One alternative open to our society is to buy time through intensive development of fossil fuels, to try to create such relatively environmentally harmless and renewable sources of energy, rather than plunge headlong into the potentially catastrophic hazards of nuclear fission.

Another major area of concern is in the manufacture of chemicals. Mankind is desperate for the development of new chemicals: for providing raw material substitutes, artificial fertilisers, pest controls and pharmaceuticals. Yet, as the side effects have become known, more and more controls have had to be introduced over such activities. The co-operation of chemical companies has been noteworthy and many of them now see the importance of ensuring that their own inherent and intrinsic practices are as safe as possible. It is good business, as well as sound social sense, because of the damage that can be caused to a company by adverse reactions resulting from its inefficiency.

The chemical industry is a classic example of the need to identify problems that we can all agree are of fundamental concern and to try and devise sensible solutions. The outcomes will vary. In some instances, the sensible solution will be not to go ahead with certain developments because the potential benefits are marginal compared with the inherent danger whereas, in other instances, the environmental issues raised may not be regarded as being of fundamental importance and the risks may be acceptable in consideration of the benefits offered.

Whatever the industry, until you identify the actual or potential environmental problems and accept that solutions must be sought and worked for, it is difficult to decide whether there is anything that can be done about them. As in the case of alternatives to nuclear power, the amount of time and resources devoted to generating alternatives has been pitifully small.

Our current methods of handling environmental issues are not very promising or productive of acceptable solutions. So far, we tend to have been locked in combat. Expert evidence (so-called) has been used by both sides to try to demonstrate the overwhelming validity of its own case. We have used the classic techniques of the English legal system, putting the defendant on trial and trying to prove him guilty, rather than the French approach of trying to discover whether a crime was committed and, if so, who was responsible. With our increasingly quasi-legal system of public inquiries, the only people who have gained from the operation seem to be the lawyers. We must develop a resource analysis rather than a legalistic approach to these problems if we are to survive.

As well as the industrialists becoming familiar with the environmentalists' case, and taking it into account when formulating business plans, it is of equal importance that the environmentalists learn to appreciate the arguments for industrial development and expansion. All too often, these are seen purely in terms of financial profit for individual firms or even individuals. The problem of 'profit' is one that bedevils society. It has become an emotive word, one which describes something which is, to many people, inherently unacceptable. We need to move towards a situation where profit is seen as being just one of the yardsticks against which to judge the efficiency of an enterprise. The argument should be on the distribution of the profit, not on the desirability of its achievement. To environmentalists, all too often the proposed developments of industrialists appear selfish. They argue that the environment is being sacrificed on the altar of profits. The implication is that things of real value are being lost simply so that firms can make money. This approach fails to appreciate that industry is geared to meet the needs of the community as expressed through demands for goods and services. It may well be that such needs could (and perhaps should) be modified in certain ways but, until they are, then the community will expect to have its requirements met, and met at the lowest possible cost.

We are constantly being reminded that 'man does not live by bread alone' but it is surely no greater a truism than the fact that man cannot live without it. You cannot preach the doctrine successfully to someone who is still going short of basic necessities. Many environmentalists are reluctant to face up to the reality of the need for further industrial development. Although, in fairness, many do not realise that this is the position they are adopting. They take the view that they are only opposing specific developments, but if each specific development is resisted on grounds of lack of need, the implicit assumption must be that industrial development is unnecessary. They hope that if it can be successfully resisted, then life can carry on as it is at present. This view totally fails to appreciate the effect of fundamental changes in population growth already taking place. Without further industrial development, more people must go hungry, be deprived of work and of standards which we would regard as being essential for reasonable living. Whether the Western ethic of personal material enrichment is morally desirable or not, there can be little doubt of its apparent persuasiveness wherever it has penetrated. To imagine a society which is prepared to give up the quest for change and growth and the pursuit of whatever it believes to be progress, seems to be asking for a change in the nature of Western man. To base a social or economic philosophy on the ossification of society would be highly unrealistic, even of the population levels of such a society were fixed. In an era of a population explosion, I suggest it is a waste of valuable time even to consider the ways in which such a result could be sought. This is not to deny the need for a continual rethinking of the objectives of mankind, but merely to accept that any profound changes cannot take place overnight. It is undoubtedly necessary to redesign the *Titanic*, but first let us build a few lifeboats.

The signpost

There is little doubt that a solution-seeking approach would demand the use of resources by companies in areas which initially seem to be unprofitable. But I suggest that it is a grave mistake on the part of businesses to assume that environmental issues are merely a form of public relations which have to be paid for, but the cost of which should be kept as low as possible. The pursuit of an acceptable environmental solution fits in with a firm's customary management objectives in four main ways:
1. By making its operations more acceptable to the community, it undoubtedly protects the long-term survival of the firm. And this is usually regarded as being the fundamental guiding precept of all company policy, this is a most important factor.
2. By compelling a closer examination of potential hazards and problems, it helps to avoid the potential dangers of environmental mishaps which, at the very least, might be extremely costly in pure financial terms to the company.[6]
3. By making the company more acceptable to the community, as a firm

---

[6] The cost of the escape of the toxic cloud at Seveso in Italy, which contained a quantity of 2,3,7,8, — tetrachlorodibenzo-para-dioxin (TCDD), is likely to be extremely expensive for somebody.

with a strong social conscience, as well as a profit motivation. This
could be of great importance in getting support for future expansion
and could give the company an edge on its competitors.

4.   On the commercial side, if the company is successful in overcoming
     particular environmental problems, then it may well gain a competitive
     edge for a period, in the market as a whole.

In carrying out their assessment of potential environmental problems,
companies must use all available techniques. Starting with the preparation of a
full analysis of the present situation in quantitative terms, they must go on to
predict what they expect will be the results of proposed developments. They
need a process of evaluation to establish what actually happens if and when
they go ahead to ensure that no unforeseen difficulties are arising. There is a
need for a new look at the possibility of providing reasonable compensation for
those people genuinely affected and therefore asked to bear an unfair share of
the social costs involved in securing a particular social benefit. Such
compensation is a legitimate cost, but it must be fairly applied. The great
danger here is that the most awkward customer will get the highest pay off in
order that the project can go ahead quickly. This is one area in which
government criteria could be of great help in establishing fair and equitable
methods of compensation for all the people involved.

Industry has to accept that it needs to live down its apparently manifest role
of being the villain of the piece. It has to be appreciated that it starts from the
disadvantage of being held responsible for creating the present environment, a
performance for which there is little praise forthcoming. The fact that in so
doing it enormously increased the living standards of the population is not
even seen as a mitigating circumstance. It is this reputation which has to be
carried and like all bad reputations it is hard to live down. The reasons put
forward by industry for carrying out this or that operation are treated with
suspicion and are considered standard diet for budding investigatory
journalists, in some cases, it must be admitted, with good reason. John
Quarles, in his book *Cleaning Up America* quotes the example of the company
president writing to Mr Nixon that compliance with a Restraining Order
issued by the Environmental Protection Agency would throw 300 people out
of work. Unfortunately, they just happened to have been dismissed three
weeks before the letter was written! Certainly not the way to win friends and
influence people.

The community is looking for clear evidence that industry and business are
genuine in their attempts to analyse and meet environmental difficulties. Lip
service will not suffice. Whereas a good reputation can be lost almost
overnight, a bad reputation, however undeserved, is very difficult to overcome
and can only be expunged by actions, not further protestations of innocence.

In carrying out this work, industry must be prepared to do more than
is required by the strict letter of the law. It will require investment of much
time, money and effort. Some will see this as attacking the profitability

of the concern and therefore being inimical to the company's real interest.

So much attention has been focussed on identifying environmental hazards, real or imaginary, that it is no longer convincing for an industrialist to hide behind a cloak of ignorance about potential problems. We all have a duty to look at any proposed development in terms of possible environmental consequences. Society has a right to expect that the risks be assessed so that a judgement can be made as to whether they are acceptable. Increasingly, companies can expect to be challenged as to whether they have fully considered the effects of their plans, to ensure that they are not changing the environment in an unacceptable way, or exposing individuals to unnecessary risks or hazards. Unless you have examined all the possibilities, you are not in a position to make this kind of judgement. Good intentions are not enough. If confidence is to be built up, companies must be prepared to put in the effort to analyse the problems. Increasingly the trend will be towards some form of environmental impact analysis. The degree and sophistication of the analysis will depend on individual circumstances and it would be quite wrong to call for the same type of analysis for, say, the building of a factory extension as for the introduction of a brand new and potentially risky chemical process.

In terms of the possible risk to employees, the new technique of hazard analysis will be used increasingly. This technique has been developed to a substantial degree in the chemical process industry. Perhaps surprisingly to the layman, studies of risks associated with chemical process operations have concluded that the occupational hazards in those areas are far less than those associated with nearly all other industries. A considerable amount of work has been done on cost effectiveness in improving safety and this requires the assessment of priorities, so that the order of dealing with risks can be established. We have to face up to the morally impossible dilemma that, at some point, it is necessary to make an objective assessment as to the amounts that can be spent to save a single life.[7] This may seem a callous approach but, in a world of finite and scarce resources, it is unavoidable. We have already looked at the way in which society accepts the appalling toll of road casualties and there, implicitly or not, society has made, or at best accepted, a judgement as to the amounts that it is prepared to spend in order to try and reduce the number of accidents on the roads. The important point here is that it is impossible and unrealistic to try to eliminate all risk from any aspect of human life. All we can do is to identify the degree of risk and assess whether it is acceptable to us or not. It is arguable that it is equally undesirable to attempt to remove all risks from life. There seems to be a compulsion to introduce some risk element: consider the popularity of such risk sports as mountaineering, climbing, sailing, motor racing and fox hunting. The distinction seems to be that we should be aware of a risk situation when we are in it.

---

[7] Elsewhere it has been established, for example, that in agriculture £2000 is spent to save an employee's life, while in the steel industry the figure rises to some £200 000, and in the pharmaceutical industry to some £5 000 000 per man.

It is also helpful for a firm to develop its own form of cost-benefit analysis. Although, the concept of cost-benefit analysis is helpful, its practice in detail, may not be. Any attempt to make this over-sophisticated, gives a misleading impression of the possibility of removing human subjectivity from decision making. You must not allow yourself to be lulled into the belief that there are arithmetical solutions to your problem of alternatives. Cost-benefit analysis tends to increase the incentives to avoid the difficult big decision by concentrating on the innumerable little ones involved in producing the cost-benefit equation. The concept of cost-benefit is of enormous value if used as a tool to clarify the issues involved and not as a substitute for the basic go/no go decisions. The idea that before embarking on any course of action we should attempt to draw up a balance sheet, setting out in detailed financial terms all the costs to the community at large, which will arise from the implementation of the scheme, and see whether these are outweighed by the benefits which will accrue, is one which must commend itself to most people. Unfortunately this cannot be done, that is, it cannot be done in *precise* terms. Attempts at precision can sometimes lead to unacceptable nonsense. On the same basis that it is impossible to weigh my additional happiness against your additional misery in quantitative terms, it is equally beyond our reach to measure communal distress as opposed to corporate happiness. How do you value the destruction of a hedgerow that has been there for over a thousand years? Or the elimination of a species of wild plant that is unique to the district? The problems that are encouraged in considering the likely effects of the development on ancient monuments have become very familiar, but we have still not been able to arrive at a satisfactory answer. Cost-benefit moves from being a useful tool into being a dangerous master when we try to ascribe some monetary value to 'immeasurable' losses which then become significant factors in the final equation.

Cost-benefit analysis is of the greatest use in trying to give a broad view of the relative magnitudes that are involved. If they are anywhere near in balance then the strong presumption must be against the development. On the other hand, if the quantifiable elements result in an overwhelming margin in favour of the project, then it follows that one has to place a very high value on the unquantifiable elements to bridge the gap. In such circumstances, the question to be asked is whether it is conceivable that the potential damage to the environment which might be incurred could be worth more than the value of the difference shown by the gap. There is no doubt that someone with a particular affection for archaeology could well regard certain buildings or remains as being literally beyond price. But, does this mean that we are never, in any circumstances, justified in doing anything that might destroy them? This is not a hypothetical question. In recent years there has been discovered, during foundation work for new buildings, a temple to the Roman God Mithras; and there has also been the major problem of the ancient Egyptian temples at Abu Simbel which were affected by the Aswan dam, part of the flood control system on the upper reaches of the Nile. In each case, compromises had to be adopted, but at what point did people decide that they could afford no more? In the case of the Egyptian temples, a major worldwide campaign was carried out to salvage as many of them as possible. But, even there, the final decision had to be reached in accordance with the funds and time that were available. If it is possible to relate firm figures to the 'cost' incurred by the destruction of such irreplaceable treaures, then it must put the whole balance sheet in question.

Cost-benefit analysis is an attempt to 'prove' the right answer in a situation where such a conclusion is by definition impossible, because whatever the result, it will still be regarded as unacceptable by those people who feel they are personally bearing more 'costs' than they are receiving benefits.

Whatever management does, it should do it in the context, not just of the environmental problems, but of the wider issues facing society as a whole. Any management that fails to appreciate the genuine concerns of their community as to the way it is handling its problems, is shortsighted indeed. As Hargreaves and Dauman put it, it is 'misleading to talk about business and society. Business is a part of society and the major force in it. The aims and standards of business cannot be allowed to diverge from those of society as a whole.'

The right road

This last sentence should be the text guiding the approach of the industrialist or businessman to the problems of how to handle the environment. I have argued that the manager is in a key position whereby, through his or her actions, the environment of tomorrow is directly influenced. The manager is in a very real sense making the future and he should be encouraged to be fully conscious of this responsibility in taking decisions. This calls for the full backing of boards of directors, shareholders and governments. In doing this, the aim should be to ensure that the standards and objectives of the manager do not diverge from those of society as a whole. In fact, I would go further and say that the manager has a responsibility to adopt the best standards in society and not the average. If we believe in the contribution of industry and commerce to our civilisation and overall well-being, then we must ensure that management becomes a vehicle for enlightened progress in all aspects of human activity, and not the vanguard of the Phillistines or the pacemakers, for purely financial ends. In doing this, individual industrialists can help to ensure the continued progress and success of their own particular enterprise by reducing the need for further interference in its affairs by governments; government intervention is usually prompted by electoral pressures which result from pressures for change.

The problems facing management are enormous and it would be foolish to underestimate them. The days of straightforward simple managerial control are over. The manager lives in a world where he is expected to persuade and to influence, rather than to order or instruct. There are growing social movements for worker participation in managerial decisions. Local authorities expect industrialists to be good neighbours, and society as a whole now strongly takes the view that it is the overriding responsibility of management to protect it as much as possible from potential hazards.

As we have seen, many of these objectives compete with each other and some compromises have to be found between them. Our mechanisms for resolving the serious conflicts of interest are far from perfect and, in many instances, far from being acceptable to the people concerned. However, this is an argument for improving the nature of the mechanisms rather than trying to abandon the machinery altogether. Finding a solution to these problems is the major challenge facing our society and our democratic way of life. I believe that the manager has a crucial part to play in these matters and that he or she should not sit on the sidelines waiting to see what the final score will be, but should participate in the game. We should not criticise the politicians for their lack of understanding if we are not prepared to make our own contribution to enlightenment. Much of the relevant information, as to the likely results of political acts, is available only to management and they have a responsibility to spell out the consequences of the more extreme propositions that are put forward. It is then up to society to decide whether it is prepared to accept them or not. The present danger is that we are not clear as to what those consequences are.

The task that I have spelt out for management is difficult in the extreme. There are no easy solutions and there are certainly no prizes for promoting the type of compromise solution that I am advocating. The 'people' influenced as they are by the press, television and radio, are far more interested in seeing a confrontation situation, with outright winners and losers than a laborious search for acceptable compromises. If we persist in this attitude, then while there will be no winners, there will certainly be an outright loser — the human race.

Selected further reading

Books

Arvill, Robert, *Man and Environment: Crisis and the Strategy of Choice*, Penguin Books (Harmondsworth 1969). (Robert Arvill is the pen name of Robert Boote, Deputy Director of the Nature Conservancy.)

Ayer, A. J., *Language Truth and Logic*, Victor Gollancz (London 1936); Penguin Books (Harmondsworth 1971).

Barr, John, *Derelict Britain*, Penguin Books (Harmondsworth 1970).

Briggs, Asa, *Victorian Cities*, Penguin Books (Harmondsworth 1968).

Brown, Wilfred, *Exploration in Management*, William Heinemann (London 1972).

Christian, G., *Tomorrow's Countryside*, John Murray (London 1966).

de Beer, Sir Gavin, *A Handbook of Evolution*, British Museum (London 1965).

Dickens, Charles, *Hard Times*, William Collins (London 1973).

Dury, G. H., *The Face of the Earth*, Penguin Books (Harmondsworth 1959).

Fairbrother, Nan, *New Lives New Landscapes*, Penguin Books (Harmondsworth 1972).

Finberg, H. P. R., *The Formation of England 550–1042*, Paladin (London 1976).

Hailey, Arther, *Airport*, Michael Joseph and Souvenir Press (London 1968) Pan Books (London 1970).

Harding, D. W., *Social Psychology and Individual Values*, Hutchinson (London 1963).

Hayek, F. A., *The Road to Serfdom*, Routledge and Kegan Paul (London 1971).

Hoskins, W. G., *The Making of the English Landscape*, Hodder and Stoughton (London 1977). Second edition.

Hyams, Edward, *The Changing Face of England*, Kestrel Books (London 1974).

Jacques, Elliot, *Measurement of Responsibility*, William Heinemann (London 1960).

Mellanby, K., *Pesticides and Pollution*, William Collins (London 1970).

Mishan, E. J., *Costs of Economic Growth*, Penguin Books (Harmondsworth 1969).

Mishan, E. J., *21 Economic Fallacies*, Praeger (New York 1973).

Nicholson, Max, *The Environmental Revolution*, Penguin Books (Harmondsworth 1972).

Pevsner, Nikolaus, *The Buildings of England*, Penguin Books (Harmondsworth).

Quarles, John, *Cleaning up America*, Houghton-Mifflin (Boston 1976).

Sampson, Anthony, *The Seven Sisters*, Hodder and Stoughton (London 1975).

Sampson, Anthony, *The Sovereign State*, Hodder and Stoughton (London 1973).

Schumacher, E. F., *Small is Beautiful*, Sphere Books (London 1976).

Simmons, J., *The Railways in Britain*, Macmillan (London 1968).

Stanton, D. M., *English Society in the Early Middle Ages*, Penguin Books (Harmondsworth 1969).

Tandy, Clifford, *Landscape of Industry*, Leonard Hill Books (London 1975).

Taylor, Rupert, *Noise*, Penguin Books (Harmondsworth 1971).

Woodham-Smith, Cecil, *The Great Hunger*, New English Library (London 1970).

Articles and reports

Alkali Inspectors, *Annual Reports*.

'Cancer experts debate whether there are threshold limits for chemical carcinogen', *Chemical Week*, 22 September, 1976.

Code of Practice for Reducing the Exposure of Employed Persons to Noise, HMSO 1972.

Committee on the Future of Broadcasting, *Home Office Report* (Chairman: Lord Annan), Cmnd 6753, HMSO 1977.

Council for the Protection of Rural England (and Scotland and Wales), *Annual Reports*.

Davison, D. J., 'Opencast coal mining — the future and the environment', *Colliery Guardian*, May 1975.

Davison, D. J., 'Restoration and reclamation of opencast sites', *Colliery Guardian Annual Review*, 1971.

Department of Commerce, USA, *A Proposed Program for Roads and Parkways*, Washington 1966.

Department of the Environment, *A Guide to Noise Units*, 1974.

Department of the Environment, *A Survey of Derelict Land in England* (annual publication).

Factory Inspectors, *Annual Reports*.

Institution of Municipal Engineers, 'Clearance of dereliction in industrial areas in relation to the work of the National Coal Board', *Monograph* No. 21, 1974.

Martindale, Roy, 'How should industry view pollution charges?', *CBI Review*, summer 1976.

Ministry of Transport, *Traffic in Towns: A Study of Long Term Problems of Traffic in Urban Areas*. Reports of the Steering Group (Chairman: Sir Geoffrey Crowther) and Working Group (Chairman: Professor Colin Buchanan), HMSO 1963.

National Coal Board, *Annual Reports*.

Neighbourhood Noise, HMSO 1972.

Noise Advisory Council, *Reports*, published by HMSO and Department of the Environment.

Noise in the Next Ten Years, HMSO 1974.

Riboud, Antoine, 'Time for the corporate social plan', *European Business*, winter 1973.

Royal Commission on the Environment, *First Report* 1971 (Chairman: Sir Eric Ashby, Cmnd 4585, HMSO 1971.

Royal Commission on the Environment, *Second Report* 1972 (Chairman: Sir Eric Ashby), Cmnd 4894, HMSO 1972.

Royal Commission on Environmental Pollution, *Reports*:

First Report (Chairman. Sir Eric Ashby), Cmnd 4585, HMSO 1971.

Second Report, *Three Issues in Industrial Pollution* (Chairman: Sir Eric Ashby), Cmnd 4894, HMSO 1972.

Third Report, *Pollution in Some British Estuaries and Coastal Waters* (Chairman: Sir Eric Ashby), Cmnd 5084, HMSO 1972.

Fourth Report, *Pollution Control, Progress and Problems* (Chairman: Sir Brian Flowers), Cmnd 5780, HMSO 1972.

Fifth Report, *Air Pollution: An Integrated Approach*, (Chairman: Sir Brian Flowers), Cmnd 6371, HMSO 1976.

Sixth Report, *Nuclear Power and the Environment*, Cmnd 6618, HMSO 1976.

Royal Commission on the 'Intermediate Areas', *Report*, Cmnd 3998, HMSO 1969.

Royal Commission on the Third London Airport, *Report* (Chairman: The Hon. Justice Roskill):

(a) Hansard, 26 April, 1971.

(b) Board of Trade Cmd on Third London Airport, 1967.

(c) Department of Trade and Industry, Siting of Third London Airport at Foulness, 1972.

Social Trends (Central Statistical Office), HMSO.

United Nations Organisation, Conference on the Human Environment, Stockholm, 5–16 June, 1972, UNO 1973:

Man's Home:

(1) The art of progress: development of the environment

(2) A watch on the earth

(3) A world of cities

(4) Pollutants poisons around the world

(5) Resources: used and abused

Index